# Transforming China's Economy in the Eighties

## Volume II: Management, Industry and the Urban Economy

Edited by
Stephan Feuchtwang
Athar Hussain
Thierry Pairault

**WESTVIEW PRESS**
Boulder, Colorado

**Zed Books Ltd**
London, England

*Transforming China's Economy in the Eighties, Volume I:*
*The Rural Sector Welfare and Employment* and
*Volume II: Management, Industry and the Urban Economy*
was first published in 1988 by:

**In the UK**
Zed Books Ltd
57 Caledonian Road
London N1 9BU

**In the USA**
Westview Press
Frederick A. Praeger, Publisher
5500 Central Avenue
Boulder, Colorado 80301

**In India**
Oxford University Press India,
Oxford House,
Apollo Bundar, P.O. Box 31, Bombay 400 001

Copyright © the editors and individual contributors, 1988.
'A Brief Outline of China's Second Economy' Copyright © 1985
by The Regents of the University of California. Reprinted from
*Asian Survey*, Vol. 25, No. 7, July 1985, pp. 715–736, by
permission of the Regents.
Map of China by kind permission of the Geographical
Association and the Editor of *Geography*.

Cover designed by Andrew Corbett.
Typeset by EMS Photosetters, Rochford, Essex.
Printed and bound in the United Kingdom
at The Bath Press, Avon.

**British Library Cataloguing in Publication Data**

Transforming China's economy in the eighties.
1. China — Economic conditions — 1976–
I. Feuchtwang, Stephan   II. Hussain, Athar
III. Pairault, Thierry
330.951'058          HC427.92

ISBN 0-86232-602-8  v.1
ISBN 0-86232-603-6  v.1 Pbk
ISBN 0-86232-604-4  v.2
ISBN 0-86232-605-2  v.2 Pbk

**Library of Congress Cataloguing-in-Publication Data**

Transforming China's economy in the eighties.
   Bibliography: p.
   Includes indexes.
   Contents: v.1. Rural economy — v.2 Urban economy
   1. China — Economic conditions — 1976–
I. Feuchtwang, Stephan.
HC427.92.C4674     1988     330.951'058     87-10631
ISBN 0-8133-0555-1 (v.1)
ISBN 0-8133-0556-X (Pbk.: v.1)
ISBN 0-8133-0557-8 (v.2)
ISBN 0-8133-0558-6 (Pbk.: v.2)

# Transforming China's Economy in the Eighties
# Volume II

# Contents

## Tables

## Figures

# Contributors

**Philippe Aguignier** Doctoral graduate at the University of Paris with a thesis on the political economy of China. Research fellow at CNRS (Centre National de la Recherche Scientifique)

**Claude Aubert** Agronomist and sociologist, presently a director of research at the Institut National de la Recherche Agronomique, Paris. Author, in collaboration with Mrs Cheng Ying, of *Les Greniers de Nancang; Chronique d'un Village Taiwanais* (Paris, 1984), and of numerous articles on the rural economy of China

**Lucien Bianco** A director at the Ecole des Hautes Etudes des Sciences Sociales, and author of *The Origins of the Chinese Revolution 1915–1949* (Stanford, 1971)

**Michel Bonnin** Researcher at the Centre Chine (Centre de Recherches et de Documentation sur la Chine Contemporaine, Ecole des Hautes Etudes en Sciences Sociales, Paris). Co-author of a book on 'educated youth': *Avoir 20 Ans en Chine . . . a la Campagne* (Paris, 1978)

**Jean-Pierre Cabestan** Graduate in Law, Chinese and Japanese; doctoral graduate in political science; now researcher at the Comparative Law Research Institute of CNRS

**Michel Cartier** Historian of pre-modern China originally; since the 1970s has devoted more attention to the demographic parameters of Chinese economy and society, at the Centre Chine

**Yves Chevrier** Co-director of the Centre Chine; co-editor of *Dictionnaire Biographique du Mouvement Ouvrier International – La Chine* (Paris, 1985); researches the intellectual history of late Qing and early Republican China as well as the reforms and society of post-Mao China

**Elisabeth Croll** Research fellow in the sociology and anthropology of contemporary China at SOAS (School of Oriental and African Studies, University of London); author of *The Politics of Marriage in China* (Cambridge, 1980); *The Family Rice Bowl* (London, 1983) and *Chinese Women Since Mao* (London, 1983)

**Delia Davin** Lecturer in History at the University of York; author of *Women Work; Women and the Party in Revolutionary China* (Oxford, 1976)

**Stephan Feuchtwang** Senior lecturer in Sociology and Principal of the China Research Unit at The City University, London; co-editor of *The Chinese Economic Reforms* (London, 1983)

**François Gipouloux** Research Officer at the Ministry of Industry, Paris, on Chinese industry, and at present resident in Beijing, PRC. Author of *Le Monde Ouvrier Chinois et la Crise du Travail Syndical en 1957* (Paris, 1983)

**Paul Hare** Professor of Economics at Heriot-Watt University. Edinburgh; co-author of *Alternative Approaches to Economic Planning* (London. 1981) and of *Hungary; A Decade of Economic Reform* (London. 1981)

**Hua Chang-ming** Researcher at the Centre Chine and author of *La Condition Feminine et les Communistes Chinois en Action; Yan'an 1935–1946* (Paris, 1981)

**Athar Hussain** Senior Lecturer in Economics at the University of Keele; co-author of *Marxism and the Agrarian Question* (London. 1981) and co-editor of *The Chinese Economic Reforms* (London. 1983)

**Richard Kirkby** China Consultant and Town Planner. Sheffield City; author of *Urbanisation in China: Town and Country in a Developing Economy 1949–2000AD* (London. 1985)

**Martin Lockett** Research Fellow at Templeton College. The Oxford Centre for Management Studies. and author of many publications on cooperative organisation of industry and the cooperative movement. in Europe and China. and on Chinese enterprise management and industrial organisation

**Thierry Pairault** Director of Research on China at CNRS. economist. and author of *Politique Industrielle et Industrialisation en Chine* (Paris, 1983)

**Michael Palmer** Visiting Research Fellow at The City University. London; graduate in sociology. anthropology and law; author of a number of recently published articles on family law and on mediation in the PRC

**Gordon White** Fellow of the Institute of Development Studies. University of Susex; co-editor and co-author of *China's New Development Strategy* (London. 1982) and author of many articles on urban–rural relations. industrial management and labour allocation in the PRC

**Wojtek Zafanolli** Research associate at the Centre Chine

# Abbreviations and Units of Measure

mu = $\frac{1}{15}$ hectare
jin = 0.5 kilogram
BMA: Bureau of Materials Allocation
CCP: Chinese Communist Party
CITIC: China International Trust and Investment Corporation
CMEA: The Council for Mutual Economic Assistance or Comecon – whose members are Bulgaria, Cuba, Czechoslovakia, the German Democratic Republic, Hungary, Mongolia, Poland, Vietnam and the USSR.
CPSU: Communist Party of the Soviet Union
EBF: Extra-Budgetary Funds
GSVO: Gross Social Value Output
ICOR: Incremental Capital–Output Ratio
NI: National Income
RMB: Renminbi – Chinese currency – yuan
SMC: (rural) Supply and Marketing Cooperative
SSB: State Statistical Bureau

# References

*BKNJ: Zhongguo Baike Nianjian* (China's Encyclopedia Yearbook) Shanghai
*BR: Beijing Review*
*Beijing Information* (as *BR* – in French)
*Caizheng* (Finance)
*China Aktuell* (Contemporary China)
*China Daily*, Beijing
*China Directory* (annual): Radio Press Inc, Japan
*CMJJ: Caimao Jingji* (Financial and Commercial Economy)
*CREA*: Joint Publications Research Service, *China Report: Economic Affairs*
*FBIS*: Foreign Broadcasts Information Service
FLP: Foreign Languages Press, Beijing.
*Congren Ribao* (Workers' Daily)
*Guowuyuan: Zhonghua Renmin Gongheguo Guowuyuan Gongbao* (PRC State Council Bulletin)
*Hebei Ribao* (Hebei Daily)
*JJGL: Jingji Guanli* (Economic Management), Beijing
*JJNJ: Zhongguo Jingji Nianjian* (China Economic Yearbook), Jingji Guanli Chubanshe, Beijing and Hong Kong
*JJRB: Jingji Ribao* (Economics Daily)
*JJXZ: Jingjixue Zhoubao* (Economics Review)
*JJYJ: Jingji Yanjiu* (Economic Research), Beijing
*Jingji Tizhi Gaige* (Structural Reform of the Economy), Sichuan
*Liaoning Ribao* (Liaoning Daily)
*Minzhu Yu Fazhi* (Democracy and the Legal System)
NCNA: New China News Agency
*NFRB: Nanfang Ribao* (The Southern Daily)
*QSND: Qishi Niandai* (The Seventies), Hong Kong
*RMRB: Renmin Ribao* (People's Daily), Beijing
*Renmin Shouce* (PRC Handbook)
*SHKX: Zhongguo Shehui Kexue* (Chinese Social Sciences)
*SWB*: BBC, *Summary of World Broadcasts: Far East*, Caversham, England.
*SYB: Statistical Yearbook of China*, 1981–85 (*Zhongguo Tongji Nianjian*), SSB, Beijing, and Economic Information and Agency, Hong Kong
*Tianjin Ribao* (Tianjin Daily)
*Wan Hui Bao* (Evening News) Hong Kong
*Wenhui Bao* (Western News) Shanghai
XH: Xinhua (New China) News Agency
*Yancheng Wanbao* (Yancheng Evening News)
*Zhengming* (Contend)

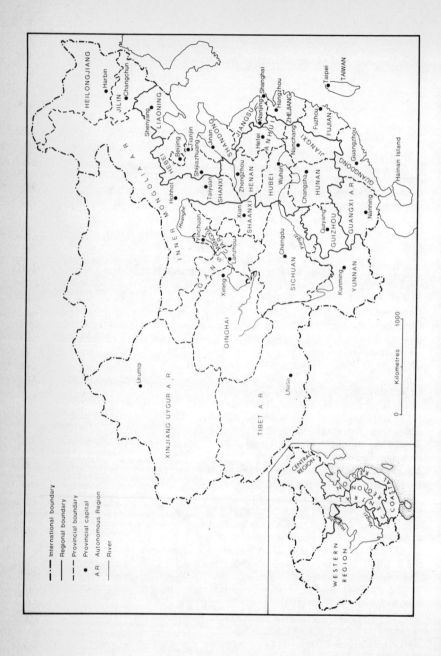

# Preface

The Chinese economy is socialist and planned. In size and resource potential for self-sufficiency it is comparable with the Soviet economy. But it is far more agrarian and far poorer. China is also the product of a distinct history whose peculiarities must be given due weight when considering the transformation it is currently undergoing.

At least one conclusion can be drawn about this transformation. It is that reforms which are similar to those which were enacted earlier in all the socialist planned economies of the eastern bloc, including the Soviet Union, have in China been more far-reaching. The result is a Chinese economy which is now far less like that of the Soviet Union than it was during the time identified with communes and with Mao Zedong, when the Chinese road to socialism was supposed to be most distinctive.

The Chinese communes were not so different from the Soviet collective farms after Krushchev's reforms had allowed them ownership of all their means of production. But now the contrast is spectacular. Soviet agriculture is organized into state and large collective farms, which are increasingly like state farms, while Chinese agriculture is organized into household farms and small enterprises bound by a national network of state purchase and supply depots (greater detail is given in Chapter 3 of Volume 1). The supply of food from plots distributed to households for their own 'private' use in conjunction with private retailing has been and continues to be vital in both economies. But the extent of rural light industry outside the state's control above county level (see Chapter 5 of this volume) is and has long been a distinct feature of the Chinese road, growing steadily under Mao and now spectacularly under Deng Xiaoping. As a result of reform since 1978 urban private and collective light and service industrial sectors have been added to this. Together they constitute a larger part of the economy than in most other socialist planned economies.

This comparative survey of the Chinese economy cannot omit planning instruments themselves. This is where the reforms are most recognizably like other socialist reforms. Chinese planning is increasingly, with pauses for consolidation, reliant on indirect, economic regulators. But it may be going further in this direction than other socialist economies.

Is China undergoing a more radical economic transformation than at any time since 1949? And if so, what peculiarity in Chinese conditions and Chinese history accounts for this? These are the questions these volumes seek to answer.

As Paul Hare (1983b) has pointed out, central capacity for planning in China has never been large compared with the Soviet Union. The number of key products and services whose balances can be calculated is much more limited and the instruments of control, such as planning commissions and banks, have far less expertise and are small relative to economic activity in the country as a whole. Decentralization of controls to lower levels of government was the chosen method of coping with these limitations until the 1978 reforms added decentralization of controls to the enterprises themselves.

Planning thus included a great deal of plan bargaining and political argument. There is nothing peculiar to China in plan bargaining. What is peculiar is the nature of the political conflict in which the centres of economic power became engaged, along with centres of other kinds of power such as the propaganda department or the military affairs committee of the Chinese Communist Party and regional military commands. For instance, much of the conflict which culminated during the Cultural Revolution (1966–76) concerned measures to deal with problems endemic to all socialist planning systems. But strong policy differences had already been manifest in the late 1950s (they are described in the introduction to Feuchtwang and Hussain, 1983). One political feature of China is the combination of a certain strength of lower power centres within a system sufficiently well integrated to centralize the differences between them, eventually, as inner party struggles. Reforms in the provinces of Anhui and Sichuan had been conducted for two years before they were adopted centrally and implemented nationally. There are also examples of local opposition to the centre successful enough to sustain opposed policies for two or three years. But they cannot remain in force for long without becoming central differences which have to be fought out. When the differences from the mid-1950s onwards were sustained and fought within the party the political stakes rose so high that they became issues of revolution and counter-revolution during the Cultural Revolution and now modernization or reversion to feudalism. One of the peculiarities of the Chinese economic reforms, then, is the political impetus behind the present ascendancy of those accused during the Cultural Revolution of seeking a reversion to capitalism.

The reforms have as a political objective the removal of whatever may be analysed as a potential source of another Cultural Revolution. This includes turning the armed forces into smaller, more specialized and technically rather than politically well equipped units, no longer enhancing their function as a model political force. The same general objective includes establishing a legal profession to depoliticize disputes that might otherwise have been collectively arbitrated. Specialization and technical renewal are also aims of economic reorganization among ministries and within enterprises. As yet they have had little success, according to Chevrier (in Chapter 1 of Volume 1), in the middle range of centres of economic state power. Similarly, a legal establishment promotes the formalization and implementation of contractual responsibilities among economic units and is a means of limiting and exposing the use of informal connections and abuses of economic state power for personal gain. This aim will take a long time to realize. Meanwhile illegalities and the second economy in general have thrived instead of being reduced by the reformed 'first' economy (see Chapter 8).

The reforms have made economic activity to some extent independent of the political administration. As some analysts have it, this is a necessary step towards the creation of a 'modern' economy, with beneficial results in raised living standards. By 'modern' is usually meant an integrated realm of economic activity where economic agents have their own power separate from state power. States may intervene and state organizations may also be economic agents, but they act in a realm with its own means of regulation and calculation. Capitalist economies are uniquely 'modern' and 'economic' in these senses. The idea that China is incompletely 'modern', on the way to completing the process of modernization but regrettably limited in its progress by internal restrictions, is an idea current among Chinese as well as among many Western descriptions of contemporary China. Is it desirable for China to be a capitalist economy with a strong state to overcome these restrictions? Some of the chapters of these volumes (see particularly Chapter 1 of Volume 1 and Chapters 1 and 2 in this volume), when examining with notes of regret the inconsistencies and apparent irrationalities of the reforms, point to an underlying logic pushing in this direction.

Many of the terms which are necessarily used are nevertheless ambivalent and have idealistic underlying assumptions. 'Modernity', 'efficiency', 'economic rationality', 'plan' and 'market' have to be read in context and in the light of the assumptions they bring with them. Take 'plan' and 'market', for instance. The occasional reference to Lange in this volume may be a reminder that in one respect the ideals of planning and of liberal market economics are identical: perfect rationality and balance. The one aims to achieve it by means of conscious representation and collective direction, the other by means of pure self-interested competition in conditions of state guaranteed peace. These means are themselves opposed aims; but the ideal economic result is the same. Any national economy being an imperfection of one or the other, we have always to ask what rationality, what efficiency, what roles do the various counsels of perfection perform, in the descriptions being offered and in the policy statements and the economic orders to which they refer. The policy statements are in any case not so much criteria by which to judge an economy's worth as political conditions in which it is working.

Some illustrative cases may be suggested by way of introduction. Take the vexed issue of price reform. Prices have many rationales, not just one ideal rationality. They can be held to signal relative costs of production and therefore, ideally, change all the time. They can also be held to act as measures of account and therefore ideally be constant over time, merely articulating qualitatively different materials and activities whose amounts and balances are changing. Of course these two selected rationales interact. Actual prices can be affected by both. In China each of these rationales has been deployed in distinct ranges of production: fluctuating prices for light industrial and non-staple consumer products, fixed prices for strategic and for staple consumer products. Most of the products of the first range have been produced by means of those in the second. None the less, the strategic and staple have an entirely distinct means of distribution in China – bureaucratic allocation – while the light and non-staple are distributed by the market, which means competitive and floating price regulation. In the context of reforms which move to reduce the fixed and extend the fluctuating price ranges, it is the fixed which are usually criticized for being historically determined and thus poor signals of cost. Yet the shortage of strategic materials means that relaxation of their pricing would result in a sellers' market and steep inflation. It is surely wrong to assume one or other rationale to be the basic law of pricing. More useful and interesting is to note the conflict and its results. The recent institution of 'indicative prices' (described in Chapter 1 of Volume 1) can be seen as the result of conflicting pressures from the two kinds of pricing policy: some of the strategic goods centrally allocated at fixed prices are passed on from their first destinations and their prices are then allowed to float.

A similar conflict arises between various measures of 'efficiency'. The production of imprecisely made goods is surely a sign of inefficiency. But it is also the result of conflicting efficiencies, such as the well known conflict between policies to maximize productivity and policies to maintain high rates of employment. Each efficiency has its own inherent notions of human resources, their use or waste. In the first place we can note that there is no absolute measure of labour efficiency; the appropriate comparator of wages paid for units produced must first be selected. But suppose that has been done. It might then be shown that procurement prices are above the costs and therefore the prices, in a different price regime, of a comparable producer. But the extra revenue from the higher price may in effect go into a wage fund for employing a larger number of workers than would otherwise be employed. Higher prices may be one of the large number of strategems for reducing urban unemployment which cumulatively had remarkable success in bringing urban unemployment down from around 20% in 1979 to around 2% in 1983, according to the estimates of Bonnin and Cartier (in Chapter 8 of Volume 1). In that sense the higher price is socially efficient. The badly made product with which this paragraph started is probably the result of a reluctance to cause frictional unemployment by reorganizing or closing factories, as well as the fault of a management used to producing for quota compliance rather than for delivery to the user.

The fact that a product has to be re-tooled before it can be put to use is certainly wasteful. It is part of what is also described as 'disguised unemployment'. But to remove the disguise and cause blatant unemployment would have its own cost in China. Most welfare comes from services bought by households from wage or self-employment earnings and from services provided by state enterprises themselves to those fortunate enough to be employed in them. So the income distributed as wages to the 'hidden' unemployed would have to be distributed in some other way to the openly unemployed unless they were to be left to starve. A major reorganization of responsibility for welfare, probably entailing the establishment of new bureaucracies and services, would be required. Reforms to increase efficiency of productivity have in fact increased pressures to find ways of achieving precisely such a reorganization, as Gordon White's discussion of labour allocation shows (in Chapter 1 of this volume). How should the costs of any such reorganization be calculated against the comparative costs of disguised unemployment to show which is the more 'efficient'?

Another, and probably more interesting question raised by this example of conflicting efficiencies, is how institutions and institutional limits are changing under the pressures pushing against them. The policy reforms and such deliberate reorganizations as have been attempted create their own repercussions.

Spheres of economic activity beyond the direct control of such crucial state administrations as those of the central bank, the industrial ministries, the finance and planning ministries and the materials allocation bureaux have grown enormously since the reforms began in 1978. Tensions among these administrations have always existed, but they are now having specific results at local (municipal and county) levels under the policy of increasing the autonomy of economic enterprises of all kinds. One intriguing result in 1981 described by Barry Naughton (1985) was what were called 'profit contracts'. As in the USSR, the setting of profit targets, rather than quotas of materials, was by then the main planning instrument. The ministry of finance set these targets, but they were often at odds with the production capacities of the enterprises, which were administered by local bureaux of the ministries of industry. As a result of the profit targets, enterprises often had too little work assigned to them. The local bureaux therefore engaged in an *ad hoc* bargaining over targets with the agents of the ministry of finance. And the results of these bargains were eventually justified centrally as a new system of profit contracts. The resulting rearrangements meant fewer remissions of funds to central government accounts than had been planned. Central budgets went into serious deficit. From 1982 onwards capital charges were placed upon enterprises through the central bank, as noted by Gordon White, and that went a little way to supporting central budgets. But more importantly, from 1983 taxes on enterprise incomes, at periodically fixed rates, began to replace profit remittance targets and to recover more funds for central budgets.

Even so, as a number of the chapters of this volume point out, funds do now accumulate for investment at the level of municipalities and county towns and beyond government control altogether. They are so great they have their own, powerful momentum. Will they, as Pairault (in Chapter 2 of this volume) asks, indicate the direction of state investments? Or will there merely be a repetition of the new, post-reforms rhythm of deregulation and reassertion of controls noted by Gordon White?

What is the relation between government controlled enterprise and economic activities beyond government control? There appears to be a process of growth within the boundaries of local markets which are forming and reforming themselves outside government control. But once an enterprise grows beyond these boundaries it becomes dependent on government controlled allocations or enterprises. When the local enterprise comes into sales competition beyond the prices of the local market, which have been to its advantage, or when the products of larger enterprises become available locally and are either of better quality or with lower prices, what happens? Or what happens when the local enterprise comes into purchasing competition with larger enterprises for centrally allocated means of production? It either becomes a loss maker or it is absorbed into the activities of larger, state enterprises, or it is itself transformed into a state enterprise.

This does not mean that the state institutions remain the same. They must be affected by what they absorb. Another change of this kind, a change which is at the same time a reinforcement of state and party institutions, can be seen in the renewal of their personnel. Cabestan (in Chapter 4 of this volume) describes the renewal at the centre which has occurred so far. A long-term project of increasing the expertise of party and state cadres is underway. Where else do the newly educated or re-educated professionals, the lawyers, the bankers, the managers, designers and technicians first go, after all, than into government offices and the large state enterprises?

Reviewing the chapters of these books, one possible prediction is that a more technocratic state will emerge with a party recruiting the new technocracy and devising new arrangements for strategic economic management and the national integration of economic activities. Local and less regulated economies would become increasingly less isolated. Another possible prediction is of a growing sphere of extra-state economic activity, but one which depends on working a system of bureaucratic controls. Growing political tensions between the use of connections and the application of technical criteria of economic performance and administration must in any case be a plausible prediction.

Neither networking nor technical criteria could be described as socialist systems of representation and accountability. Yet what seems quite implausible is any change of state and party controls entailing the abandonment of reference to socialist norms and ideology. They may be redefined in the process of justifying new practices, but not abandoned. At the same time they act as a moral dynamic, reminders of principles capable of other interpretations. China's socialism is now less predictable and more distinctive than it has ever been before.

# 1 Evolving Relations between State and Markets in the Reform of China's Urban–Industrial Economy[1]

**Gordon White**

One of the fundamental aims of Marxian socialism has been to replace the 'anarchic' markets of competitive capitalism with the 'scientific' determination of social needs through planning. Early radical theorists of Soviet socialism, such as Bukharin and Preobrazhensky, held that, as the new socialist society arose, it would displace the 'economic categories' characteristic of capitalist markets (value, price, wages, profits), (Bukharin and Preobrazhensky, 1920 (1969)). The plan would impose a 'teleological unity' on society; economic development would become the object of conscious direction.

In this tradition, the relationship between socialist planning and markets is zero sum, the former competing with, and eventually displacing the latter during the period of 'socialist transition'. This competitive view of the relationship between planning and markets underpinned the orthodox version of socialist political economy which emerged in the Soviet Union in the 1930s and was transmitted to the new socialist countries which emerged after World War II, both in Eastern Europe and the Third World. This position was defined by Stalin (1952) who, while admitting that 'commodity production without capitalists' and the 'law of value' continued to exist in socialist society, emphasized that both were subordinate to the plan and would gradually be replaced. Later forms of revolutionary socialist ideology, such as Maoism in China and Guevaraism in Cuba, while taking issue with certain aspects of the official Soviet tradition, preserved this competitive view of plan–market relations. Radical Maoists, for example, viewed the market and its characteristic features (notably prices and profits) with suspicion, as mechanisms for the restoration of capitalism.

In the traditional Soviet model, a pervasive state regulates industry and agriculture by means of centralized directive plans, enforced by a network of political and administrative agencies. The role of markets is limited to four sectors: first, in foreign trade, which is perceived as a necessary but ancillary element of a development strategy aiming at self-sufficiency (Koves, 1981); second, in the distribution of consumer goods whereby individuals use money to exercise consumer choice and prices operate to some extent to balance supply and demand; third, in relations between the (state) industrial sector and the (collective) agricultural sector, whereby industrial goods and agricultural produce are bought and sold with prices playing a role in regulating exchange; fourth, to the extent that labourers exercise a degree of control over their choice of occupation and workplace, and labour power is mobile and responds to wage signals, there is a labour market of sorts. None of these four processes reflects a market in any full-fledged sense characteristic of neo-classical modelling; each is heavily circumscribed by political and administrative controls, the role of price in particular being very weak.

Historical experience suggests that whereas classical directive planning can play a positive role in the initial stages of industrialization in certain circumstances, this potential for success is highly contingent, subject to severe limitations, and purchased at considerable cost (for a general discussion, see White, 1984). Evidence from the more mature socialist economies of Eastern Europe suggests several conclusions. First, success in one economic sector (heavy industry) has been purchased at the cost of other sectors (light industry, agriculture, commerce and services), where directive planning methods are less effective. The resulting constraints on the growth of popular living standards have reduced work incentives and overall productivity. Second, the very success in industrialization meant that, as the economy grew more complex and sources of extensive growth dwindled, the characteristic problems of directive central planning multiplied. Third, to the extent that a more complex economy leads to greater reliance on foreign trade (especially in smaller countries such as Hungary), international competition exerts pressures for more flexible economic management and more dynamic technological progress. In successful socialist industrializers, these pressures combine to create a new strategic policy agenda, issues of micro-economic efficiency and technological change taking on cardinal significance.

These problems have forced a reconsideration of the role of markets in socialist economies, with profound implications for the economic role of the socialist state. Economic reformers drew on another tradition of socialist political economy which argued that markets were a crucial feature of the period of socialist transition and that planning could, indeed must, be harmonized with markets to serve socialist ends. I shall call this the complementary view of plan–market relations. It provided the theoretical underpinning for the economic reforms which gathered pace in Eastern Europe in the 1960s. Its intellectual origins can be traced to certain defeated protagonists in the Soviet industrialization debates of the 1920s, such as Sokolnikov, Bazarov, Kondratiev and (the later) Bukharin (Brus, 1972b, pp. 41–60) and to inter-war discussions among Western socialists, notably Lange and Lerner, about the ideal functioning of socialist economies (Lange and Taylor, 1938; Lange, 1936–7 (1972)). It was first put on the practical policy agenda by the Yugoslav break with Stalin in the late 1940s and the gradual evolution of 'market socialism' in that country.

The debate between the competitive and complementary views of the relations between plan and market has double relevance to Third World countries adopting a socialist development model. First, in contexts where commodity production is weakly developed, there would seem to be a strong case for incorporating vigorous markets in the *earliest* stages of socialist transition (Mackintosh, 1984). The development of markets is crucial because they provide incentives for stimulating productivity and increase the density of social exchange which can underlie dynamic economic growth. In such contexts the imposition of a comprehensive, centralized, directive planning system is not only very difficult, but also unwise because it may in effect be replacing one form of natural economy with another. Second, in countries which have applied the Soviet model with some success in the early stages of industrialization, the arguments of the Eastern European reformers are compelling since the very advance of industrialization has multiplied the intrinsic problems of directive planning.

China is an interesting case on both counts. In this chapter, I shall investigate evolving relations between plan and market, state and economy, in the context of the Chinese economic reforms of 1978–85. I shall begin with a brief overview of the analysis of plan–market relations taken by economic reformers (an example of the complementary position). I shall then focus on the urban and industrial sector, and attempt to assess the success which Chinese reformers have achieved in introducing market mechanisms and the political and economic problems they have encountered along the way in the areas of finance, commerce and labour allocation. I shall conclude with an evaluation of the reforms, both in terms of their impact on China's future and their implications for the theory and practice of socialist development in general.

## The Theoretical Basis of Economic Reform

Reform economists in the post-Mao era concentrated their fire on the economic irrationalities of the previous pattern of state involvement in industry.[2] The central elements of their critique have been covered extensively elsewhere, so I shall be content here with a rapid overview. They are careful to acknowledge that the socialist state *can* play a positive role in regulating (directly or indirectly) the structure and direction of the macro-economy, especially in the early stages of industrialization. But the economic advantages of planning originally posited by the Marxian socialist tradition are now seen as contingent, not automatic, thus raising serious questions about the nature and degree of state involvement.

Reformers argue that the previous planning system imposed a statist logic on the economy which impeded or distorted economic development. Historically, it was a fusion of two forms of statism: the 'feudal' (i.e. imperial Chinese and Tsarist Russian) and the 'socialist' (i.e. Leninist–Stalinist). In consequence, the economy is transformed into a politico–administrative system, giving rise to two basic problems. First, the imperatives of *political* mobilization and conflict distort economic processes. Reform economists argue that there is an independent economic sphere in society governed by 'economic laws'. Hu Qiaomu, for example, maintains that 'politics itself cannot create other laws and impose them on the economy', rather, the function of political leadership is 'to see to it that our socialist economic work operates within the scope of these objective [economic] laws' (1978, Part I, p. 8). This insistence on the 'relative autonomy' of the *economy* in socialist society is a paradoxical inversion of Western Marxist arguments about the 'relative autonomy' of the *state* in capitalist society.

Second, the state apparatus imposes its own *administrative* logic on the economy, with several ill effects. To the extent that state power is concentrated and hierarchical, the economy becomes rigidified and its productive elements, the enterprises, are rendered inert. Conversely, to the extent that authority in the state apparatus is diffused and overlapping, 'semi-anarchy' reigns, which hampers economic planning and coordination. In both cases heavy state intervention is irrational because it imposes 'a "net"-like system of administration whereby countless vertical and horizontal restrictions break up the natural relations of the objective economy' (Ji Chongwei and Rong Wenzuo, 1979, p. 14). Skinner (1964–5, Part III) has identified the problems caused by this tension between natural and state economic systems in his analysis of the massive disorientations caused by the commune movement in 1958–9. In the industrial sector, the economic costs of this kind of administrative segmentation are a familiar feature of directive planning systems elsewhere. The Polish economist Balcerowicz, for example, points to the problem in an Eastern European context, arguing that it embodies a constant tension between the economy's 'material ties' and 'organizational ties', which is particularly harmful to technological innovation (1980, pp. 160–1).

Reformers have drawn four policy conclusions from their analysis of administrative segmentation. First, there should be greater separation between the spheres of administration and economics, the latter having more scope to operate according to its own organic logic. This implies the formation of natural economic zones crossing administrative boundaries and the promotion of inter-plant integration, particularly through cross-boundary companies or associations. Second, central planning organs should be strengthened to curb branch-based departmentalism and establish a more rational division of labour between central and local departments. Central planners would henceforth concentrate on macro-economic management, regulating the micro-economy less by directive means and more by economic levers or guidance methods. Third, market processes were to be resuscitated, with a new ideological outlook which recognized the commoditized character of socialist economy. Fourth, the bedrock of the reform programme, the decision-making autonomy of industrial enterprises, should be expanded (see White, 1983b).

These were the central ideas which have underlined the specific policy innovations of the past eight years. We shall now examine in detail the progress of reform policies in the three areas of finance, labour and commerce.

## The Impact of Economic Reforms

### The Financial System
Perhaps the area of reform policy which has had the greatest impact on the urban–industrial economy has been that of finance. Financial reforms set out to redefine the process of capital aggregation and circulation, specifically to diversify sources of capital provision and redefine the terms on which capital is allocated. In this section, I will be interested in the extent to which this has led to the emergence of capital markets, characterized by decentralized sources of supply and allocation

according to supply and demand conditions measured by variable interest rates.

The first main thrust of reform in industrial finance has been the attempt to impose market-like discipline by moving away from the previous practice of supplying all of the fixed and much of the working capital funds of enterprises as interest-free budgetary allocations. Under the new system, the bulk of capital advances would be in the form of bank loans, subject to repayment and carrying a cost in the form of interest. The previous system, argued the reformers with considerable justification, had generated an essentially political struggle between enterprises to obtain more investment with little pressure to use these funds effectively once acquired (Wang Chuanlun, 1984, p. 61). The scramble for extra investment fostered a tendency towards extensive rather than intensive industrial development, allowed slack management of equipment and raw materials and encouraged managers to conceal their true capital assets as part of their strategy of bargaining with state agencies. The reforms, it was hoped, would raise the efficiency of capital utilization by introducing more caution and cost consciousness into managers' calculations about the acquisition and use of capital.

During 1979–85, therefore, there has been movement towards greater commercialization of capital provision along several fronts. The role of the banking (as opposed to the budgetary) system was expanded and its autonomy increased. During the Cultural Revolution decade, the People's Bank of China had effectively been under the control of the Ministry of Finance and the banking system had reflected fiscal priorities and processes. In the early stages of the reforms, the People's Bank was allowed to increase its role as a provider of credit. As of 1984 its role was changed to that of a Central Bank in charge of monetary policy and overall financial policy. Most of its commercial functions were transferred to a new Industry and Commerce Bank charged with providing credit for enterprises and managing bank deposits.[3] The banking system underwent further institutional changes: a number of specialized banks were established (to operate under People's Bank supervision), there was a significant devolution of decision-making power from central to local bank branches, and other types of investment trust or corporation were encouraged to set up, at both national and local levels.[4] A special company, the China International Trust and Investment Corporation (CITIC), was also established in 1979 to encourage and channel foreign investment.

Banking institutions were charged with the role of using economic, rather than administrative, methods to stimulate industrial development in two senses. First, they could use their capacity to aggregate and channel credit funds to promote industrial expansion and implement current planning priorities (for example, by directing loans preferentially to light rather than heavy industrial projects, the collective rather than the state sector, and export-oriented rather than domestic enterprises). Second, through their ability to provide or withhold loans, set their conditions through differential terms and interest rates and enforce credit contracts through an expanding framework of financial laws, banks could act as a stimulus to industrial efficiency. In effect, they were to play a major role in supervising enterprise finances: they could act to encourage efficient and penalize inefficient enterprises, monitor the implementation of state plans, improve the quality of financial accounting, stimulate technical innovation, speed up the turnover of working capital, curtail unproductive or duplicating investment projects, monitor the level of bonus payments and so on.

The second major thrust of the financial reforms has been to devolve more financial power to the enterprises themselves by changing the previous practice of syphoning off enterprise revenues into state coffers. This reform has gone through three stages, each of which has brought greater financial power to enterprise managers. I have discussed these in detail elsewhere (White, 1983b) so I shall be less interested in their precise nature and more in their effects on the system of industrial finance as a whole.

The introduction of these reforms led to claims and counter-claims about their effectiveness in improving industrial efficiency. Though there was some improvement in certain financial indicators of industrial performance, by 1982–3 considerable disappointment was expressed by senior financial officials about the effectiveness of the reforms (see Wang Bingqian, 1982). In fact, the impact of the reforms was uneven and contradictory. Certain problems arose from their lack of impact. Though the institutional reforms in the banking system did reduce the monopolistic character of the old system to some extent, the new system was still oligopolistic and imposed powerful obstacles to the fluidity of capital. Some economists criticized 'the endless game of administrative changes' and called for decisive steps to establish more lively financial markets (*China Daily*, 9 June 1984). Moreover, many enterprises resisted the move from budgetary to credit provision of investment funds and, in the five years from 1979 to 1984, bank credit only amounted to 10% of the state capital construction budget (*XH* domestic, 4 July 1984, *FBIS*, no. 133). The potential for using interest rates as a weapon of economic policy was not exploited and the overall level of industrial loans was too low to have a significant effect on enterprise behaviour (Byrd, 1983, p. 77).[5] Banks also found it difficult to supervise enterprise activities given the difficulties they encountered in enforcing repayment of loans (in the absence of effective legislation on contracts) and in securing accurate information on enterprise activities, their continued vulnerability to political and administrative pressures (for example, to give loans to inefficient enterprises) and their lack of properly trained professional cadres.

Other problems, however, arose from the very effectiveness of certain elements of the financial reform programme. Between 1979 and 1984 there was indeed a major diversification of sources of industrial finance and considerable decentralization of financial decision-making power: power flowed to individual economic departments, local governments, industrial enterprises, rural co-ops, specialized banks, local bank branches, investment trusts, individuals (in joint stock ventures) and foreign interests. The proliferation of 'extra-budgetary funds' (EBF) from these sources created what has been called a 'second budget' (Wang Chuanlun, 1984, p. 65) or an 'unorganized capital market'. As a proportion of state budgetary funds, EBF rose from 4% in 1953 to around 60% in 1981. Of total EBF the proportion actually managed by state financial departments fell from 15% in 1953 to 6.9% in 1981 (Wu Renjian, 1983). Apparently a large proportion of EBF were used for investment; already by 1980 EBF provided 55% of gross fixed investment in state enterprises (compared with 40% in 1979, 38% in 1976 and only 11% during the First

Five-Year Plan) (Byrd, 1983, pp. 27–8).

The state lost a good deal of its ability to control the money supply in general and the expansion of investment funds in particular. In 1982, for example, gross national investment in fixed assets reached 84.5 billion yuan, exceeding the plan by 15 billion yuan – a trend which continued into 1983 (Wang Jiye, 1983). Over-investment was accompanied by over-distribution as enterprises poured money into productivity bonus schemes which were often poorly conceived and outstripped improvements in labour productivity. For example, though full capacity labour productivity in state enterprises in 1982 was 2.3% up on 1981, wages rose 7.6% and the total amount of bonuses and extra piece-work wages by 19.8% (Rong Zihe, 1983). Along with problematic fiscal policies which created large budget deficits in 1979 and 1980, these financial pressures contributed to the inflation which had risen to alarming levels (by Chinese standards) by 1980 (Dai Yuanchen, 1981). This situation provoked a strong response from the financial authorities who attempted to recentralize financial allocation during 1981–3, with only limited success (Wang Jiye, 1983). There was a concomitant drive to cut back on capital investment programmes, particularly by local authorities, again with very limited success. The banks were also impelled to reduce the monetary disequilibrium by limiting credit expansion, increasing personal savings and withdrawing currency from circulation. These measures, along with increases in the output of consumer goods and price controls, eased the growth in the money supply and reduced inflation. But with the renewed reform impetus which built up during 1984–5, the same pressures emerged and there were various signs of overheating in the economy in 1985. In fact, there was a rhythm of stop–go financial policy throughout the 1978–85 period: financial liberalization followed by overheating followed by government attempts to restore controls.

It would be misleading to attribute these problems to an extension of financial markets in any strict sense. To the extent that the role of credit money was expanded, the regulating power of interest rates was increased, sources of investment finance proliferated and investment decisions were decentralized (particularly to industrial enterprises), certain elements of a capital market were introduced. However, many of the sources of investment funds remained bureaucratic (local governments and functional economic departments) and allocations continued to be made on politico–administrative grounds. Moreover the impact of certain key mechanisms of a true capital market – notably variable interest reflecting supply and demand conditions, the vetting of loans on commercial criteria and legally enforceable contracts – still remained weak. Indeed, it could be argued that this initial attempt to combine planning and market in the financial sphere led to a situation which combined the worst of both worlds: on the one hand, the state's capacity to control and coordinate capital flows was severely weakened; on the other hand, the reforms brought much of the disorder of a market system without much of its capacity for self-equilibration and allocative efficiency. However, problems of this kind are to be expected in such an important economic transition. Though they reappeared in the renewed reform push of 1984–5, the CCP leadership pressed ahead undeterred. But this next step involved not merely more decisive steps towards the establishment of financial markets (probably including the appearance of share markets and further erosion of the oligopolistic control of the central banks) but also towards strengthening the capacity of the state to regulate an increasingly complex financial system (see Li Chengrui, 1985).

## Labour Recruitment and Allocation

As in the case of capital, the issue of 'labour markets' is politically sensitive in China since, in the Marxian classics, the existence of a market in labour power is a defining characteristic of capitalism. Up till very recently, therefore, economic reformers have been careful to avoid direct advocacy of labour markets. Many of their proposed reforms in the labour system, however, are clearly designed to move in that direction.

They argue that, of all aspects of the previous system of industrial planning, 'the allocation of labour resources is by far the furthest from the market mechanism'. Following the principle of 'unified employment and assignment', state labour bureaux had exercised a virtual monopoly over the allocation of urban labour (including both the state and the 'big collective' sectors). There was a pressing need to reduce the span of direct controls, simplify the technical and administrative requirements of labour planning by more selective intervention and encourage a greater degree of labour mobility (while retaining a commitment to full employment).

There is considerable evidence that the previous system of administrative allocation had a bad effect on workers' motivations and productivity. It was too 'top down', imposing (often unreasonable) 'plan' requirements on (often unwilling) individuals. Refusal to 'obey allocation' to one's first job assignment could be interpreted as disloyalty to the nation and the socialist cause. After initial job assignment, moreover, the individual found it difficult to move laterally to other units or areas. Administrative labour allocation had also encouraged overmanning, argued the critics. State enterprises had expanded extensively by taking on fresh labour rather than intensively by using technical and managerial innovation to raise the productivity of the existing workforce.[6]

Restrictions on labour mobility meant that most workers and staff on the state payroll had lifetime tenure in their original units with job promotions or wage increments based heavily on seniority. This was the notorious iron rice-bowl which reformers identified as a major impediment to improving labour productivity. Though enterprises could achieve some degree of flexibility by taking on temporary or contract labourers for limited terms, these workers resented the differential, and pressured managers to grant them an iron rice-bowl too. When successful, they became less productive, as senior researcher, Feng Lanrui, points out (interview in White, 1983a, p. 148):

> [All] temporary workers wanted to be full workers; you told them to go and they would refuse. The state tried to control this by allowing *planned* temporary workers to change over, but not those outside the plan, but this approach was ineffective. The trouble is that, when they became fixed workers, they slacked off.

Finally, argued reform critics, state monopoly over urban labour allocation had contributed to unemployment by obstructing the emergence of alternative job agencies and reduced the motivation of the urban unemployed to find jobs for themselves, inuring them to dependence on the state.

Labour reform policies since 1978 have sought to rectify these problems by improving labour planning, changing the degree and forms of state involvement in labour allocation and encouraging more spontaneous labour mobility. The principle of state planning was to remain the dominant element in a new system of labour allocation: state labour bureaux would determine the overall proportions of the national labour force but would use direct administrative controls more selectively; independent cooperative labour agencies would help people find jobs; enterprises would have a greater say in recruiting and dismissing their own workers; and individuals would be encouraged to find or create their own jobs.

If we turn now to the impact of these proposals, progress in the first wave of reform up to 1981 was very slow and disappointing (White, 1983a; 1985). The ability of enterprise managers to select new workers has increased to some extent: for example, enterprises could select individual workers so long as they observed numerical quotas; they made increasing use of advertisements for job vacancies and applicants were vetted by examinations. Very little progress was made in increasing the power of enterprises to dismiss workers. One exception was the 'special economic zones' in the south-east where management powers over hiring and firing were greater than elsewhere. Where the power was exercised elsewhere, it only applied to workers who repeatedly violated labour discipline, relatively infrequent cases. State labour bureaux still controlled numbers of personnel and wage funds, often with little reference to what enterprises themselves wanted. Labour bureaux were under pressure to alleviate urban unemployment; thus they padded their quotas and enterprises had to accept unnecessary labour. Though there had been some progress in diversifying channels of labour allocation through the new labour service companies, their impact on the state industrial sector was negligible and they remained under the control of local labour bureaux. The methods used by central personnel agencies to allocate 'strategic' groups (notably college graduates) had not changed. The degree of individual choice was still very limited and levels of 'misallocation' remained high.

As of early 1982, therefore, labour system reforms in the state sector had been far less effective than their counterparts in finance. State controls were still tight, labour flexibility in the state sector had hardly changed and the iron rice-bowl was as strong as ever. Indeed, in some aspects the situation had got worse: labour productivity was stagnant and even falling in some cases; overmanning actually increased to the extent that by mid-1983 economists estimated that between 20 and 30% of the workforce of state enterprises was unnecessary (White, 1983a, pp.12, 147); the practice of job inheritance had spread (ibid., pp. 120, 130); the number of 'strategic' categories subject to central state 'unified allocation' had increased (ibid., p. 16). Clearly labour reform remained a pressing priority.

A second wave of reform, more deliberate than the first, began in early 1982, spearheaded by Premier Zhao Ziyang. The aim was to push forward elements of reform which had stalled and launch a frontal attack on the iron rice-bowl through the introduction of a labour contract system. I shall concentrate on the latter here, given its importance in increasing flexibility in labour circulation within the state sector. The contract system was designed to change the status of state workers, 97% of whom had previously enjoyed job security. Henceforth they would be employed on contracts of varying length, agreed between themselves and enterprise management and enforceable through new labour legislation. At the end of the contract, if job performance had been unsatisfactory or if the labour requirements of the enterprise had changed, the contract need not be renewed. Ideally, this system would improve productivity by concentrating the minds of the workers; it would give enterprise managers more flexibility in adjusting their labour force to changes in market demand and production process. The enterprise, labour service companies and local governments would each play a role in guaranteeing welfare benefits (sickness or injury pay, pensions, etc. which had formerly been the sole responsibility of the enterprise) and for redeploying and retraining redundant workers. Thus the state's role would become more 'parametric', with the key elements of labour allocation based on the relationships between enterprise and worker (see White, 1985, pp. 19–21).

This is a radical change in labour policy and is a political hot potato, a fact reflected in the cautious way in which the policy was introduced during 1983–5. By mid-1985, only a very small percentage of state workers were on contracts, mostly the new intakes of 1984 and 1985. There was little movement towards extending the principle to the established workforce. Interviews revealed that, though the Ministry of Labour was apparently committed to generalizing the contract system, as of mid-1985 there was still considerable disagreement among policy makers and their advisers about how to proceed (White, 1985). It was easier in sectors where the contract principle was already established and fitted specific job conditions (notably in mining and construction). Interviews and press reports suggest considerable scepticism and opposition, not only from academics such as Jiang Yiwei (1985) (then head of the Institute of Industrial Economics in the Chinese Academy of Social Sciences), from state industrial workers and their organizations (White, 1983a, p. 147) who could complain of a return to wage labour, but also from industrial managers who, like senior managers in a Shenyang woollen mill interviewed in 1983 (ibid., p. 120), or in Taiyuan Iron and Steel Company interviewed in 1985 (White, 1985, p. 32), felt that the system was inappropriate to specific conditions in their own factories.

Political constraints apart, however, successful introduction of the contract system requires local governments to improve their capacity to deal with frictional unemployment and establish complementary systems of social welfare, housing and education. While the contract system further reduces the direct role of the state in labour allocation, it also requires government to take on new functions (along welfare state lines) for which it is as yet ill prepared.

Economic conditions are also unfavourable for introducing the contract system. So long as there is a significant level of urban unemployment and the rewards for non-state employment remain inferior, state workers will resist the contract principle with vigour. Though official sources claimed to have brought the unemployment rate down to 2.6% by 1983, this was certainly an understatement. Pressures on the state workforce, moreover, do not stem merely from unemployment: many workers in the urban collective sector would dearly like a state job, even on a contract basis (because there is always the chance of converting it into a 'fixed' position); and outside and over the cities looms the problem of rural surplus labour, estimated at present to be about one-third of the rural workforce (or about 100 million people: White, 1985, pp. 2–4).

Thus for these powerful reasons it will be difficult to make headway in improving industrial performance by increasing labour circulation. In the state sector at least, it is unlikely that there will be any significant shift in the direction of labour markets in the near future: the principle of job tenure will be hard to budge, lateral mobility will increase slowly if at all and state labour bureaux will continue to dominate labour allocation. In the non-state urban sector, however, there is much more of a labour market with far greater freedom of entrance and exit, and lower job security. Thus the question of planning and market in labour allocation must be situated in this dualist economic structure, each sector operating according to different economic principles, not unlike the industrial structure of a capitalist economy such as Japan. If the rewards for work in the non-state sector increase (and there is some evidence that this is happening), this will not only reduce the demand for state jobs but will tempt state workers out into the informal sector, trading security for higher immediate incomes. On the other hand, the defensiveness of state workers may be reinforced if greater numbers of peasants are allowed into the cities (an increasing trend), adding a third tier to the dualist urban economy.

### Commodity Circulation and Price Policy

We can separate this topic into the two broad areas of commodity circulation and commodity exchange. Taking commodity circulation first, the previous system essentially had three components: (1) a centralized system of materials supply which planned and allocated basic raw materials and capital equipment to state enterprises; (2) the state commercial network which handled the wholesale and retail distribution of industrial goods; and (3) rural supply and marketing cooperatives (SMCs) which bought farm produce and supplied industrial goods to the countryside.

Reformers argued that this system had been monopolistic and cumbersome: the materials supply system was prone to the usual miscalculations of centralized directive planning; the state commercial system was an ineffective link between producers and consumers since it had insufficient outlets, was poorly managed, and operated along lines of distribution which followed administrative rather than economic logic (e.g. Wan Dianwu, 1983); and the SMCs, which were originally envisaged as providing a supplementary channel to state commerce, were cooperatives in name only, in fact being merely appendages of local commercial bureaux.

Reformers proposed several avenues of improvement. The materials supply system should be carefully deregulated, centralized allocation being retained only over a few strategic goods, others being handled by local authorities or marketed freely either by specialized agencies of the Bureau of Materials Allocation (BMA) or by producing units themselves. The degree of monopoly exercised by the state commercial system over the distribution of consumer goods was to be reduced and channels of commercial circulation made more rational (the principle was 'increase the channels and cut down the links'). These aims were to be achieved by encouraging the development of independent cooperative and private trading concerns, by allowing enterprises to market a portion of their output directly, and by organizing the flow of commodities according to natural marketing systems, bypassing the bureaucratic network of state wholesale stations (including the move towards city-based 'economic zones'). To improve their capacity to link changing patterns of supply and demand, state commercial enterprises and SMCs were to be granted more independence and put on a better business footing.

Turning now to commodity exchange, reformers argued that the previous commercial system failed either to create an effective link between production and sales or to reflect real conditions of supply and demand. They devoted particular attention to the irrationality of planned prices. In the sphere of production, the relationship between the price of a commodity and its costs of production was vague and prices failed to register differences in enterprise efficiency. In relations between state enterprises, prices played a 'passive' accounting role, reflecting 'planned' relationships between physical goods. In the sale of consumer goods, prices were inflexible, too often reflected non-economic considerations and were only seldom used to readjust patterns of production or demand.

Certain fundamental changes were required, argued reform economists. First, planned prices should be rationalized to relate them more closely to actual costs of production. Second, prices should be deregulated by decentralizing price administration from central to local agencies, reducing the range of goods subject to state price controls, and diversifying price forms, with a range from fixed to negotiated, floating and free market. Third, the state should use price policy more actively as an economic lever to regulate demand and supply. The central aim was to increase the allocative role of price, the main operating principle of market regulation. However, it was still assumed that the state would continue to fix prices for strategic producer and essential consumer goods and be responsible for maintaining overall price stability.

How have these proposed reforms fared? Taking *circulation* first, there was progress on several fronts. First, there were some (limited and uneven) changes in the system of materials supply. Commodities deemed in good supply (for example, in 1982–3, machinery and electrical equipment, certain steel products) have been to some extent deregulated (White, 1983a, p. 24). They are increasingly allocated through direct relations between producing and consuming enterprises or by special materials trading markets specializing in certain groups of products (such as the Shanghai Chemicals Materials Trading Market, see White, 1983a, pp. 87–93). Deregulation varies considerably across sectors: the First Ministry of Machine Building has been a pace-setter. Some factories (such as the Shanghai High Pressure Oil Pump Factory which I visited in 1983) (ibid., p. 58) now purchase most of their own materials. There has also been some progress towards decentralizing allocation, with more power going to local governments and greater use of specialized supply stations or shops. Barter trading between local governments also expanded formally (i.e. an undiscoverable proportion of it had existed before informally) with some provinces obtaining as much as 20% and some counties as much as 50% of their material needs through barter (ibid., pp. 25, 65–6).

In spite of this movement, however, the dominance of administrative allocation has been difficult to dent. The materials allocation bureaucracy was still enormous (Beijing officials estimated a total staff of 700,000 nationwide!) and, as one BMA official put it, 'some small commodities can be freed, but we really can't open up much' (ibid., p. 30). The central problem is that, as Kornai (1980a) has pointed out for Eastern European economies, the system of administrative allocation of producer goods operates according to a logic of shortage. As long as the basic system is unreformed, the amount of products in good supply will be relatively marginal. Though there has been a certain degree of organizational decentralization and a number of buyers' markets have emerged over recent years, the principle and practice of bureaucratic allocation and systemic scarcity still dominate. This in turn has hindered progress towards organizing the flow of materials along more rational, natural channels of circulation.

On the other hand, there has been more striking progress in improving circulation through management reforms and a diversification of channels in the state commercial system. In the past, state commercial agencies had usually been obliged to sell whatever factories produced, including goods of dubious quality and unsaleable lines. From 1979 on, they were able to exercise greater discretion in choosing factory products, reserving the right to reject unsatisfactory items. Within commercial units, though, 'responsibility systems' and productivity schemes helped improve efficiency to some degree but, as in the case of industrial enterprises, the overall impact of such measures was disappointing (see Wan Dianwu, 1983).

A much more effective impetus for greater efficiency was the increasing competitive pressure arising from a diversification of marketing outlets. Enterprises were allowed to market a portion of their output independently, they signed contracts with other enterprises, set up their own shops and advertised their own products. The overall level of self-marketed output had reached about 15% of total non-agricultural retail sales by 1983. But the levels of self-marketing vary greatly across regions (much higher in pace-setting cities such as Shanghai or Chongqing), across sectors (higher in consumer than producer goods sectors), across sub-sectors and individual enterprises within sectors and across products (varying according to their officially defined importance, categories 1, 2 or 3 being progressively more marketized). This is all at the formal level, of course; additional informal market procurement and sales may well be substantial.

There has also been a rapid expansion of cooperative and private commercial businesses in the cities. By the end of 1984, they were handling about half the country's total retail sales (urban and rural) (XH, 24 December 1984). Urban commerce has been enlivened by the spread of farm produce markets where peasants sell their produce in a (regulated) free market environment (such as the one in the north-eastern city of Shenyang, see White, 1983a, pp. 109–13). The benefits of this diversification have been considerable: stimulating agricultural and industrial production, speeding flows of circulation, raising levels of service in commerce, and meeting demands arising from the sharp increase in mass purchasing power over the past five years and thus reducing inflation. In spite of successive stop–go clampdowns by the authorities, therefore, the process is likely to continue at a steady pace. In Shanxi province, for example, it was planned, as of early 1983, to reduce the state share to 70% of wholesale and 60% of retail industrial and agricultural trade within three to five years; in the urban service and catering sectors, the state share was set to drop to 30% (Shanxi radio, 15 February 1983, *FBIS*, no. 35).

One major dimension of commercial reform, however, is still in an embryonic stage: the desire to redirect commercial flows, both state and non-state, from following the logic of administrative regions and departments to natural marketing zones based on principles familiar to economic geographers. While some progress has been made in breaking down barriers to inter-regional trade, the thrust towards central city-based economic regions is in its early stages. The pace-setters are Chongqing in the south-west and Shanghai (as the hub of the Lower Yangtze Region) in the east. While the process is as yet not far enough advanced to hazard a judgement, progress appears to have been slow and patchy so far, dogged by bureaucratic recalcitrance, local rivalries and poor policy coordination.

Turning now to questions of commodity exchange, movement on the price front has been fitful and slow. Planners have been unwilling to grasp the nettle of comprehensive reform of the official price parities of state industrial products, confining adjustments to a very few cases of (mainly) consumer goods. Moreover, limited attempts to deregulate prices (for example, in 1979–80 and 1985) have fuelled inflation and popular discontent, leading to administrative backlash. Fluctuations apart, however, there has been some limited movement towards granting greater power over price regulation to local authorities, and expanding the range of commodities allowed to circulate at non-fixed 'floating' or 'negotiated' prices, especially for less important consumer items (see White, 1983a, p. 41). In the producer goods sector, movement towards more flexible price forms has been more cautious. The main experimental unit has been the First Ministry of Machine Building which implemented a system of floating prices for certain types of machinery and electrical goods in early 1980. But this experience has apparently not been generalized.

Though there have been some attempts to use price policy to adjust supply and demand, these have not necessarily been thought through and the results have been ambiguous. The most important measure was a dramatic increase of 40% in agricultural procurement prices between 1978 and 1982, which served to stimulate agricultural production and, through higher peasant incomes, increase demand for industrial (especially consumer) goods. On the other hand, it raised an inflationary wave throughout the economy, which the authorities failed to foresee and found difficult to manage. Compared to this major change, other efforts to use price policy have been more incremental: for example, cutting the price of durable consumer items in oversupply (such as wristwatches) to clear stocks, reducing the price of synthetic in relation to cotton fibres to reflect changing cost conditions and increase demand for the former. Some price increases (such as cigarettes and wine) were purely for revenue purposes or to reduce inflation by soaking up excess purchasing power (for example, through injections of expensive imported consumer goods such as Japanese cassette-recorders, televisions or refrigerators). In general, however, price policy has been treated with caution like a loaded weapon and used sparingly.

To what extent do these changes in circulation and exchange contribute to 'marketization' of the Chinese urban–industrial economy? The answer is ambiguous and reflects a basic indecision in the Chinese conception of market regulation, between the market as a form of commodity circulation and as a method of regulating commodity exchange. In the first sense, the reforms have brought considerable movement by diversifying commercial channels, breaking down administrative barriers and promoting more direct contacts between producers and consumers. Even without significant price competition, the expansion and diversification of the commercial network has been economically and politically important in meeting rapidly rising consumer demands, exerting salutary pressures on the state commercial system and alleviating urban unemployment. Yet periods of dynamic commercial change (such as 1979–80) have tended to provoke official counter-measures; why is this?

In the second sense, the operation of prices as indices of changing conditions of supply and demand for industrial goods has in the event been marginal. But if scarcity prices are the essence of 'real' markets and the economic reforms, to be effective as a package, depend on a properly functioning price system, why has there been so little progress?

First of all, many officials in the party–state apparatus viewed expanding markets (in both senses) with alarm, as subversive forces which spread economic anarchy and social unrest and undermined the plan rather than complementing it. From one point of view, this perception reflects the competing interests of state and non-state economic sectors. Politocratic and bureaucratic interests showed through in various ways, partly through sheer inertia and red tape, partly through clashes between state commercial and service agencies which were being undercut or outperformed and partly through a generalized (and sometimes apparently pathological) organizational ideology, nurtured by millennia of bureaucratic dominance and anti-commercial ideology and by decades of directive planning, which defined social fluidity as indiscipline, economic autonomy as potentially subversive and sought to reimpose control before 'chaos' set in.

From another point of view, the conflicts which have emerged between state and commerce reflect the contradiction between the (still largely unreformed) operational logic of the previous system of planned circulation and exchange on the one hand, and of emerging real markets reflecting actual conditions of supply and demand on the other hand. The state wished to expand markets in industrial goods incrementally, without any significant attempt to free the terms on which they exchanged through price reform. But prices in the new channels of circulation (often in sellers' markets) clashed sharply with the official price system and, to the extent that industrial and commercial enterprises had more autonomy, they could use it to raise prices, formally or informally, directly or indirectly.

There were many manifestations of these tensions after 1978 as repressed real markets burst into the open. Enterprises and trading outlets expanded the frontiers of officially sanctioned negotiated and floating prices. Enterprises were often able to use oligopoly power, sometimes reinforced by local protectionism, to raise prices as a way to increase profits and bonuses. Even if nominal prices were not raised, moreover, real prices were increased by using inferior materials, adulteration or giving shorter measure. In one publicized case in Beijing, for example, a snack-bar had responded to increases in the price of pork by reducing the number of meatballs in their soup from 12–14 to 6–7, while keeping the price the same. There was also a good deal of arbitrage with traders taking advantage of price differentials between localities or between state fixed and free market prices.

Though sharp practices were no doubt widespread, the basic problem was that the state, for all its talk about the need for market regulation, could not manage real markets when they surfaced. There were of course problems which needed corrective action: the rush into profitable lines led to overproduction; enterprises concentrated on their self-marketed, floating price output, directing attention away from planned production tasks and reducing the quality of planned output. Evasion of price controls also fed the general rise in prices during 1979–81 and 1985, contributing to the economic and political problems of inflation to which the CCP has been extremely sensitive.

But the state's reaction cannot be analysed merely as a rational response to problems arising from reform policies; it reflects the conflicting interests and operational logics of state and non-state political economies, planning and market processes. Activities which reflected real patterns of supply and demand and which might, in other contexts, be perceived as normal market behaviour were thus defined as 'speculation', 'profiteering', 'extortion', 'economic criminality' and so on. The resultant policy cycle is depressingly familiar: extension of market freedoms in circulation and exchange; official complaints about economic chaos, illegality and excess, reinforced by public complaints about sharp practices; the reimposition of administrative controls; a stifling of markets which drives them underground, stimulates new forms of evasion and has a harmful effect on public morality; shortages created which lead to public unrest; a new attempt to liberalize and so on. One major cycle occurred between 1978 and 1981, the clampdown coming at the end of 1980. It looked as if another cycle was under way in 1985. The administrative backlash involves efforts to control price increases and limit the range of commodities targeted for deregulation; reimposition of rationing; controls over the content of advertising; mobilization of the population to supervise the activities of traders; tightening of the licensing arrangements for non-state trading enterprises; 'corralling' free markets (such as urban farm produce markets) within stout bureaucratic fences; police measures against 'smugglers', 'profiteers', and the like. But much of this bureaucratic furore was useless. Officials of price control teams complained that they went into shops or factories, lectured the miscreants who promised to be good in future but who reverted to their previous behaviour as soon as the team was out of sight.

A similar logic operated in the specific area of price policy; the big bugbear here was inflation. The existence of generalized shortages drives up the prices of extra-plan industrial commodities and, given the shallow effect of the reforms overall, the lack of effective competition between state industrial enterprises allows them to pass on price increases to the consumer with impunity. Market blockades between localities help to prevent the entry of competitively priced commodities from more efficient regions like Shanghai.

Though inflation posed economic headaches for the reformers, the main problem was political. The CCP had been helped to power in 1948 by hyperinflation under the Nationalist regime and had prided itself on maintaining price stability since then. The ability to control inflation, a phenomenon avowedly characteristic of capitalist economies, was one of the CCP's most significant claims to legitimate rule. The issue was thus very sensitive and when considerable urban discontent over prices emerged (for example, during 1980), the state reacted strongly with a battery of administrative controls.

Inflation thus provided an important political impetus to slow the pace of reform. It also helps to explain the Chinese authorities' reluctance to deregulate prices and use price policy as an economic lever. An even more basic problem, however, was the politicization of prices, an endemic feature of all state socialist societies. Xue Muqiao has pinpointed the problem well (1981, p. 146): '[prices] are a concentrated expression of the contradictions among different social groups which, in their own interests, wish to see certain products sold at prices higher or lower than their values'. Since price decisions can be directly traced to governmental action and not to the impersonal processes of a market, they are politically loaded. Thus the CCP has been very reluctant to tamper with prices, however economically irrational they might be. Consider this familiar policy cycle when price reforms, however marginal, are introduced: rumours about an impending price increase of commodity $x$; panic buying of $x$ which drains government stocks and drives up the price of $x$ on informal markets; the government either relents, deciding to postpone the increase (and subsidize the price of $x$ if contributing costs have risen), or goes ahead but attempts to cushion its impact through non-price subsidies to affected groups. Thus when agricultural procurement prices were raised after 1978, price rises were either not passed on to urban consumers or, where they were, a monthly supplement was paid to compensate urban wage earners. In the case of cotton textiles, for example, while the average procurement price of cotton rose by 50% between 1978 and 1982, the price of cotton textiles did not increase. The result was that, in some regions, the price of the finished product was lower than the cost of the raw material. Yet when the price of cotton textiles was adjusted in 1983, it was done with considerable preparation and caution, and sweetened by better prices for synthetic substitutes. Even then, the state paid subsidies to 50 million people living in poor rural areas in eight provinces who relied upon bought cotton textiles.

Public discontent is thus avoided at the cost of increasingly heavy burdens on the public purse. As of mid-1983, subsidies swallowed up about one-third of state budgetary expenditures (White, 1983a, p. 5). The government is thus caught in a vice between price paralysis on the one side and escalating subsidies on the other. For both economic and political reasons, this situation cannot be maintained; yet how to escape from it?

Clearly, if the logic of the reforms is to be pursued consistently and if reform policies are to achieve their desired effects across the board, comprehensive changes in commodity circulation and exchange are necessary and the nub of these is the price question. Steps must be taken to lay a rational basis for price policy, to establish an economically sensible foundation for setting official price parities and develop a capacity for flexible adjustment (notably through decentralization of price decisions to local governments and state enterprises); to clarify the respective spheres of operation of fixed, intermediate and free market prices and establish a complementary rather than contradictory relationship between them (the expansion of enterprise autonomy and the establishment of mutually beneficial relations between state and enterprises is crucial here); to find ways to manage the economic repercussions and reduce the political sensitivity of price decisions; and to draw up a programme of reform which coordinates price with other aspects of the reforms (financial, fiscal, wages and welfare).

The experience of China and other socialist countries (including Hungary) suggests that progress on the price front will be slow and uneven: the political costs are potentially high and the economic 'ripple' effects potentially unmanageable. The prospect for the short and medium term is that the Chinese government will continue to be reluctant to embark on any comprehensive price reform, will seek policies which are functional substitutes for price policy and are easier to implement (for example, through differential tax rates on enterprise revenues designed to counter profit distortions arising from irrational price disparities) and, to the extent that price reforms are introduced, the government will proceed with extreme caution, like infantry in a minefield (using basic level party organizations and economists as two different kinds of geiger counter), introducing changes in a relatively marginal and piecemeal fashion. This scenario does not augur well for the future of the economic reform programme as a whole.

## Conclusion

What is the future likely to hold for the relationship between planning and markets in China's urban–industrial economy? Though reforms have achieved considerable progress over the past years, their impact has been very uneven and, in overall terms, fairly superficial, in sharp contrast to the countryside. The mould of the bureaucratic command economy has yet to be broken. The scope of 'directive' plans has not contracted as much as reformers would have liked; though the importance of 'guidance' planning is strongly asserted, there is still little clarity about what this means in both theory and practice. The fundamental nature of the relationship between state and enterprise has changed little. Nor have market processes expanded as much as the reform blueprints of 1978–9 envisaged. Though the scope of markets varies across sectors, in general they have not taken on the full characteristics of competitive price systems and have not generated the salutary efficiency pressures and allocational benefits which reform analyses promised. Indeed, liberalization in a context of partial reforms (in which enterprise budgets are still soft) has proven to be a recipe for profligacy at the micro-level and overheating at the macro-level, imparting a stop-go, cyclical rhythm to the reform programme.

The process of moving towards a more productive relationship between state and economy and greater complementarity between plan and market is likely to prove more tortuous. While the experience of the post-Mao era has brought greater clarity about the analytical and practical problems of combining plans and markets, the constraints on reform have also become clearer. Efforts to implement reform policies have run into serious economic problems, notably budgetary deficits, inflation and over-investment. There has also been formidable political opposition from former supporters of radical Maoism and from entrenched interests both inside and outside the state apparatus. There has also been the familiar clash between 'efficiency goals' and 'socialist ethics' which Kornai has analysed for the Hungarian reforms (Kornai, 1980b). It is much to the credit of the Dengist leadership, however, that they have been willing to brave opposition and court unpopularity in their desire to carry the reforms forward.

Since both state and markets are matrices of differentiated interests, historically and structurally determined, a fundamental change in the state–economy relationship affects the balance of power between social groups. Thus, the problems in building a stable and productive relationship between the socialist state and markets are not merely technical or managerial; they may reflect a structural contradiction at the heart of state socialist political economy.

Indeed, the post-Mao reform era has highlighted one of the basic dilemmas of a socialist developmental state. The record of the 1960s and 1970s suggests the growing incapacity of the state institutions to direct the economy productively through the traditional mechanisms of political mobilization and bureaucratic control. To respond to escalating economic problems by strengthening traditional methods could only make matters worse. On the other hand, to embrace the reform programme fully would bring about such a radical shift in relations between state and society as to undermine the very basis of Leninist socialism. Thus the competitive view of the state–market relationship may well be vindicated.

## Notes

1. The author would like to thank the British Academy and the Chinese Academy of Social Sciences for their financial support and academic assistance which has been invaluable in carrying out the research on which this chapter is based.

2. This section on the reform critique is based heavily on analyses by the following authors: He Jianzhang, 1979; Jiang Yiwei, 1979, 1980; Liu Shinian, 1980; Liu Guoguang, 1980; Sun Xiaoliang, 1980; Ma Hong, 1981; Xue Muqiao, 1981.

3. *XH*, English service, 28 September 1983, in *SWB*, p. 7452. For a detailed analysis of this reform see Lu Baifu and Qian Zhongtao, 1984.

4. For a review of institutional changes in the banking system, see 'Banking reform favours centralisation', *BR*, vol. 27, no. 15 (9 April 1984), pp. 16–18.

5. For a discussion of interest rate policy, see Jiang Weijun, 1984.

6. *XH*, English, 13 December 1980.

# 2 Ideology and Industrialization in China 1949–83

## T. Pairault

In a country where ideology dictates every ordinary act and where developing the economy is more often than not synonymous with industrializing, analysis of the relationships between 'ideology' and 'economic development' is a vast field that we cannot hope to cover in its entirety in this chapter. We shall instead restrict our examination to the consequences for Chinese economic development of the application of the law of the priority growth of the producer goods department (department I)[1]. We shall first present this law and then set out its consequences.

## Birth and Survival of a Law

In Book II of *Capital*, Karl Marx analyses the processes of the simple and expanded reproduction of capital by attempting to show the process by which capital consumed during production is replaced. Marx divides the gross social product (in Chinese: *shehui zongchanzhi*) into the gross social product of department I (means of production) and the gross social product of department II (means of consumption); from his analysis he deduces functional relationships that must occur for the process to happen. His conclusion is that department I must grow more rapidly than department II.

Marxian analysis, elaborated for the capitalist economy, was taken up and developed by Lenin in a little work written in 1893 entitled *The So-called Market Question* and in his book *The Development of Capitalism in Russia* written between 1896 and 1899. Lenin's main contribution was to introduce into the initial Marxian pattern a new factor: technical progress. In Lenin's mind, if we refer to his work *Characterisation of Economic Romanticism*, written in 1897, it seems that the phenomenon of the priority growth of department I is characteristic of economic development in capitalism (Lenin, 1967, p. 28).

Despite its rudimentary character – and the fact that it is erroneous, as we shall see below – this model of economic development was enormously influential. No doubt because it implied a mode of extensive economic growth and promoted the formation of a basic economic infrastructure vital to development, this model was adopted by the USSR and the phenomenon of the priority growth of department I was erected by Stalin into an economic law[2] imposed on Soviet planners – and later on those of other socialist countries. The definitive formulation of this law was set out by Stalin in a text of 22 May 1952 concerning the *Errors of Comrade L. D. Yaroshenko*.[3]

In this article Yaroshenko is presented as one of the economists who had taken part in a conference organized in November 1951 to assess the draft *Textbook on Political Economy* of the USSR; the proceedings of this conference and thus the speech Yaroshenko is said to have made there were never published, nor indeed was a letter from Yaroshenko addressed to the Political Bureau of the CPSU on 20 March 1952.[4] Yaroshenko is said to have distinguished two types of social systems: pre-socialist systems and socialist systems. In the first type of system, the object of political economy is said to be the analysis of the relations of production, whereas in the second type its object is said to become the study of the productive forces with a view to optimizing their effectiveness through a better organization of the factors of production making it possible to obtain an abundance of products and, consequently, to move to communism. As the conclusion of his analysis Yaroshenko is said to have rejected the law of the priority growth of the producer goods department. Stalin presents his condemnation of this rejection and, in a supreme irony, accuses Yaroshenko of wanting to promote 'production for the sake of production', an aphorism by which Karl Marx[5] summarized precisely the essence of the priority growth of department I. And Mao Zedong, that eminent economist – who may have been Marxist but was certainly not Marxian, followed this by judging, in 1958, that Yaroshenko and some other economists 'do not enjoy [sic] economics'.[6]

As a result of the application of this law, Chinese planning – like Soviet planning before it – is still today mainly drawn up according to the 'ratchet principle': after postulating growth rates and taking into account a number of hierarchies, it simultaneously derives final output and the output essential to the material outlays of the various sectors of the economy. The logic of this procedure is to maximize output in order to maximise final consumption (of producer goods and secondarily of consumer goods). For some Chinese economists – and some Soviet ones too – this type of teleological planning, which consists in deriving from the planned targets for heavy industry – in particular for steel – those for light industry and then those for agriculture (a mode of planning called *zhong, qing, nong*: first heavy industry, then light industry, finally agriculture), leads to irrational choices in resource allocation. They argue in addition that it is possible to find a more coherent method of planning aiming no longer at maximizing final output but at optimizing it in the light of economic conditions and long-term goals; whence the proposals made by some Chinese economists as early as the mid-1950s.[7]

It took the unhappy experience of the Great Leap Forward and Mao Zedong's subsequent partial political eclipse for these economists, in opposition to Mao Zedong's 'voluntarism', to be able to impose a more 'pragmatic', even 'anti-Maoist', mode of planning, consisting in 'planning the national economy by defining successively the targets of agriculture, light industry and heavy industry' (*yi nong qing zhong wei xu, anpai guomin jingji de jihua*) (on Mao Zedong's attitude see Appendix 1). It should be noted that this new mode of planning, called *nong, qing, zhong* in contrast to the previous one, in no way rejects the law of the priority development of department I. As the slogan adopted by the Tenth Plenum of the

Eighth Congress in September 1962 stressed, 'take agriculture as the foundation and industry as the dominant factor' (*nongye wei jichu, gongye wei zhudao*).

The first part of this slogan means that planning must be done on the basis of the possibilities of agriculture then light industry then heavy industry and it is accepted that the growth rate of industry may depend in part on that of agriculture and that of department I in part on that of department II; however, and the purpose of the second part of this slogan is to recall it, this method of planning must not be interpreted as an abandonment of the priority growth of department I.

This policy was called into question, if not before, at the latest by the Cultural Revolution which gave rise to the New Flying Leap *xin fei yue*, (1968–73), which was itself followed by the New Leap Forward, *xin yue jin* (1975–78) (see Pairault, 1980, pp. 19–31).

Following the Third Plenum of the Eleventh Congress (December 1978) and in the climate of so-called liberalization that followed, a number of theoretical articles published in 1979 mainly in the journal *Jingi yanjiu* (*Economic Research*) attempted to reassess the law of the priority growth of department I. These criticisms were on two levels. On the mathematical level, they showed that this law is only confirmed because Marx, and later Lenin, postulated a number of technical constraints to define the mode of development of capitalist societies (constancy of the rate of accumulation of constant (fixed) capital in relation to surplus-value for Marx, constancy of the rate of investment of surplus-value in department I for Lenin). If there is nothing to justify these constraints, the appearance of a growth rate in department I higher than that in department II becomes one possibility among others. On the historical level they showed that, contrary to the assertions of Marx and Lenin, the capitalist countries did not make developing their heavy industry a priority nor had they even experienced a notable increase in the capital–labour ratio.[8]

This research concluded that rejection of the law of priority growth was the precondition for the abandonment of the dogmatic priority accorded to the development of heavy industry, whether this priority be absolute – the 'voluntarist' slogan of the Maoists, *zhong, qing, nong* – or relative – the 'pragmatic' slogan *nong, qing, zhong*. Consequently, in order to restore its purpose to socialist production, planning must no longer ignore everything to do with consumption and wages and must cease considering them as byproducts of the system of production. That is why these economists proposed planning based, not on a view of the economy divided into three departments (agriculture, light industry, heavy industry) of production arranged in a hierarchy that always favours the development of production for the sake of production, but on a forward looking view starting from the evolution of the population in order to derive its consumption and consequently the obligations of the productive departments. We should note that if this proposal signifies the abandonment of a socialist planning whose targets expressed social preferences transcending individual preferences in favour of a planning whose targets would express revealed individual preferences, then this proposal condemns itself: since planning would lose any normative aspect and ideology any justification. If it means the abandonment of a normative planning of maximum output in favour of a normative planning of optimal consumption, then would not this proposal reintroduce a metaphysical planning and, so to speak, what Mao is supposed to have claimed: better to be poor in a socialist country than rich in a capitalist one?

But in an editorial dated 20 October 1979 the *People's Daily* called these economists to order, and thus put an end to their heretical speculations, by reaffirming, invoking Stalin, the transcendence and universality of the priority growth of department I which must henceforth be respected through a 'pragmatic' mode of planning, *nong, qing, zhong*, that is defining planning targets in the order 'agriculture, light industry, heavy industry'.

Let us see, from an historical–economic viewpoint, how the application of this law in China worked. Table 2.1, Net Output and Regression Coefficients, shows that during the period 1953–80 the net output of heavy industry rose at an average annual rate of 11.6%, that of light industry at an average annual rate of 8.4% and that of agriculture at an average annual rate of 5.0%.

We have used the criterion of net output, *jing chanzhi*, in preference to that of gross output, *zong chanzhi*, since net output corresponds to the net value-added of each department (i.e. is equal to gross output less material outlays less depreciation of fixed capital). Consequently, using net output makes it possible to measure the effective contribution of each sector and its actual evolution avoiding the effects of double counting (for example in so far as it consumes industrial goods the gross output of the agricultural sector is increased by that much by including part of the value added of the industrial sector).

**Table 2.1**
**Net Output and Regression Coefficients**

| | Average annual growth rate (%) | | | Regression coefficient | |
| | Agriculture[a] | Light industry | Heavy industry | Industry/ Agriculture | Heavy industry/ Light industry |
|---|---|---|---|---|---|
| First Plan (1953–7) | 4.5 | 13.9 | 21.5 | 1.6 | 1.3 |
| Second Plan (1958–62) | 0.9 | 0.6 | 5.7 | 2.4 | 10.5 |
| Readjustment (1963–5) | 13.0 | 24.2 | 13.8 | 1.0 | 0.6 |
| Third Plan (1966–70) | 4.4 | 6.5 | 10.9 | 1.7 | 1.8 |
| Fourth Plan (1971–5) | 4.4 | 6.8 | 8.2 | 1.3 | 2.9 |
| Fifth Plan (1976–80) | 5.6 | 4.0 | 8.2 | 1.3 | 2.9 |
| | | | | | |
| *Average 1953–80* | 5.0 | 8.4 | 11.6 | 1.5 | 1.6 |

[a] Agriculture includes not only agriculture narrowly defined but also water and forests, stock-raising, meteorology, etc.

*Source:* Pairault (1983, p. 34).

If we use the criterion of gross output, we observe that by 1954–5 gross industrial output had already reached the level of gross agricultural output, whereas it was not until 1975, twenty years later, that the value added by industry equalled that added by agriculture. In other words, the criterion of gross output, unlike that of net output, exaggerates the effect of changes and tends to create the impression of a rate of industrialization that does not exist.

Table 2.1 also shows that on average between 1953 and 1980, when net agricultural output grows by one point, that of industry grows by a point and a half and, when net output of light industry grows by one point that of heavy industry grows by more than a point and a half. In other words, the law of the priority growth of department I has effectively been applied in China and has led to a mode of industrialization whose features we shall now try to analyse.

## The Law of the Priority Growth of Department I and Industrialization in China

A first logical consequence of the law of the priority growth of department I is that Gross Social Value Output (GSVO) grows faster than National Income (NI): in China for the period 1952–83 the GSVO grew at an annual average rate of 7.7% against 6.7% for NI (see Table 2.2, Gross Social Value Output, National Income and Capital–Labour Ratio).

In fact, if we stay with the theory and accept that technical progress leads to a faster growth of material outlays ($c$) than of the remuneration fund ($v$) in the GSVO, it is inevitable that ($c+v+m$), the GSVO,[9] should grow faster than ($v+m$), the NI. However, in the case of China, the reason might be different. We should observe that the ratio ($c/v+m$) almost doubles in thirty years on the one hand and that provision for depreciation has always been (much) too low on the other hand: these facts suggest that the increase in the ratio ($c/v+m$) may be due to a rise of material outlays as a result of a waste of resources. Two facts confirm this hypothesis.

First, the policy of small-scale industrialization certainly did not make for technical progress but, on the contrary, encouraged technological backwardness since the sums invested in outdated processes were diverted from investment in modernization. In 1979, small-scale steelworks produced 27% of Chinese pig iron. Because of the techniques used, these units consumed on average 400 tonnes of coke more per tonne of pig iron than modern units and this to produce grey pig iron, poorly adapted to the fabrication of modern steels; but production of these modern steels is the precondition of modernization in a country that bases its development strategy on the priority growth of its heavy industry. In other words, investments in small-scale industries perpetuated technical backwardness as well as a structure of supply of steel products comparable to that of Western countries on the eve of the First World War and, hence, hindered the modernization of this sector and thus that of China (Pairault, 1983a, pp. 89–110).

Second, for the period 1960–77 the ratio between the index of the GSVO at constant prices at time '$t$' and the index of the NI at constant prices at the same time '$t$' for the East European socialist countries reveal a tendency to a low level of inflation of the GSVO relative to the NI (on average 1.1) whereas that of China for a similar period (1957–80) is 1.5. Comparison does not of course prove anything; but it remains the case that a group of countries following the same strategy as China shows different results.

**Table 2.2**
**Gross Social Output, National Income and Capital–Labour Ratio**

| *Billions yuan* | *1952* | *1957* | *1965* | *1975* | *1980* | *1983* | *G* |
|---|---|---|---|---|---|---|---|
| Gross social value output ($c+v+m$) | 101.5 | 160.6 | 269.5 | 537.9 | 849.6 | 1105.2 | 7.7 |
| National income ($v+m$) | 58.9 | 90.8 | 138.7 | 250.3 | 368.8 | 467.3 | 6.7 |
| Material outlays ($c$) | 42.6 | 69.8 | 130.8 | 287.6 | 480.8 | 637.9 | 8.8 |
| Remuneration fund ($v$) | 47.7 | 70.2 | 98.2 | 162.1 | 252.1 | 331.1 | 6.2 |
| $c/v+m$ | 0.72 | 0.77 | 0.94 | 1.15 | 1.30 | 1.36 | |
| $c/v$ (capital–labour ratio) | 0.89 | 0.99 | 1.33 | 1.77 | 1.90 | 1.92 | |

$G$ = average annual rate of growth $m$ = net additional product.

*Source: SYB*, 1984, pp. 20–33.

A second logical consequence is the increase of the capital–labour ratio (the organic composition of capital, *ziben youji goucheng*, in Marxist terminology). In China this ratio appears to have almost doubled between 1957 and 1980 (see Table 2.2). This evolution is quite normal in a country which emphasizes capital investment. The American researcher Rawski notes the following phenomenon:

> The correlation between capital intensity and rapidity of growth is striking . . . all industries with above average capital intensity grow at above average rates, whereas sectors with relatively low capital intensity experience below average growth. As a result, structural change alone can be identified as an important cause of capital deepening within the industrial sector (1979, pp. 46–7).

The sectors where capital intensity is above average are precisely those in department I.

Let us analyse the consequences of this correlation using Domar and Harrod's formula: $g = s/k$ ($g$ is the growth rate, $s$ is the savings ratio – here the investment ratio – $k$ is the capital–output ratio).[10] Domar and Harrod's formula is used by the Chinese themselves and leads them to observe that the capital–output ratio is too high in China (*JJYJ* 7, 1980, pp. 16–17). In fact the Chinese do not use the expression capital–output ratio (which is a measure of the profitability of capital) but efficiency of accumulation (*jilei xiaoguo*), which amounts to the same thing. This difference of vocabulary arises because, in Marxist theory, capital does not itself create value; only labour does. The consequence is that the Chinese have always sought first to increase labour productivity through investments giving the highest labour productivity, whence the development of capital spending industries, which are essentially those in department I.

Domar and Harrod's formula teaches that if the planner, aiming at maximizing production, is confronted by a resistance on the part of the factors of production which prevents him reducing the capital–output ratio, accumulation will rise with the increase in the weight of the denominator in the equation. In other words, the law of the priority growth of department I has as a corollary a high rate of accumulation, and the higher the share of the production of department I devoted to department I the higher that rate of accumulation will be.

Table 2.3, Accumulation and Growth of National Income, does indeed show an increase, period by period, of the capital–output ratio (average for a period), from 2.8 for the First Five Year Plan to 4.0 for the Fifth Five Year Plan; an increase correlated with a high growth of the rate of accumulation. Table 2.3 gives a national level picture and does not take account of the productive or non-productive use made of accumulation. Table 2.4, ICOR and Industrial Enterprises, shows this ratio to be on a rising trend in those industrial state enterprises which are accounting units.

[a] $P$ = plan; [b] RA% = rate of accumulation as a % of National Income; [c] in billions of yuan; [d] trend before the launching of the readjustment policy.

*Sources:* Ma Hong, 1981, p. 727; *SYB*, 1981, p. 21 and author's calculations based on these data.

## Table 2.3
## Accumulation and the Growth of National Income

**First Plan**

|  | 1953 | 1954 | 1955 | 1956 | 1957 | *average* | *RA%*[a] | *average capital-output ratio* |
|---|---|---|---|---|---|---|---|---|
| Accumulation[b] | 16.8 | 19.5 | 18.5 | 21.7 | 23.3[c] | 20.0 | 24.2 | 2.8 |
| Growth of National Income[b] | 12.0 | 3.9 | 4.0 | 9.4 | 6.0 | 7.1 | | |

**Second Plan**

|  | 1958 | 1959 | 1960 | 1961 | 1962 | *average* | *RA%*[a] | *average capital-output ratio* |
|---|---|---|---|---|---|---|---|---|
| Accumulation | 37.9 | 55.8 | 50.1 | 19.5 | 9.9 | 34.6 | 30.8 | 11.5 |
| Growth of National Income | 21.0 | 10.4 | -2.0 | -22.4 | -7.2 | 3.0 | | |

**Readjustment**

|  | 1963 | 1964 | 1965 | *average* | *RA%*[a] | *average capital-output ratio* |
|---|---|---|---|---|---|---|
| Accumulation | 18.3 | 26.3 | 36.5 | 27.0 | 22.7 | 1.7 |
| Growth of National Income | 7.6 | 16.6 | 22.1 | 15.4 | | |

**Third Plan**

|  | 1966 | 1967 | 1968 | 1969 | 1970 | *average* | *RA%*[a] | *average capital-output ratio* |
|---|---|---|---|---|---|---|---|---|
| Accumulation | 47.0 | 30.4 | 29.8 | 35.7 | 61.8 | 40.9 | 26.3 | 3.7 |
| Growth of National Income | 19.9 | -9.9 | -7.2 | 20.2 | 30.9 | 10.8 | | |

**Fourth Plan**

|  | 1971 | 1972 | 1973 | 1974 | 1975 | *average* | *RA%*[a] | *average capital-output ratio* |
|---|---|---|---|---|---|---|---|---|
| Accumulation | 68.4 | 64.8 | 74.1 | 74.1 | 83.0 | 72.9 | 33.0 | 4.3 |
| Growth of National Income | 15.6 | 5.8 | 18.6 | 25.0 | 15.4 | 16.8 | | |

**Fifth Plan**

|  | 1976 | 1977 | 1978 | 1979 | 1980 | *average* | *RA%*[a] | *average capital-output ratio* |
|---|---|---|---|---|---|---|---|---|
| Accumulation | 75.6 | 83.2 | 108.3 | 116.1 | 116.4 | 99.9 | 33.4 | 4.0 (5.3)[x] |
| Growth of National Income | -7.0 | 22.4 | 35.2 | 38.1 | 36.8 | 25.1 | | |

[a] RA% = rate of accumulation as a % of National Income: [b] in billions of yuan: [c] trend before launching of the readjustment policy.

*Sources:* Ma Hong, 1981, p. 727; *SYB*, 1981, p. 21 and author's calculations based on these data.

Table 2.4
ICOR (Incremental Capital Output Ratio) and Industrial Enterprises
(in billions of yuan)

|  | 1952 | 1957 | 1965 | 1975 | 1978 | 1979 | 1980 | 1981 | 1982 | 1983 |
|---|---|---|---|---|---|---|---|---|---|---|
| Fixed capital | 14.9 | 33.7 | 104.0 | 242.8 | 319.3 | 346.7 | 373.0 | 403.2 | 437.5 | 476.7 |
| Net income | 3.7 | 11.5 | 30.9 | 58.2 | 79.1 | 86.4 | 90.7 | 92.3 | 97.2 | 97.2 |

*Sources: JJNJ*, 1981, p. VI–18; 1982, p. VIII–22; 1983, p. III–24; *SYB*, 1984, p. 262.

Trend of the ICOR: let $K$ = fixed capital, let $R$ = net income (profits and taxes) and the production function will be defined by $R = aK^B$ from which the first derivative is $R^1 = dR/dK = ßaK^{B-1}$. The ICOR $k$ will thus be equal to $dK/dR$ or $1/R^1$.

Our calculations give the following formula:

$$R = 0.35K^{0.94}$$

The ICOR will be defined by the following formula:

$$k = 1/0.33K^{-0.06}$$

According to this formula the ICOR would be equal to $k_{52} = 3.5$ for 1952 and $k_{83} = 4.4$ for 1983, whence a rising trend of the ICOR between 1952 and 1983.

To return to Domar and Harrod's formula, during the two quinquennia 1971 to 1980, National Income increased at an average annual rate of 6.9% and the average ICOR for this period was 4.15. In other words, it should only have taken an accumulation rate of 28.6% of National Income to guarantee the realization of the growth rate observed; but the effective accumulation rate was on average 33.2% of National Income during this period. There was thus over-investment.

The strategy of growth induced by the dogma of the priority growth of department I pushes the planner to set a high growth rate. Since the objective is to maximize output, he associates it with a level of investment (accumulation rate) that is all the higher because it aims at the development of heavy industry where, precisely, the ICOR is highest. But there is not necessarily any consistency between a plan of finances derived in this way and the material resources available (raw materials, equipment, etc.); so an excess of demand for producers' goods will appear (as a result of the investment plan) compared to the supply of these same goods, and this will be for reasons both of absolute quantity (volume of output too low) and of relative quantity (quality too poor).

Let us take the example of laminated products. Since 1949, imports of laminated products have constantly increased, but never been able to meet demand. From 1953 to 1962, annual imports were on average 800,000 tonnes, then from 1966 to 1970 they rose to two million tonnes a year on average and later reached an average of four million tonnes a year between 1971 and 1975, six million tonnes between 1976 and 1980, seven million tonnes in 1981, 3.7 million tonnes in 1982, and 9.6 million tonnes in 1983.

While these massive imports are at first sight a sign of serious under-production, they in fact conceal a very serious crisis of unsuitable over-production: at the end of 1982, there existed in China stocks of 18 million tonnes of unsold and unsaleable laminated goods (equal to 70% of recent annual output and after having reached fifteen months of production); this was so despite cheap sales authorized under the policy of readjustment.[11]

It will therefore be difficult to achieve the programmes envisaged and launched under the plan. Considerable resources are thus frozen for an uncertain period and the installation of new production capacities will take longer and longer. The sums locked up, for failure to implement projects, were equal on average to 63% of annual investment during the First Five Year Plan; this figure rose to 175% during the Third Five Year Plan, then fell to 165% during the Fourth Five Year Plan rising again to 210% for the years 1976 and 1977 (*JJYJ* I, 1982, p. 49). The average time of execution of large and medium-sized projects rose from 6.5 years during the First Plan to 13.2 during the Fifth Plan (*JJYJ* I, 1982, p. 39). This situation was aggravated by the use for investment of frozen funds.[12] In addition, since in order to ensure the construction of new units, the replacement and modernization of the equipment of existing units is neglected, the productivity of capital cannot but decrease (see Table 2.5, Capital Productivity). Let us return once again to Domar and Harrod's formula. We have seen that, being required to set high rates for the growth of National Income, the planner is obliged through the raising of the ICOR to impose rates of accumulation that are higher and higher. But, consumption being the difference between National Income and accumulation, the higher the rate of accumulation is, the weaker the rate of consumption. In a country where the population is growing at a steady rate, heavy levies in favour of accumulation strengthen inflationary tensions. These show themselves less in price rises, although today there is a certain degree of open inflation resulting from both the disorganization of the economy and the rises decided by the government and those following the enlargement of the free market. They are seen more in the length of the queues at shops which are soon sold out, the general fall in the quality of goods and a general increase in the volume of savings.

**Table 2.5**
**Capital Productivity (%)[a]**

| 1957 | 1961 | 1965 | 1966 | 1975 | 1976 | 1978 | 1979 | 1980 | 1981 | 1982 | 1983 |
|------|------|------|------|------|------|------|------|------|------|------|------|
| 23.6 | 10.3 | 20.9 | 24.2 | 15.0 | 12.2 | 15.9 | 16.2 | 15.7 | 14.4 | 13.7 | 13.4 |

[a] For state industrial enterprises that are accounting units. The criterion used is the ratio of profit (attributable to management, unlike taxes) to fixed capital (original value).

*Sources: JJNJ*, 1981, p. VI–18; 1983 p. III–24;
Shigeru Ishikawa, 1983, 258; *SYB*, 1984, p. 262.

Statistics on savings in the form of bank deposits (hence excluding cash holdings) exist for China. However, in these bank savings it is difficult to distinguish between desired savings (savings with a view to a definite but deferred consumption) and forced savings (the fraction of income that it is impossible to consume for lack of products satisfying the desire to consume). It is these forced savings that would be the most suitable measure of suppressed consumption resulting from high rates of accumulation.

Table 2.6 and Fig 2.1 illustrate this phenomenon. In this table and figure two periods can be distinguished, one 1970–78 and the other 1978–83.

Between 1970 and 1978 we observe a slight rise in consumption as well as a parallel increase in the pressure on consumption, while total deposits rose from index 100 in 1970 to index 200.8 in 1978. What happened during that period?

Table 2.6
Pressure on Consumption (non-peasant; index: 1970 = 100)

| | 1971 | 1972 | 1973 | 1974 | 1975 | 1976 | 1977 | 1978 | 1979 | 1980 | 1981 | 1982 | 1983 |
|---|---|---|---|---|---|---|---|---|---|---|---|---|---|
| Accumulation (non-peasant workers) | 110.6 | 104.8 | 119.9 | 119.9 | 134.3 | 121.0 | 134.6 | 175.9 | 187.8 | 188.5 | 178.9 | 200.0 | 229.7 |
| Personal consumption | 102.8 | 113.0 | 117.2 | 119.5 | 123.2 | 128.7 | 132.9 | 140.0 | 145.9 | 156.6 | 158.8 | 160.0 | 164.0 |
| Personal savings | 111.4 | 127.4 | 137.1 | 151.7 | 159.8 | 167.2 | 181.2 | 200.8 | 244.9 | 330.1 | 392.6 | 472.8 | 530.7 |
| Pressure[a] | 104.6 | 107.8 | 114.9 | 122.9 | 127.9 | 129.7 | 136.7 | 142.4 | 165.1 | 193.9 | 231.2 | 271.9 | 329.9 |

[a] The index of the pressure on consumption is the ratio of personal savings to personal income.   *Source: SYB*, 1984, pp. 32, 81, 401, 403, 425, 426, 454, 459, 482.

We should first observe that between 1952 and 1978 potential demand in China went up 4.7 times while the supply of consumer goods went up only 4.5 times. The inflationary gap appears to be weak (0.2); it nevertheless suggests a tendency to the underdevelopment in the volume – let us ignore here the fall in quality – of the supply of consumer goods. More precisely, for the period we are dealing with, we shall note that in 1972 total demand increased by seven billion yuan compared to 1971 whereas the supply of consumer goods increased by only three billion yuan, an inflationary gap of four billion yuan; similarly in 1974 potential demand increased by 4.7 billion whereas supply increased by only two billion, an inflationary gap of 2.7 billion yuan; similarly in 1976 demand increased by 5.3 billion yuan whereas supply decreased by one billion, an inflationary gap of 6.3 billion. We may thus conclude that during the period 1970–77 the increase in the volume of savings resulted in large part from a shortfall in supply compared to demand and, therefore, that the savings of employees' and workers' households were essentially forced savings (Liu Guoguang, 1981, pp.276–96). The existence of an inflationary gap continued until 1982, when there appeared for the first time in a long time an equality *in value* between total potential demand and total supply; since however the structure of supply has scarcely altered, a hidden inflationary gap continued to exist, although it is difficult to put into figures.[13]

From 1978 to 1983 there was some progress in the consumption level of city dwellers following the realignment of salaries decided first in 1977 and a second time in 1979; in fact the improvement in the purchasing power of employees and workers was expressed in a very strong surge of savings: in 1983, the average propensity to save of city dwellers was 0.24 (savings/income, i.e. 12.5 billion yuan/52.3 billion yuan) and the marginal propensity to save 1.4 (growth of savings/growth of income from 1982 to 1983, i.e. 3.2 billion yuan/2.3 billion yuan). In other words, city dwellers saved a quarter of their incomes and devoted an amount equal to 140% of the increase in their incomes to increase the volume of their savings.

From 1978 to 1982 overall potential demand for consumer goods increased by over 140 billion yuan, but only 52.4% of this sum was devoted to the purchase of consumer goods, while 33.1% was deposited in banks and 14.5% was used to build up cash holdings. In addition the amount of consumer goods unsold during this period reached about 11% of the stocks of commercial services (*CMJJ* 5, 1983, p. 47).

To what extent does this phenomenon demonstrate the existence of forced saving? In Shanghai, between 1978 and 1982, the amount of bank deposits more than doubled and 95.8% of these deposits were term deposits whose average length rose from 356 days in 1979 to 416 days in 1982. In addition, two surveys carried out among five hundred urban households revealed that between 1981 and 1982 these households' income rose by 3.5% but their consumption diminished by 1.5% while their savings (deposits and cash) increased by 59% (Shanghai, 1983, pp. 826, 1268).

Another survey of a hundred depositors in the city of Chengdu in Sichuan reveals the purpose of their deposits: 10.71% of the deposits constitute savings with a view to short-term deferred consumption (less than a year: for example expenses in

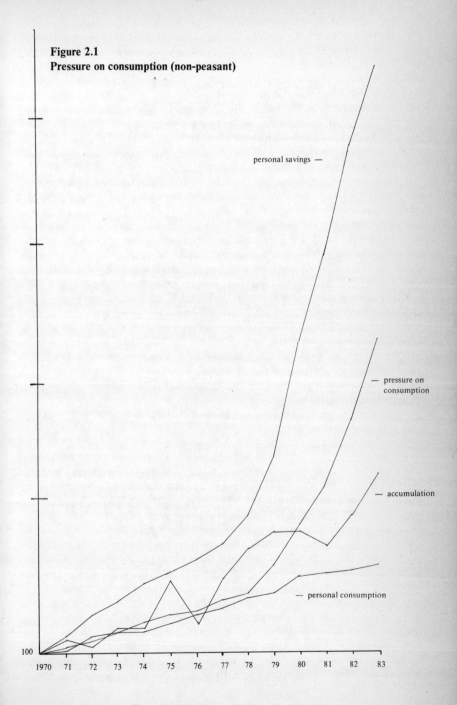

**Figure 2.1**
**Pressure on consumption (non-peasant)**

personal savings —

— pressure on
consumption

— accumulation

— personal consumption

100

1970  71  72  73  74  75  76  77  78  79  80  81  82  83

connection with the Chinese New Year, etc.); 49.20% of the deposits constitute savings with a view to long-term deferred consumption (purchase of consumer durables, children's clothes, etc.); 14.42% of deposits constitute nest eggs made necessary by the small amounts granted by the sickness and old age insurance systems; 25.67% of the deposits had no definite purpose (*CMJJ* 11, 1983, p. 24). We can conclude from reading these figures that forced savings in the narrowest sense, and not taking into account cash holdings, are equal to about 26% of bank deposits; to this we can add money set aside for sickness and old age if we consider that it results from an inadequate supply of social services compared to actual demand. On this hypothesis the forced savings would be equal to more than 40% of bank deposits (again not including cash holdings).

If we use this last figure for illustrative purposes, we can calculate that the cumulative total of forced savings, in other words unsatisfied demand, was 35.7 billion yuan, at the end of 1983, or a sum equal to about 16.5% of the supply of personal consumer goods during 1982[14] – again not including cash holdings.

The fact is that it is not by reducing the accumulation rate that the Chinese leaders will overcome the structural imbalances in their economy since such a reduction, provoking an increase in the rate of consumption of National Income, would only fuel inflationary tendencies without satisfying the population's needs for consumer goods; on the contrary, the unsatisfied demand would grow and the resulting extra bank deposits might lead the banks to convert these deposits into investments outside the plan,[15] something that would work against the planned reduction of the accumulation rate.

Nor is it by favouring the production of consumer goods without first transforming the structure of supply of these goods (in quantity and *quality*) that the forced savings, a real sword of Damocles hanging over them, will find outlets satisfying the consumers.

Thus the Chinese leaders have no choice. They have to pursue a policy of high rates of accumulation in order to

1) Maintain pressure on consumption. We should remember that the rate of accumulation, which was on average 33.4% of National Income during the Fifth Five Year Plan, was planned to stay at a still high average level of 29% during the Sixth Five Year Plan (1981–85). This is still far short of the magic figure of 25% that was the object of the reformist incantations of the years 1979–80.

2) Stabilize 'forced' saving through the granting of higher interest rates the longer the term of the deposits. Since 1979, interest rates have been raised four times: in 1979, 1980, 1981 and 1983. These rates vary from 2.9% a year for immediate deposits, to 10.4% a year for eight-year deposits (*Guowuyuan*, 27, 1982, p. 895). At the end of 1983, term deposits (more than six months) represented about 80% of deposits as against 77% in 1982; however, the amount of deposits for terms of more than three years has diminished precisely because depositors have the hope of being able rapidly to acquire goods that are currently unavailable on the market (*JJNJ*, 1983, pp. III–192, III–94).

3) Modify the ratio of so-called productive investment to so-called unproductive investment.[16] The distribution between these two types of investment shifted from

80/20 in 1978 to 55/45 in 1982. This shift especially benefited property construction whose share rose from 8% to 25%; however bottlenecks are appearing: whereas investment in this sector has risen by 260%, output has only risen by 34% – another source of forced savings (*JJNJ*, 1983, pp. III–17, III–30).

4) Modernize existing production units. This is a matter of diverting a portion of the amount of investment in the construction of new production capacities towards the re-equipment of production capacities already in service. In the framework of the state sector, the Sixth Plan allocated a third of planned investment to such modernization. However, here again we observe bottlenecks. The machine building industries particularly affected by this policy saw their output stabilize overall between 1978 and 1982, declining and then rising slightly again in 1982 for machinery and equipment intended for industrial use, and declining significantly, until 1981, for railway machinery and equipment, which is supposed to be one of the priorities of the Sixth Plan.

In fact, today the Chinese are questioning the purely extensive aspect of this development strategy, still centred on heavy industry. Alongside a model of extensive growth, they are putting in place the following elements:

1) An intensive growth through modernization. The consequences of this intensification should be: a) to increase the productivity of capital and so make possible a reduction in the ICOR and allow higher growth rates of National Income at unchanged accumulation rates; b) to increase the capital–labour ratio, an increase which is the corollary, as we have noted, of the law of the priority development of department I.

2) A lateral growth through pushing back the limits within which investment is carried out. Here the object of investment is not to increase productive capital in proportion to the labour force directly, but to accommodate growth by meeting individual (clothing and household durables) and collective (housing, health and education) consumption needs. But then is not the characteristic of any investment to open up new outlets for the means of production sector and hence to strengthen its growth potential?

A year and a half after writing most of this chapter, it would appear that the situation has not fundamentally changed, despite the appearance of new tendencies resulting from the reforms. Available data on rates of accumulation and rates of growth in the different sectors – agriculture, light and heavy industry – show how fixed are the structures I have described. Yet, if the CCP and central government hope to maintain effective control over the direction of investment they will have to take cognizance of the important increase in the funds invested outside the state sector, be they private or merely exclusive. In 1984 these funds came to 35.3% of total investment. Within this new development can be seen a new hope for China discreetly, which is to say without a serious political or ideological crisis, to combat a Stalinist dogma which, despite its official standing, will then fall unofficially into abeyance.

# Appendix I

## Mao Zedong and the Strengthening of the Law of the Priority Growth of Department I

The divergences, if any, between Stalin and Mao Zedong do not bear on the existence of the law of priority growth but rather on its role in the evolution towards communism. Stalin considers this law as the principle of social change, whereas Mao Zedong sees in it only a planning tool and reserves for 'politics placed in command' the role of the principle of social change. This postulate has as a corollary that 'First the production relations have to be changed, then and only then the productive forces can be broadly developed', which is precisely made possible by having politics in command (Mao Zedong, 1977, pp. 93, 58).

This contribution by Mao Zedong to the evolution of Marxist thought proves to be very important since Mao Zedong saw in it the means of resolving a contradiction in the evolution of China. The law has as a corollary that the growth rate of department II (consumer goods) is a function of the growth rate of department I (capital goods) fixed by the planners and, consequently, that the growth rate of agriculture is a function of that of industry; in other words the rate of accumulation in the economy is a function of the planned growth rate of department I. It is this logic that Mao Zedong expressed in his speech of 11 October 1955 by saying that 'the general task for the transitional period demands that agriculture adapts to industry',[17] a demand which could only be satisfied through a rapid development of the agricultural sector which had just experienced two consecutive years of poor harvests (1953 and 1954).

At the time of this speech, the vast majority of peasants were working in the framework of non-socialist structures which ensured them sufficient decision-making autonomy with regard to the central government to be able to refuse to deliver their grains to the state (Mao Zedong, 1977, p. 212), and Mao Zedong writes elsewhere:

> the policy of 'unified purchase and sale of private output' could not have been persevered in. The reason is that that policy could be maintained and made to work thoroughly only on the basis of cooperativization [meaning the socialist cooperatives – author] (Mao Zedong, 1977, p. 46).

Mao Zedong realized very clearly that if the supply of agricultural goods were insufficient to absorb the supply of industrial goods, agriculture would determine industrial growth and, consequently, the growth rate of department I, whence the need for an alliance with the peasants. Similarly, he understood very clearly that, if the supply of industrial goods were too low to meet the supply of agricultural goods, the peasants would prefer to increase their subsistence consumption – whence the need for a temporary alliance with the industrial bourgeoisie (Mao Zedong, 1977, pp. 196–201). In such a conjuncture, the growth rate of department I constantly risks being a function of that of department II and more precisely of that of the agricultural sector.

If we stay with classical Marxist theory, this situation cannot change so long as the productive forces have not attained a sufficient degree of development to necessitate a change in the relations of production: tractors precede collectivization, to use an image dear to Mao Zedong. Conversely, Mao Zedong's theory, by reversing the order of the propositions, allows an immediate move to the higher system which, suppressing the autonomy of the peasants and subjecting them rigidly to the directives of the plan, should make possible the proper functioning of the law and thus guarantee that the growth rate in agriculture is a function of that in industry, and that in department II a function of that in department I; in other words, planning that takes into account first heavy industry, then light industry and finally agriculture. Such was the purpose of Mao Zedong's imposition of first socialist cooperatives and then people's communes which are no more than social structures of agricultural production deemed to be more efficient in achieving maximum accumulation with a view to accelerated industrialization. According to Mao Zedong, some comrades 'consider the present rate of the development of industry to be adequate, they consider that it is not necessary that industrialization go hand in hand with agricultural cooperation which can get along with a particularly slow rate'. That, he continued, was to forget that 'the industrialization of China [demands] enormous sums, and a very large part of these can only come from the agricultural sector'. There follows a plea for accelerated collectivization. (Mao Zedong, 1977, pp. 181–3).

Mao Zedong's analysis, in one and the same breath, permits a definition of ambitious targets and high accumulation rates – over 30% of national income, he specifies (Mao Zedong, 1977, p. 96) – and, hence, legitimates 'a simultaneous development of agriculture and industry on the basis of the priority development of heavy industry', makes it possible to deny any regulatory role, even any role at all, to the law of value[18] and, lastly, above all, does so without undermining the principle of planning: heavy industry first, then light industry, finally agriculture postulated by the Stalinist exegesis of the law. In other words, by his theoretical contribution, Mao Zedong justifies Stalinist dogmatism and encourages its 'voluntarist' side.[19]

# Appendix 2

## An Example of the Non-Dogmatic Proof of the Law of the Priority Development of Department I

In 1956, a work by Xiao Daiyun made the following four points:

### Definition of the Growth Rate of Industry
The growth rate of industry must depend on objective factors and not on political factors (an allusion to the 'voluntarism' that led Mao Zedong to launch the small 'leap forward' of 1956).

### Priority Development of Department I (Producer Goods).
The author comes down in favour of such a priority not for 'orthodox' theoretical reasons but for reasons of: a) economic strategy – in an underdeveloped country, this priority growth is necessary to build up an industrial base; b) international strategy – political independence presupposes economic independence.

### Relations between Department I (Capital Goods) and Department II (Consumer Goods)
Economic development demands a strong growth of department I, but rapid population growth demands a strong growth of department II. What therefore is needed is to find growth rates for each of these two sectors such that they take account of objective constraints and ensure a balance in the distribution of resources (relative character of the priority).

In a poor country, the demand for consumer goods is low; in addition in a country with a subsistence agricultural economy, the share of marketable agricultural output is necessarily small. For these reasons, the growth rate of department II cannot but be lower than that of department I.

### Relations Between Industry and Agriculture
The growth of agricultural output is low. The development of the agricultural sector, thanks to the development of the industrial sector, will enable the marketing of agricultural products to grow. The growth rate of marketed agricultural output will be higher than the growth rate of global agricultural output; but the growth of industry is a function on the one hand of the marketed agricultural output and, on the other, of the manufacture of the means of industrial production: the growth rate of industry will necessarily be higher than that of agriculture, but not necessarily much higher.

# Appendix 3

## Statistical Aspects of Industrialization

**Table 2.7**
**Accumulation and Investment in Three Major Branches (in %)**

|  | Rate of Accumulation | Agriculture[a] | Light industry | Heavy industry | of which metallurgy | Heavy industry/ light industry & agriculture[b] |
|---|---|---|---|---|---|---|
| First plan (1953–7) | 24.2 | 7.1 | 6.4 | 36.1 | 10.5 | 268 |
| Second plan (1958–62) | 30.8 | 11.3 | 6.4 | 54.0 | 14.8 | 307 |
| 1963–5 | 22.7 | 17.7 | 3.9 | 45.9 | 9.3 | 213 |
| Third plan (1966–70) | 26.3 | 10.7 | 4.4 | 51.1 | 11.8 | 339 |
| Fourth plan (1971–5) | 33.0 | 9.8 | 5.8 | 49.6 | 10.6 | 317 |
| Fifth plan (1976–80) | 33.4 | 10.5 | 6.7 | 45.9 | 9.3 | 267 |
| Sixth plan (1981–5) |  |  |  |  |  |  |
| – 1981 | 28.5 | 6.6 | 9.8 | 39.0 | — | 238 |
| – 1982 | 29.0 | 6.1 | 8.4 | 38.5 | — | 266 |
| *Growth 1982/1981* |  | *+16.8* | *+7.1* | *+24.1* |  |  |

a By agriculture must be understood water and forests and meteorology as well as agriculture;
b this column gives the ratio between the amount of investment in heavy industry and the amount of the sum of investment in light industry plus agriculture (defined as above) in %.

NB: for a given period the total of the columns agriculture, light industry and heavy industry is not equal to 100 as the Chinese distinguish other sectors.

*Sources:* Pairault, 1983, pp. 33–37; *SYB*, 1982; *JJNJ*, 1983.

Table 2.8
Working Population and Net Output of Three Major Branches (in %)[a]

| | 1949 | 1952 | 1957 | 1962 | 1965 | 1970 | 1975 | 1978 | 1979 |
|---|---|---|---|---|---|---|---|---|---|
| Working population | | | | | | | | | |
| – agriculture | — | 93.3 | 93.2 | 92.6 | 92.8 | 90.8 | 87.3 | 85.5 | 84.9 |
| – light industry | — | 4.7 | 4.1 | 3.4 | 3.4 | 3.8 | 4.9 | 5.3 | — |
| – heavy industry | — | 2.0 | 2.7 | 4.0 | 3.8 | 5.4 | 7.8 | 9.2 | — |
| Net output[a] | | | | | | | | | |
| – agriculture | 84.5 | 74.7 | 62.3 | 59.5 | 55.9 | 50.7 | 47.0 | — | 45.9 |
| – light industry | 11.0 | 14.5 | 18.6 | 17.5 | 21.9 | 22.0 | 22.9 | — | 20.7 |
| – heavy industry | 4.5 | 10.8 | 19.1 | 23.0 | 22.2 | 27.3 | 30.1 | — | 33.4 |

[a] It is the much more significant figure of net output, in fact the added value of each sector, that is given here; the publication of these figures is exceptional since the Chinese usually give those of gross output which, since they do not take account of double counting, give a distorted picture of the contribution of each sector.

NB: the totals for each period of the working population, on the one hand, and net output on the other, are equal to 100: the other sectors have been excluded from the breakdown in order to grasp more clearly the relative importance and evolution of each of the three sectors in relation to one another.

**Table 2.9**
**National Income and Net Output (in %)**

| *Average annual growth rate of* | *National income* | *Agriculture*[a] | *Light industry* | *Heavy industry* |
|---|---|---|---|---|
| First plan (1953–7) | 8.9 | 3.8 | 16.0 | 24.0 |
| Second plan (1958–62) | –3.1 | –5.9 | –2.0 | 3.0 |
| 1963–5 | 14.5 | 11.5 | 27.0 | 17.0 |
| Third plan (1966–70) | 8.4 | 3.0 | 10.0 | 14.0 |
| Fourth plan (1971–5) | 5.6 | 3.5 | 7.5 | 9.0 |
| Fifth plan (1976–80) | 8.0 | 3.3[b] | 4.0[b] | 10.0[b] |
| *Average 1953–80* | 6.0 | 2.5[c] | 9.5[c] | 13.0[c] |

[a] see Table 2.7 for the definition of agriculture; [b] for the first four years; [c] for 1953–79.

**Table 2.10**
**Composition of Gross Industrial Output Value by Major Branch of Industry (in %)**

| Industry | 1952 | 1957 | 1965 | 1975 | 1978 | 1979 | 1980 | 1981 | 1982 |
|---|---|---|---|---|---|---|---|---|---|
| Metallurgical | 5.9 | 8.5 | 10.7 | 9.0 | 8.7 | 8.9 | 8.6 | 8.8 | 8.7 |
| Power | 1.3 | 1.7 | 3.1 | 3.9 | 3.8 | 3.8 | 3.8 | 3.8 | 3.7 |
| Coal | 2.4 | 2.9 | 2.6 | 2.8 | 2.8 | 2.6 | 2.3 | 3.0 | 3.0 |
| Petroleum | 0.5 | 1.1 | 3.2 | 5.6 | 5.5 | 5.4 | 5.1 | 5.4 | 5.2 |
| Chemical | 4.8 | 6.8 | 12.9 | 11.3 | 12.4 | 12.2 | 12.5 | 11.4 | 11.8 |
| Machine building | 11.4 | 16.9 | 22.3 | 27.7 | 27.3 | 27.1 | 25.5 | 20.9 | 22.0 |
| Building material | 3.0 | 3.2 | 2.8 | 3.1 | 3.6 | 3.6 | 3.6 | 3.8 | 4.0 |
| Forest | 6.5 | 5.8 | 2.9 | 1.9 | 1.8 | 1.8 | 1.7 | 2.0 | 2.0 |
| Textile | 24.1 | 19.7 | 12.6 | 12.0 | 11.2 | 11.3 | 11.4 | 13.3 | 13.6 |
| Paper-making | 27.5 | 20.4 | 15.8 | 12.3 | 12.5 | 12.9 | 14.7 | 20.5 | 19.1 |
| Other | 2.2 | 2.2 | 1.8 | 1.3 | 1.3 | 1.3 | 1.3 | 1.3 | 1.3 |
| Total = 100 | | | | | | | | | |

NB: the percentages have been derived on the basis of gross industrial output at constant prices for 1952, 1957 and 1965; on those of 1970 for 1975, 1978, 1979 and 1980; on those of 1980 for 1981 and 1982.

# Notes

1. Formally, department I embraces the means of both industrial and agricultural production; however there has been a shift towards identifying department I with heavy industry as the key producer of the means of production. So this law often becomes the law of the priority development of heavy industry.

2. Economic laws, like the laws of nature, as understood by Soviet philosophy, have an existence of their own; they are transcendental and universal; they force man to carry out acts and policies without him being able to avoid them.

3. Extracts in Bruce Franklin (1973). On the role of Stalin and his acceptance of the model of the economist Eugene Preobrazhensky, see Alexander Erlich (1960).

4. Various Western researchers have wondered about the true identity of this economist of whom no trace has ever been found, unlike other challengers criticized by Stalin during 1952 such as A. I. Notkin, A. V. Sanina and her husband V. G. Venger. Yaroshenko may well have been a fictional character invented by Stalin, a sort of distillation of the opposition to the theses advanced by Stalin; or was he a man of straw through whom Stalin was aiming at other targets?

5. In Lenin (1967, p. 79), referring to *Theories of Surplus Value*, Vol. II, Part I, p. 304.

6. *Concerning Economic Problems of Socialism in the USSR*, in Mao Zedong, (1977, p. 132).

7. See Pairault 1983, pp. 23–7. Before his disgrace in 1958, Chen Yun was in the vanguard of this movement.

8. In an ironic twist, Stalin himself criticized his own law in a speech to the electors of the Stalin constituency in Moscow (9 February 1946). He observed that the USSR 'has rejected the "usual" path [Stalin's quotes] of industrialization' which is industrialization through the development of light industry, as the capitalist countries had done, in favour of industrialization through the development of heavy industry. This recognition of a historical fact ought to have led Stalin in 1952 to accept that the priority development of the means of production be considered, not as a law, but as a strategy of economic development dictated by circumstances – something that he explains very clearly in the 1946 speech.

On the Chinese critique see *JJYJ*, 1979, no. 9, pp. 16–21; no. 12, pp. 17–22 particularly.

9. $m$ is surplus value renamed 'net additional product' for the socialist countries.

10. The capital–output ratio $k$ is equal to $dK/dR$ (growth of fixed capital over growth of output) or $I/dR$ (investment over growth associated with output). $k$ is the ICOR or incremental capital–output ratio.

11. See Pairault, 1983, pp. 97–9. We have been able to estimate the elasticity of the gross industrial output of the machine building industries as a ratio of investment by state units in machinery and equipment and have observed that from 1975 to 1981, when investment rose by 1%, output rose by only 0.03%. Similarly, we have estimated the elasticity of the output of industrial machinery and equipment as a ratio of investment in state industrial enterprises during the period 1978 to 1982 and calculated that when investment rises by 1% output only increases by 0.76%.

12. On the financial aspects of the plans and their inflationary consequences see Pairault, 1983, pp. 95–101.

13. In fact the situation is more complicated: potential demand equals supply, but effective demand (potential demand – savings + dissaving of unassigned funds) will

be higher than supply, but again *a fortiori* effective demand will be much higher than desired supply (total supply minus supply of unsaleable goods), whence the inflationary gap.

14. Note an increase from 1982 (15%) to 1983 (16.5%).

15. The total amount of investment outside the plan financed by the banks reached 3.7 billion yuan in 1982; see the report on the draft plan for 1983 in *Guowuyuan*, 14, 1983, p. 641.

16. By 'productive investment' must be understood investment that aims directly at increasing output and thus results in an increase in National Income. Unproductive investment refers to investment made in sectors which have no material output (health, leisure, services, etc.) and whose output value is not taken into account in calculating National Income. This distinction is the result of the ontological pre-eminence of the material over the immaterial and consequently of production over consumption.

17. Mao Zedong, 1977, p. 201; Stalin said the same thing, in 1977, p. 388.

18. Mao, 1977, pp. 58, 132. On the problem of the law of value in China, see Pairault, 1982, pp. 1041–54.

19. It should be noted that Mao Zedong's analysis is identical to Stalin's such as it appears in his speech of April 1929 aimed at condemning Bukharin's economic policy (Franklin, 1973, pp. 320–437). The only difference between these two theoreticians is that Mao Zedong draws these conclusions from his analysis: evolution of the relations of production preceding those of the productive forces.

# 3 What Can China Learn from the Hungarian Economic Reforms?

## Paul Hare

At first sight, we might expect any connection between the processes of economic reform in Hungary and China to be tenuous. For Hungary is a relatively advanced, industrialized socialist country, while China, for all its recent successes, remains a poor, predominantly agricultural country. Moreover, Hungary, given its smallness in general and lack of raw materials in particular, is an exceptionally trade dependent country which in 1983 exported over 40% of its gross domestic product (*Statisztikai Evkönyv*, 1983); in contrast, although China's foreign trade has recently been growing very rapidly, exports still only amounted to 9.9% of national income in 1982 (Yeh, 1984). Finally, Hungary's population of about ten million is just 1% of China's billion, the latter being ethnically and linguistically extremely diverse (though with a preponderance of Han Chinese), as compared to Hungary's remarkable homogeneity.

Despite these important differences between Hungary and China, the countries do nevertheless have enough in common to make the comparative analysis set out in this chapter a worthwhile and fruitful exercise. For present purposes, their most significant common feature is that in the early 1950s both countries adopted the centralized Soviet-type model (often called the Stalinist model) of planned economic management and development. For different reasons, and by following somewhat divergent routes, both countries are now groping their way towards the development of fundamental, economic reforms, Hungary since 1968 and China since 1979. Both Hungary and China found that the traditional, Stalinist model had such severe shortcomings that beyond a certain point it retarded rather than promoted further development. The two countries therefore sought to introduce reforms which made planning and economic management more flexible than in the past and did so by introducing some market-type mechanisms. In both cases the ability to do this (as opposed to making more cautious reforms that might have been introduced without threatening the traditional framework of economic relationships) relied on a particularly favourable political conjuncture. It is interesting to note that both Hungary and China found it politically and economically expedient to begin their reform process in agriculture, for reasons that we discuss below.

Since Hungary's reforms are a decade ahead of China's (and even further ahead in agriculture), it is to be expected that China could learn something from Hungary's experience. This expectation is indeed correct and we shall see that there is scope for learning in the following areas (China has already recognized, and taken advantage of, some of these possibilities): 1) procedural aspects of reform; 2) market-oriented reforms in agriculture; 3) problems of investment planning; 4) enterprise autonomy; 5) reforming the institutional structure; and 6) political and social aspects of reform.

In this chapter, we begin in the next section by giving a brief sketch of Hungary's position within Eastern Europe, its traditional economic system and various attempts at economic reform: partial and usually ineffective reforms in the early 1960s, more comprehensive reforms from 1968 onwards. Section three then covers substantially the same ground for China, laying the groundwork for the next section which discusses the six areas given above in relation to Hungarian experience and Chinese possibilities. From this discussion it will become clear that Hungary has a number of positive lessons for China, in the sense of reforms that appear to be effective and successful; but it also reveals some serious lacunae in the theory and practice of a market oriented socialist economy, areas where Hungary has made mistakes and China may well do the same.

# Hungary

By about 1950, in common with the other Eastern European countries, Hungary had adopted the Stalinist model in its entirety. This not only meant that Hungary introduced the same institutional structures and hierarchical, centralized planning arrangements as prevailed in the USSR, but also that the direction of economic policy was virtually the same, with taut, overambitious planning, an industrialization drive emphasizing heavy industry and forced collectivization of agriculture (see Berend and Rankin, 1985). The result was a rapid growth of output but a fall in living standards, as resources were shifted into the investment drive, and increasing political tension.

Following the 1956 Revolution and its defeat by Soviet intervention a new government was established under Janos Kador, a government which rapidly consolidated its position by adopting a conciliatory and pragmatic approach to economic and social policy. In the aftermath of 1956 most of the cooperative farms collapsed, the earlier, overcentralized planning in industry was heavily criticized (see Kornai, 1959, for instance) and radical reform proposals were put forward. As it turned out, however, agriculture was the only sector in which reforms occurred at that time, the rest of the economy returning to the centralized model, albeit with some important modifications.

In agriculture, compulsory delivery quotas were abandoned to give farms more flexibility about what to produce, but a new collectivization campaign soon got underway. On this occasion, some important lessons had evidently been learnt from the earlier attempts. The main one was the realization that collectivization could not be done 'on the cheap': to make the new forms of farming succeed required massive investment, and this was reflected in the much higher share of investment going into agriculture as compared to the early 1950s. Similarly, to make the cooperatives attractive they had to ensure a reasonable income in the present as well as offering security in the future for the members. The new farms achieved this partly by developing regular wage payment and pension systems as their productivity grew, a process essentially completed by 1977; and partly by adopting a flexible attitude to ancillary activities and private plots. The latter have provided almost a third of agricultural output (inclusive of on farm consumption) and generated nearly half of farmers' income. As Swain (1985) interestingly observes, Hungarian agriculture nowadays can be regarded as a remarkably fruitful symbiosis between 'socialist wage labour' and traditional 'family labour'. From the standpoint of the remainder of the economy, the most notable features of this success story are as follows: first, sustained growth of agricultural output both assures the domestic food supply and provides a surplus for export; secondly, rural incomes have risen to urban levels and sometimes even above them, so that the countryside provides a major component of Hungary's demand for manufactured consumer goods; thirdly, many households have workers in industry as well as agriculture and to some extent the symbiosis mentioned above is not therefore merely confined to agriculture. It is worth noting that Hungary has been the only Eastern European country to adopt such a flexible approach to agriculture.

Reform came more slowly to industry and other branches of the economy. The centralized system of economic management re-established in the late 1950s differed from its predecessor in several ways: plans were much less rigid, the pattern of investment was changed in favour of light industry (and agriculture, as mentioned above) and real wages soon began to grow steadily. Nevertheless, the familiar inefficiencies of overcentralized planning rapidly appeared again and numerous partial reforms were instituted in an effort to make the traditional system function more efficiently. These included reductions in the number of centrally fixed plan indicators, more emphasis on profitability and organizational changes such as the formation of industrial trusts and large enterprises by extensive amalgamation in the early 1960s.

Although the economy was functioning reasonably well, it was clear by the mid-1960s that Hungary was reaching the limits of the traditional model. Unlike other countries where economic reform has been brought about by crisis, Hungary was able to take its time to devise the most appropriate reform package, a process that took three years from the initial decision in 1965 to implementation in 1968. In the absence of economic crisis, what led Hungary to introduce such radical reforms? Several factors are relevant here, though growth rates that were declining and expected to decline further were probably the most important. Associated with this was the realization that the incentive structures in the traditional model were not very effective at delivering productivity increases: a good deal of Hungary's post-war growth was achieved by throwing additional resources of capital and labour into new areas of production, with minimal attention to productivity. With a shortage of labour becoming ever more severe (and little labour available for transfer from agriculture), growth could only proceed on the basis of faster productivity growth. A third factor was the country's persistent failure to achieve a sustained convertible currency surplus, indicating a highly uncompetitive output mix and poor marketing practices: again it was concluded that the traditional model could not resolve this problem; but equally a trade dependent economy like

Hungary could not afford to leave it unresolved. (As we shall observe in the next section, these reasons for reform are quite different from any that may be adduced for the Chinese case.)

The 1968 reform package (for details, see Hare, Radice and Swain, 1981, and Marer, 1984), initially referred to as the New Economic Mechanism, abolished the practice of breaking down plans to enterprise level. Enterprises were expected to work out their own plans and arrange for their own input supplies and output marketing in a major shift to reinstate a form of market mechanism into the economy. Macro-economic planning went on very much as before, but enterprise activity was to be guided by so-called economic regulators: wage policy, profits taxation, price policy (prices were reformed in 1968 as part of the package), credit policy and so on. There was some decentralization of authority in relation to foreign trade transactions as well as investment, but in both these areas the centre chose to retain substantial control. In principle, therefore, the result was a dramatic decentralization of decision-making regarding current inputs and outputs, with much less change where decisions could influence the future structure of the economy significantly. Strangely, there was virtually no institutional change to accompany this major reform, a fact which turned out to impede the progress of the reforms in a number of ways, as well as facilitating some recentralization in the 1970s in response to the economy's problems. Despite this particular limitation, Hungary's reform was much the most radical to be carried out in Eastern Europe in the 1960s (or since). Other countries such as Poland and Czechoslovakia considered similar reform proposals but stopped short of introducing them.

While the economy enjoyed some years of faster growth following the reforms, and living standards rose quite sharply, it was quickly evident that some of Hungary's long term, persistent problems had not been resolved. The reform process had given rise to greater difficulties than the more optimistic reformers had hoped and the country's economic behaviour and performance could not be changed overnight. According to Marer's (1984) useful review, the New Economic Mechanism still had to contend with considerable inflexibility in the price system, insufficient competition, an extremely rigid system of wage determination and a weak and circumscribed operation of the profit motive. The problem of how to integrate Hungary's more liberal domestic economic arrangements with the CMEA's bureaucratic foreign trade mechanism was scarcely addressed, let alone resolved, and the serious shortcomings of the investment sphere were also virtually untouched by the reforms.

The mid-1970s was a period of limited recentralization, combined with rapid growth based on heavy foreign borrowing. By the end of the decade it was plain to all that the insulation of domestic producers from world market pressures had led to some costly economic errors and that this could not continue in the face of a deteriorating external environment (two oil crises and a major recession in under a decade). In much less favourable conditions than the 1968 reforms, Hungary's leadership therefore decided that market oriented reforms must be resumed, and this second round of reforms began in 1979.

The first step was a price reform, making domestic producer prices correspond much more closely to world market prices, and this was followed by some of the institutional changes neglected in 1968, such as breaking up many trusts and large enterprises into their constituent units, and making it much easier to set up a variety of types of new production and service unit. In addition, branch ministries within industry were abolished, with the formation of a new Ministry for Industry, and foreign trade was further decentralized so that more enterprises had independent foreign trading rights. There were also some tentative steps in the direction of facilitating financial intermediation.

Although this latest phase of reform basically built on the 1968 reforms by strengthening its competitive, market oriented features and weakening the more traditional, vertical links within the planning hierarchy, it is not yet possible to evaluate its effectiveness. This is partly because institutional reforms necessarily take some time to have their maximum effects, but also because the hard currency debt crisis forced Hungary to impose domestic recession to cut imports and release resources for exports. It is only in the last couple of years that growth has been resumed.

# China

China's political and economic experience since the Second World War is rather different from that of Hungary but, as much of the necessary background information for China is given elsewhere in this volume, it will be possible for us to be brief in this section.

Following the 1949 revolution, economic stabilization and recovery were impressively rapid in China. With the help of Soviet advisers a system of national economic planning was established which almost exactly mirrored the Soviet model (see Lardy, 1978). The system was based on branch ministries located in Beijing, though some role was also assigned to provincial and other lower level administrations. Price fixing, materials allocation and the distribution of final products, investment decision-making, credit allocation and so on were all in the hands of state bodies, while enterprises received increasingly detailed production plans. The whole process of economic administration soon became extremely centralized and bureaucratic, with less and less scope for market forces to operate within the system.

China's first Five Year Plan covered the period 1953–7, though it was not actually published until 1955 (see Howe, 1978). It embodied the traditional Soviet priority for heavy industry, an emphasis that undoubtedly made more sense for China than it ever did for Hungary, especially as agriculture and light industry were not entirely neglected. During the early 1950s, almost all production units were transformed into state enterprises or cooperatives. In agriculture, following the land reform that dispossessed the landlord class (see Hinton, 1966), the development of agricultural cooperatives was encouraged and in many areas several stages of cooperativization succeeded one another very rapidly.

While the first plan was broadly fulfilled and laid a solid foundation for subsequent development to build on, serious planning was about to be swept aside by a wave of absurdly overoptimistic projections and policies from China's political leadership. The success of the first plan, together with the unexpectedly rapid establishment of the commune system in agriculture led to the Great Leap Forward of 1959. This was an attempt to accelerate economic development by achieving a massive rise in grain output, promoting small-scale rural industry (of which numerous backyard steel furnaces are the best known example) and boosting urban industrial output, all at the same time. Although it had some successes to its credit, the Great Leap caused extensive disclocation in both agriculture and industry and a complete breakdown of the planning system, the latter caused to some extent by the large-scale falsification of economic statistics during this period. The combination of dislocation and disruption, followed by natural disasters in the period 1960–62 produced a major recession, as well as serious famine in parts of China. Meanwhile, the second Five Year Plan covering the years 1958–62 was completely overtaken by these horrific events.

Not surprisingly, the early 1960s were years of consolidation and recovery; but in 1966 Mao launched the Cultural Revolution. Initially an attack on so-called bourgeois education and culture, directed also against 'revisionists' within the Party, the revolution soon extended into a general challenge to established authority in all areas of economic and social life. For the economy, the result was an actual fall in output in 1967, though by the end of the 1960s growth resumed. In addition, material incentives – bonuses – were attacked as 'unsocialist' and foreign trade stagnated.

The 1970s saw order restored and central planning, at least on an annual basis, re-established; but serious political conflict within the leadership continued to have adverse effects on the economy (Howe, 1978). Moderates (Zhou Enlai and Deng Xiaoping) thought in terms of a long term development plan to promote the 'Four Modernizations' while the left attacked planning as a whole and criticized proposals to use China's resources (notably oil) to pay for imported machinery. Only Mao's death in 1976, shortly afterwards followed by the downfall of the radical left 'Gang of Four' allowed a new leadership to unite around the moderates' programme. Foreign trade began to expand rapidly once again and material incentives were restored throughout the economy as the tempo of development accelerated once more. Signs of overheating in the economy were widespread by the end of the 1970s so the announcement of a period of consolidation and restructuring came as no surprise. This period marked the first stage of what is turning out to be a comprehensive economic reform, to which we now turn.

It is important to consider, first of all, why China should embark on major reforms at its present stage of development. For despite the political turmoil and dramatic reversals of policy referred to above, the economy as a whole has grown very rapidly since 1950, with industry doing especially well; there has not even been clear evidence of a secular decline in the growth rate, one of the factors that stimulated Hungary's reforms. Moreover, China is so poorly integrated into the world economy and so self-sufficient in essential materials, that the arguments for reform based on foreign trade efficiency, which were so important for Hungary, carried very little weight. But China's traditional central planning system has failed to achieve any significant advance in popular living standards since the early 1950s, and it is this glaring failure which the present reforms are seeking to rectify.

Two aspects of the living standards issue are germane to the question of economic reform: food supply and consumer goods. Agricultural output did expand from 1950–79, but it only just kept pace with population growth and food availability per capita only increased a little. Not only that, but the average performance masks disparities between provinces and smaller areas, with some areas suffering significant malnourishment in years of relatively poor harvests. As for consumer goods, output did of course increase but supplies of modern consumer goods to the countryside remained poor and even in the cities, real wages per capita hardly increased at all after the mid-1950s. The traditional, Soviet-inspired planning system generated enormous growth in heavy industry and sustained a huge rate of accumulation (over 30% of national income in some years). It also generated a great deal of economic waste and inefficiency, though unlike in Hungary this can scarcely be regarded as a major factor stimulating reform: for in China's case it is likely that there remains significant scope for improving the efficiency of the existing planning system without fundamental reform (see next section) and the resource mobilizing abilities of the centralized model have probably not yet exhausted their full potential. For China, the principal reason for the present programme of reforms is the perceived political imperative to raise living standards after decades of stagnation, together with the conviction on the part of China's top leadership that the centralized planning system alone is too unwieldy and cumbersome to deliver the goods.

In contrast to Hungary, China's reforms are being telescoped into a much shorter period. Whereas Hungary's all-important and highly successful agricultural reforms preceded industrial reforms by a decade, in China the two stages have proceeded in parallel. In agriculture the development of the responsibility system gathered pace from 1979 onwards, while in industry a variety of economic experiments were underway at the same time, and were soon extended to the whole country (Gray and Gray, 1983, and Hare, 1983b). The apparent success of the new arrangements in agriculture, securing and improving both the food supply and the supply of agricultural raw materials for industry, is the main reason for the recent Central Committee decision to extend economic reforms in urban areas (Central Committee, 1984).

The responsibility system, in effect, involves the end of the commune system as it has been known since 1958. The local government responsibilities of the communes are being transferred to new township governments, whereas agricultural production itself (as well as sidelines and some small scale industry) is being decentralized to small groups – sometimes single families but more usually a group of families, sometimes a group as large as the old production teams – who contract to supply specified quantities of output to the collective. Land ownership normally resides with the production team and contracts under the new system, initially issued for short periods of three years or so, can now be offered for 15 years. Thus cultivators have an incentive to introduce new, improved production methods, and to invest in buildings and equipment since they can expect to enjoy the returns at least until their current contract terminates. A benefit claimed for the responsibility system is that personal incomes are much more closely linked to individual effort than under the earlier arrangements; the system is also more democratic in the sense that the opportunities for day to day interference in production decisions by communist party cadres should be greatly reduced. On the other hand, there is some risk that open rural unemployment could emerge, instead of being hidden as before (for a very useful study of employment and productivity in China, see Rawski, 1979), though this is being countered by the vigorous promotion of township industry and services to provide additional, non-agricultural jobs. Also, one would expect rural inequality to increase as a result of the responsibility system, which is confirmed in Li Chengrui, in *BR* (1985), reporting a small increase in the rural Gini coefficient from 0.237 in 1978 to 0.264 in 1984. Nevertheless, the reforms in agriculture have undoubtedly been accompanied by a remarkably strong upsurge in output, both of food crops and of industrial raw materials; the improved security of China's food supply makes it easier for the leadership to undertake the risks involved in industrial reform. What is not yet clear, however, is whether recent agricultural growth rates can be sustained, or whether the recent improvement in performance is simply a once and for all effect of the shift to the responsibility system (see Walker, 1984, and Lardy, 1984).

In industry, the initial reform steps – experiments – were not unlike measures that have been introduced in the Soviet Union and Eastern Europe (including Hungary before the mid-1960s). Such experiments are typically stimulated by two considerations: firstly, the recognition that, whether they like it or not, the central planners *cannot* control every detail of enterprise activity; since, therefore, some decentralization is unavoidable, the planners might do better to choose what form it should take; secondly, a recognition that attempts to control production in too much detail are likely to stifle enterprise level initiative and severely blunt incentives, hence giving rise to much inefficiency. Reforms involve cutting back on the number of compulsory plan indicators, in the Chinese case focusing on a single one, profits; allowing enterprises to retain and use for approved purposes certain proportions of planned and above plan profits; and formulating rather looser plans, allowing enterprises to make their own marketing arrangements in respect of above plan output.

From 1979 onwards, measures such as these were applied to selected enterprises in certain areas such as Sichuan, Shanghai and elsewhere, and were found to be successful in that profitability of experimental enterprises improved sharply, the supply position on the market was said to be better and product mix also improved. Although it is not clear how representative these findings were, for it seems probable that, just as in the Soviet Union, experimental enterprises would be the ones that were doing well under the traditional system, the experiments were soon extended to the whole country.

Above enterprise level, the rather complex system of ministerial and provincial planning and supervision of production remains in place (for details, see Hare, 1983b), although some steps are being taken to simplify it. At present, this basically means a reduction in the number of commodity groups being centrally allocated in 1985, from 120 to 60 (also, the number of agricultural and sideline products subject to state purchasing falling from 29 to 10), with the scope of guidance planning (similar to Hungary's concept of plan implementation through the use of economic regulators) and market regulation correspondingly increased. The products still subject to mandatory planning are principally basic materials and important categories of machinery. To some extent, this kind of reform can be regarded as merely a recognition of reality, in that China's capacity to allocate centrally the range of commodity groups attempted previously must be open to some doubt. Aside from deficiencies in statistics and a serious shortage of skilled staff to deal with resource allocation matters, it is also likely that some of the centrally allocated products would be better dealt with either by provincial or lower level administrations, by the supplying enterprises if these are very few (in effect, this is what often happens in Hungary) or through unregulated market transactions where products are no longer persistently in short supply.

Finally, the Central Commission decision on economic reforms (Central Committee, 1984) clearly saw China's agricultural success, together with substantial overfulfilment of most output targets for the first four years of the Sixth Five Year Plan (1981–5) as a favourable environment in which to push ahead with reforms focusing on urban areas. Aside from points already noted above, these include the extension of something like the responsibility system to urban enterprises, comprehensive wage and price reforms, and a recognition of the need for diverse economic forms though still retaining a leading role for state enterprises.

As yet it is not obvious just what the proposed extension of the responsibility system will entail. But it may well be rather like some of the latest measures in Hungary involving the formation of so-called economic working groups, both within enterprises or operating independently (see Hare, 1983a). These are small groups of workers to whom enterprises sub-contract particular items of work for an agreed fee. The arrangement is partly a device to avoid the normally stringent wage regulations but it has the merit of allowing the better workers to earn much more than the average; it also makes more effective use of both labour and capital than the usual employment arrangements make possible. The second point, wage and price reforms, has been seen as an area needing reform for a long time – wages to improve work incentives and to differentiate more between different skills and qualities of work and prices to establish a better relationship between prices and costs so that a more decentralized, profit-oriented economy might function reasonably well. Both wages and prices are seen as matters of great sensitivity in China so that although some tentative moves towards reform were undertaken in 1985 (Zhao Ziyang, 1985), the general approach is much more cautious than it has been in Hungary. The last point, on diverse economic forms, belatedly concedes one of the key weaknesses of the centralized model of a socialist economy, whether in China, the Soviet Union, or elsewhere. This is the tendency, for reasons of administrative convenience as much as anything, to compress the richness and variety of economic life into a small number of standardized organizational forms, e.g. state enterprises and cooperatives. Many socialist countries, including Hungary some years ago, and now apparently China, have recognized the error of this policy and permit (in some cases, encourage) more varied economic forms to function. Such forms are especially important in the provision of urban services and in small-scale production, indeed anywhere where it is efficient to operate on a small scale and absurd for remote central planners to get involved.

## Lessons

We are now equipped with sufficient background information on the Chinese and Hungarian reforms to enable us to return to the question of lessons that Hungary's reform experience can offer China. As noted in the introduction to this chapter, these lessons will be reviewed under six headings.

### Procedural Aspects of Reform

Strangely, this feature of an economic reform programme is almost totally ignored in most discussions. Yet reforms do not just materialize out of thin air and nor are they implemented merely by waving a magic wand. Instead, reform proposals are typically conceived and elaborated by individuals – belonging to committees representing various economic and political interest groups; agreement on a programme normally requires some major compromises to be accepted by certain groups; and its implementation – whether in stages or as a single, coordinated package – depends on complex economic policy measures as well as constant monitoring and review to ensure that the desired effects are being achieved. Not many countries have successfully gone through all of these phases with a major reform programme. In most cases, particular interest groups committed to the traditional, centralized model have proved sufficiently strong either to resist anything but relatively minor reforms, or at least to block the effective implementation of more fundamental ones. Hungary, however, is one country which, despite some setbacks in the 1970s, has now sustained radical reforms for a decade and a half: it is not, therefore, surprising that China found it could learn a great deal about the procedural aspects of reform from Hungary.

To this end, a Chinese delegation visited Budapest in 1979 specifically to study reform procedures. Indeed, some Hungarian economists were apparently amazed by this concentration on procedures: for the Chinese were not so much interested in Hungarian reforms *per se*, but rather in what committees the Hungarians set up, who belonged to them, what sorts of research were undertaken to assess the problems of the traditional system and so on. These are very important questions, however, and this author thinks the Chinese were quite right to ask them. Moreover, both China and Hungary (in 1968, not so much in 1980) have been in the fortunate position of being able to consider reforms against a background of already reasonable economic performance. This makes it possible to prepare reforms carefully and both countries have taken advantage of this opportunity. No doubt other contacts between Budapest and Beijing have been more concerned with the content than with the procedure of economic reform: to this we now turn.

### Market Oriented Reforms in Agriculture

We have seen that Hungary successfully collectivized its agriculture and developed a prosperous farming sector on the basis of a combination of socialist wage labour and family labour. China, on the other hand, completed its collectivization in 1958 with the establishment of the commune system. However, after functioning for over two decades, this system has now been allowed to collapse altogether, with the almost universal adoption of the responsibility system. It appears that China failed to achieve Hungary's mix of collective and private work because labour productivity on the communes remained low, indeed according to Rawski (1979) it even declined slowly with time: the communes effectively absorbed, and provided employment for everyone living in the countryside who needed work, but generated extremely low per capita incomes. For this reason, collective work was attractive neither in relation to what people could earn from their private plots or sideline activities, nor in relation to typical urban earnings.

In the late 1970s many Chinese officials spoke optimistically of achieving a high level of mechanization of the country's basic agricultural operations within a very short period. If successful, this would have released huge numbers of workers for other sectors of the economy, while also sharply raising agricultural collective incomes. However, it was quite impossible to proceed at the anticipated rate. For even with a faster rate of investment in agriculture, China's level of technical development was so low compared to Hungary of the 1950s and 1960s that it would have taken decades to reach an adequate level of mechanization and, in any case, the ability of other sectors to absorb displaced workers was itself fairly limited. In addition, the limited capacity of factories producing agricultural equipment and shortages of people with the skills required to operate and maintain it were important factors constraining the pace of agricultural development.

Thus although, given enough time, China's experiment with collective agriculture might eventually have produced results something like Hungary's, the Chinese turned instead to draw on the one resource they possessed in abundance: labour. The wage payment system that took root in the communes, based on workpoints, established an extremely weak nexus between individual effort and reward and within any given accounting unit (usually a team, but sometimes a brigade) ensured an almost uniform income distribution. Hence the introduction of the responsibility system was an attempt to strengthen work incentives by making the family, or some other small group of workers, the basic accounting unit. The system also relaxed many limitations on private trading and other small-scale private economic activity.

While China's most recent agricultural reforms therefore took a very different direction from Hungary's, the principal reason for the difference was more a matter of practical reality than fundamental principle: Hungary had the investment resources to make collective agriculture succeed and China did not. Despite this difference, the two countries share a strong market orientation in their agricultural policy and both managed to elicit high work effort through an appropriate incentive system. As a result, food supply is ample and still expanding or diversifying. Probably correctly in view of other countries' experience (e.g. Poland), the political leaders in Hungary and China have judged that successful agriculture is a *sine qua non* for effective reforms elsewhere. One cannot claim, in this case, that China has learned much directly from Hungarian policies, but China has nevertheless worked its way around to a policy with some common features and with a similar outcome to the Hungarian one. It only differs from the latter because of the enormous difference in relative resource endowments (i.e. capital, labour and land).

## Problems of Investment Planning

As compared to the 'anarchy of the market', we might expect investment planning in a socialist country to result in a steadier rate of development, with less waste and fewer mistakes along the way. However, the basic problem with investment is that it necessarily involves casting a glance into the future, and socialist countries find this scarcely easier than capitalist ones. Moreover, Kornai (1980a) has argued that certain institutional features of socialist countries, notably the predominance of state enterprises which are only subject to very mild financial pressure (the so-called soft budget constraint), makes investment appear to be costless to lower level units: hence the effective demand for investment is virtually unlimited. At the same time, the inability of the central institutions (ministries, bureaux etc.) to coordinate the total volume of investment because they tend to disagree about relative priorities creates a situation in which they may well permit a large number of projects to start. The resulting dispersion of investment leads to low efficiency, as well as periodical crises when the centre finally recognizes that resources are overstretched and puts on the brakes. These investment cycles (which, unlike in capitalist countries, are not accompanied by employment cycles) have been well documented for several Eastern European countries, including Hungary, in Bauer (1981); but they have also been a feature of China's economic development since 1950 (as is clear from *SYB*, p. 323). Interestingly, contrary to the optimistic hopes of reformers, investment cycles in Hungary have continued since the 1968 reforms, albeit with somewhat lower amplitude than before; it is too early to judge whether China's current round of reforms will have any effect on the Chinese cycles.

There are, however, some important differences between China and Hungary, which afford grounds for greater optimism in regard to Chinese investment performance. In China, relatively fewer investments are dependent for economic success on the vagaries of overseas markets and this may make it a little easier than in Hungary to select viable projects. Secondly, China has far more enterprises, so that even within a fairly bureaucratic system of investment selection and regulation there is more chance that limited competition within any given branch will give rise to reasonably efficient investment choices. Thirdly, China's partial decentralization to provinces makes it possible that provincial investment cycles may not be perfectly synchronized with each other, in which case interprovincial transfers of investment resources could help to even out fluctuations in investment at the overall, national level (though it must be conceded that there is little indication of this happening in the past). On the other hand, China has more branch ministries (over 30), as compared to Hungary's three (industry, construction, agriculture and food production), so it may be harder to arrive at an agreed, coordinated investment policy; also, investment criteria, accounting practices related to investment and the general level of technical expertise are all fairly unsophisticated, compared to Hungary. On balance, however, I would still consider it likely that investment planning in China has the potential to proceed more smoothly than in Hungary.

As for lessons from Hungary there are a few worth noting. The first and most important is that a substantial decentralization of current production decisions to enterprises is not sufficient to improve the economy's investment performance.

While enterprises continue to regard investment as almost costless and while central agencies struggle to increase their shares of the investment 'cake' it is actually unrealistic to expect much change in the investment sphere. This was and still is the situation in Hungary and appears to be in China as well. Secondly, however, attempts in Hungary to make more investment dependent on repayable credits rather than non-repayable budget allocations, and to focus on specific economic criteria such as the generation of additional hard currency net exports have been rather more successful than the general picture might suggest and I would expect this to hold for China, too. Thirdly, both in China and Hungary the most difficult problem for the authorities is to restrain the persistently excessive demand for investment. It is worth remarking that this problem is almost unknown in capitalist countries except for occasional brief boom periods, a contrast which hints that the locus of the problem may be found in the differing status and structure of the bodies that generate most of the demand, namely enterprises. This observation brings us to the next point.

**Enterprise Autonomy**
In most countries that have implemented or considered economic reform there have been calls for greater enterprise autonomy. Sometimes this is just a natural reaction against the rigid overcentralization of the traditional Soviet-type models; but it can also be justified in terms of improving lower level incentives and economic efficiency, and making possible some degree of enterprise democracy. To be effective, arguments along these lines are usually linked with proposals for price reform, strengthening competition and developing enterprise responsibility: in extreme cases, the last of these would allow for enterprises to go bankrupt in the event of economic failure, a nettle that socialist countries, for quite understandable reasons, have been slow to grasp. However, such an insistence on enterprise responsibility would undoubtedly result in a more disciplined approach to investment.

Hungary's measures to strengthen enterprise autonomy have been far-reaching, especially concerning control over current production, as we saw earlier. But in 1968, little was done to enliven competition, either by breaking up existing large enterprises into smaller units, or by relaxing controls over imports; nor was much done to enforce financial responsibility, that is, harder budget constraints (see Kornai, 1980a) and enterprises continued to suffer from a great deal of intervention from their ministerial superiors (see Bauer, 1976); finally, there was no move to make management more democratic.

During the late 1970s, it was increasingly recognized that a new round of reforms would be needed to rectify these 'errors' and this has gathered momentum from 1979–80 onwards, though some of the new steps being taken are admittedly quite cautious and hesitant (see Hare, 1983a). What this experience indicates is that the business of breaking down the fetters imposed on enterprise activity by the centralized model of a planned economy is not at all as easy as the Hungarian reformers once imagined. After some decades of operating that model, certain modes of behaviour on the part of central planners and enterprises become deeply entrenched: they do not change easily even after such a radical reform as Hungary put in place in 1968.

For China, despite the political turmoil and economic disruption that has featured periodically in the last three decades, the same resistance to change on the part of central agencies and, to some extent, enterprise management, can be anticipated. One reason for this is that planners and other officials in the bureaucracy tend to look back to the 1950s, the heyday of the centralized model, as a golden age of planning and moreover feel that a centralized approach to economic management is far from having outlived its usefulness in China. Moderate reforms that merely reduce or simplify plan indicators will have no more long-term effect in China than elsewhere: at best they will merely improve the system's flexibility. The reforms introduced in China to date, devolving modest additional powers to enterprises but with only promises of price reform and other more fundamental changes, must be regarded as exceedingly cautious. There is the possibility of a real increase in enterprise autonomy in due course, as a coherent package of reforms is implemented. However, the Chinese decision to proceed in stages runs the risk that later stages in the process may be stalled, as happened for instance in Poland (see Hare and Wanless, 1981). Ironically, this must be considered especially likely in China, at least for the bulk of the state sector, in view of the astonishingly good economic performance of the last few years. Concerning enterprise autonomy, therefore, it seems likely that China could make the same mistakes as Hungary, but that because of China's earlier stage of economic development and lower dependence on efficient foreign trade these mistakes could have far less serious adverse consequences and may not create pressure to advance the reforms to a more radical stage.

## Reforming the Institutional Structure

From the above remarks about enterprises it is apparent that the effect of an economic reform depends at least as much on the institutional framework within which enterprises, for instance, are embedded, as on the formal changes in policy measures (e.g. changes in plan indicators or enterprise taxation) which constitute the subject matter of most discussions of reform. Hungary certainly learned this lesson during the 1970s and an important element of the more recent reforms concerns the institutional structure of economic management.

At present, China is not moving in the same direction, at least within the state and large-scale cooperative sector. Instead, there is some indication that China might be developing a number of parallel systems subject to different 'rules of the game'. One is the traditional state system, controlled largely by plan directives issued by ministry or provincial authorities; here the reforms so far announced are relatively modest, seeking merely to improve flexibility and simplify existing operating procedures, but without changing institutional structures at all. Secondly, industrial cooperatives, most of which are supervised by municipal or prefectural authorities, can expect a somewhat more relaxed operating environment. In the past cooperatives have effectively been assimilated to the category of state enterprises despite formal differences in their legal status and property ownership. It is now becoming more likely that their property rights and managerial autonomy will be respected. The third system is the burgeoning, small-scale private sector.

Suppressed for decades, private business is now encouraged as a way of absorbing people whom the more capital-intensive state sector cannot absorb, and also to provide goods and services not supplied (or not supplied efficiently) by the state and cooperative sectors of the economy. Small-scale private business is subject to little official regulation, though of course the firms concerned must make their own supply and selling arrangement through market rather than plan channels.

Thus China's institutional framework, though initially based on the Soviet model just like Hungary's, is not at present changing in the same way. While Hungary faces pressures to strengthen competition and improve the effectiveness of trade, China has a massive job creation problem and a state sector that is currently functioning rather well. These different situations and pressures are sufficient to explain the two countries' divergent approaches to institutional reform.

## Political and Social Aspects of Reform

Economic reform is never a purely technical matter, isolated from political and social issues. The erratic course of the Hungarian reforms provides a vivid illustration of this fundamental point. Although the 1968 reform was expected to worsen the income distribution by allowing certain groups to get much better off very rapidly, when it actually had this effect many in the leadership expressed surprise and concern, and some recentralization was put into effect to restrain these tendencies. Moreover, worries about income distribution allowed opponents of reform to gain in influence for a time during the early 1970s until it became evident that centralized, imposed solutions were unable to resolve Hungary's critical economic problems. But this complex interplay of economic, social and political aspects of life has been a constant theme in Hungarian life since the 1968 reforms.

The same is also the case for China since 1979, though the official facade of unity and agreement tends to mask it. For example, while it is clearly recognized that China's agricultural reforms in the countryside will raise inequality of incomes (see above) by allowing some people to become much better off, there is little public awareness that some families will do badly under the new arrangements, either through bad luck or poor work. Yet for two decades the poorest in China have been assured of at least a minimal level of income. What happens in a society when such important guarantees are removed, or seriously undermined? It seems to me that this aspect of the rural reforms is fraught with serious political risks; nor will the situation be any better in the towns if the responsibility system is extended there as planned, unless some sort of social security mechanism is developed. In addition, if decentralization in industry proceeds far, many bureaucrats will lose power and the less capable managers will feel threatened. Accordingly, we can expect enormous resistance from these groups to all but minor reforms and it is not clear what is being done to overcome it. So industrial reforms could very well be blocked just as they have been in Poland and the Soviet Union: it is hard to see why we should expect China to be very different. Hungary's reforms are still going ahead because all major interest groups are agreed, or at worst reluctantly accept, that the old centralized style of economic management has little to offer. While recognizing past mistakes, and conceding that limited decentralization could help to improve economic performance, the fact remains that for China this line of argument is invalid.

## Conclusions

Since most of the available theory of a market socialist economy (e.g. see Cave and Hare, 1981) is concerned with a one-period model containing a given collection of enterprises, it is not surprising to note that the most glaring lacunae are in the two areas of investment and the institutional framework. From our discussion in the above section the reader will also realize that these are areas which have given rise to the greatest difficulty for the Hungarian and Chinese reformers: both countries are groping their way towards viable solutions consistent with reasonably efficient production and an acceptable degree of control from the central authorities, and theory offers little help.

In other areas there is a stronger theoretical consensus about the likely effects of particular sorts of economic reform, buttressed by evidence from Hungary's own earlier experience in attempting to implement comprehensive reforms from 1968 onwards (and as early as 1959–60 in the all-important agriculture). All this provides guidelines for Chinese practice, in the ways outlined earlier in this chapter.

Lastly, when discussing radical reforms in Hungary and China in the same chapter, we should beware of hasty conclusions. We have already remarked that China's present economic success makes the extension of radical reform from agriculture to industry rather less imperative than it has appeared to be for Hungary. In the last section we also noted the obvious sources of opposition to major reforms in China, which will not be easy to overcome. Hence what may be the most crucial lesson from Hungary's experience is simply the following: that it is not worthwhile accepting the serious political risks of a comprehensive economic reform until the economic case becomes far more compelling. In agriculture, the economic case surely was considered to be quite overwhelming, but for industry, we are not convinced that it is.

# 4 The Modernization of Élites:

## The evolution of leadership recruitment in the central state administration of the People's Republic of China from 1965 to 1985

**Jean-Pierre Cabestan**

The economic development of China cannot rest solely on a relative decollectiviza-tion of agriculture, a relaxation of industrial planning and a policy of opening up to the outside world; it must include adaptation and a modernization of the élites responsible for carrying out this programme. While Chinese leaders were aware of this as early as 1978–9, the period when the real change in direction of the regime occurred, this latter reform was only introduced with extreme slowness; this was so for essentially political reasons. At that time, Deng Xiaoping was not sufficiently in control to get rid of the leaders who had survived the Cultural Revolution relatively unscathed and who had helped him to regain power, and *a fortiori* those he had just rehabilitated. Only the most fervent supporters of the 'great helmsman' were quickly removed.

At the time of the restructuring of the State Council (March and May 1982) and the Twelfth Congress of the CCP (September 1982), a partial renewal of the governing teams occurred. But it was not until 1985 that implementation of this reform was somewhat accelerated, and it still remains incomplete, especially at the provincial and local levels.

Nevertheless, a preliminary assessment of this evolution at the central level is already possible. Unlike numerous quantitative studies of Chinese leaders, this analysis does not use the Central Committee of the CP and its Political Bureau as its basis but the government, i.e. the State Council, which has seldom been considered a subject for research in its own right.[1]

Yet this body is not only an executive body carrying out the decisions of the party leadership, that is of the secretariat and to a lesser extent of the Political Bureau (and not of the Central Committee), but is also at the apex of the state administration, and more particularly of the economy. In fact, the economic departments of the Central Committee, dismantled in 1966, were not re-established after the Cultural Revolution. The secretariat of the CP, provided apparently only with a few departments responsible for carrying out surveys and background studies,[2] is obliged to use the departments under the State Council to implement policies that it has adopted. That is why the standing committee of the State Council (the premier, vice-premier, state councillors and secretary-general of the State Council), a vital link in the decision-making chain between the highest political organs of the party and the central government departments, is composed of leading members of the Political Bureau and secretariat of the CP. The State Council thus includes most of the decision-makers of a Chinese administration, which still plays a frontline role in the economic development of the country.

But is the present government better equipped to deal with the challenges of this enormous task? In order to respond, at least in part, to this difficult question, we have attempted to assess in detail the changes – or lack of changes – in modes of recruitment to leadership positions in the central state administration. Are the rules for promotion laid down by the present leadership actually implemented or not? What are the unwritten laws of advancement?

We have chosen to compare the leading personnel of the State Council after the September 1985 reshuffle with those of five earlier State Councils: that of 1965, formed on the eve of the Cultural Revolution; that of 1975, appointed after the end of that period of domestic upheavals; that of 1978, headed by Hua Guofeng, Mao Zedong's 'designated successor'; that of 1980, controlled by Zhao Ziyang, a close associate of Deng Xiaoping; and that of 1983, after the restructuring of the central state administration was completed.

There is little biographical information on Chinese leaders and the sources are sometimes contradictory.[3] That is why we had to limit our study to ministers and directors of organs directly subordinate to the State Council who have the rank of vice-minister, but whose decision-making autonomy is more extensive than that of a deputy to a minister. Moreover, some of these organs have become ministries (for example the Xinhua News Agency in 1982) and vice versa (for example, the Ministry of Materials Allocation which reappeared as a state bureau after the Cultural Revolution).[4] But the dearth of information on vice-ministers and the large number of them in each ministry up to 1982 (sometimes more than 20 and usually about 10) obliged us to exclude them from our study. Conversely, we have included the heads of all the departments which were in one of the governments studied and of some state bodies which do not formally come under the State Council.[5] The personnel studied are as in Table 1.

We then distributed these leaders into 14 areas of activity based on the UN's classification (1981) of the functions of government, with some slight modifications made necessary by the nature of the Chinese political system. We grouped the 14 sectors in three broad areas of activity: 1) economic and social, 2) political and 3) military (see Appendix 1). The first is the principal activity of government and formally no longer has any corresponding departments in the central party apparatus. The second area, in contrast, remains closely supervised by specialist organs of the Central Committee. There are not many representatives of the third area in government, whose military organs have as their main function to coordinate the activities of economic ministries with those of the army, which remains directly under the control of the Party Central Committee's Military Affairs Commission.

Finally, we have used two types of factors or 'criteria' of promotion:

**Table 4.1**
**The Organs and Leaders Studied**

| Government formed in | Commissions, ministries, staff officers and other organs of ministerial rank | Bureaux and other organs of bureau rank (leading groups, banks, etc.) | Premiers, vice-premiers, state councillors without portfolio | Total of multiple office holders | Total of leaders | Total of leaders of rank of minister or higher | Total of leaders of rank of vice-minister |
|---|---|---|---|---|---|---|---|
| January 1965 | 60 | 28 | 5 | 6 | 87 | 61 | 26 |
| January 1975 | 43 | 27 | 10 | — | 70 | 43 | 27 |
| March 1978 | 43 | 36 | 8 | 1 | 86 | 51 | 35 |
| September 1980 | 57 | 51 | 2 | 7 | 103 | 56 | 47 |
| June 1983 | 50 | 49 | 6 | 11 | 94 | 56 | 38 |
| September 1985 | 51 | 74 | 7 | 19 | 113 | 57 | 56 |

1) *Political and sociological criteria*: These are by nature subject to the vagaries of the Communist Party line, the basic source of the functioning rules of Chinese institutions: do the leaders of the 1980s have the same education and political experience as their elders, especially those who controlled the administration before the Cultural Revolution? To what extent may provincial and social origin, sex and nationality handicap or advance the career of leaders in the central state administration?

2) *Administrative criteria*: Do government leaders still tend to spend all their career in one or a group of sectors, that is in a 'functional system' as observed by A. Doak Barnett (1967, pp. 67, 456–7). The rules governing the mobility and career of cadres are unfortunately unknown. Some are secret and variable, others do not exist. The aim of this study consists precisely in trying to grasp some of them and to see whether they promote the rise of more competent officials to the top of the Chinese administration.

## Political, Educational and Socio–Cultural Background of State Council Leaders

### New Cadres versus Veterans

The revolutionary experience is a decisive factor in the career of Chinese communist cadres. Depending on whether you are a veteran cadre (*lao ganbu*), that is whether you joined the Communist Party before 1949, or a new cadre (*xin ganbu*), promotion, prestige and privileges – pension arrangements, for example – are totally different. That is why, in 1985, the first group still held 61% of leadership positions in the central state administration.

Of course, between 1965 and 1985, the percentage of veterans in central government declined and that of new cadres increased. But this shift was limited and uneven. In 1983, the number of new cadres was still practically identical to that in the 1975 government (15%). It was not until 1985 that these accounted for one-third of the government. In fact, the rehabilitation of leaders removed during the Cultural Revolution significantly increased the proportion of veterans in leadership positions in the administration, especially after the Third Plenum of the Eleventh Central Committee (December 1978).

Nevertheless, within this latter category, the generation of the Long March and Yen'an, that is of cadres who had joined the CP before 1938, has been slowly but surely disappearing since 1980, after remaining relatively preponderant until 1978 (mainly because of the peculiar prestige accorded by the Maoists to those who had followed their leader from Jiangxi to Shaanxi in 1934–5. The number of veteran cadres from the 1938–49 period remains virtually stable and it is likely that a good proportion of the leaders whose career before 1949 we do not know (30% in 1985) belong to this category, given their age.

'Rising cadres'[6] were relatively numerous in 1965 (eleven, nine of whom were not members of the Chinese Communist Party) but disappeared from the leadership of departments during the Cultural Revolution. However, the appointment in 1982 of two who had come over after 1949, He Dongchang and Lu Jiaxi – the latter does not belong to the Communist Party – to head the Ministry of Education and the Chinese Academy of Sciences respectively, underlines the current leadership's openness and might be followed by other examples.[7]

Excepting 1975, veterans have consistently been more numerous among leaders in the political area because of the promotion of activists and the transfer to the head of industrial ministries of military leaders, most of whom had participated in the Long March. The 'rising cadres' virtually all held industrial and commercial portfolios, and gave way twenty years later to new cadres promoted from within their areas of activity (Rui Xingwen in the construction sector, Wu Wenying, Li Tieying, Jiang Xinxiong, Zou Jiahua, Li Xu'e in the industrial sector, etc.).

In 1965 all the leaders of the military sector of the government had taken part in the Long March and until 1982 they belonged to the oldest generation of the CP. The appointment, in August 1982, of Chen Bin, born in 1921, and then in June 1985 the appointment of Ding Henggao, born in 1931 and son-in-law of Nie Rongzhen, to the chairmanship of the National Defence Scientific, Technological and Industrial Commission certainly marked a turning point in the recruitment of leaders of state military departments.

The new cadres are thus far from occupying a dominant position at the head of central state organs. The proportion of leaders who joined the Communist Party during the anti-Japanese war or during the civil war, and who have been moulded by the regime, ought logically to rise. However, length of party membership remains one factor determining appointment to the highest positions of responsibility in the state administration. This situation is bound to have an effect on the implementation of the policy of rejuvenating the leadership of the State Council.

## What Rejuvenation?

The rejuvenation of the leadership, which over-60s continued to dominate after 1982, seems, to say the least, limited. While it ceased getting older, 1985 still did not mark a return to 1965 when most leaders were under 61.[8]

**Table 4.2**
**Average Age of Leaders of the Central State Administration**

|  | 1965 | 1975 | 1978 | 1980 | 1983 | 1985 |
|---|---|---|---|---|---|---|
| Average age in years | 60.3 | 62.6 | 65.5 | 66.1 | 64.0 | 62.7 |

The 1982 reform obliged ministers and vice-ministers to retire at 65. According to the figures supplied by Beijing for 38 ministries and commissions, the average age of ministers and vice-ministers fell from 64 to 58 in May 1982.[9] But many ministers obtained waivers, which is why their average age fell by only three years between 1980 and 1985. The trend, observed in all socialist countries, towards the ageing of the leadership had been contained ten years after 1965, when the average age had risen by only 2 years, but it was accelerated in China by the return of victims of the Cultural Revolution between 1978 and 1980.

While the number of septuagenarians had fallen slightly from over a quarter in

1980 (28%) to 22% in 1985, the proportion of over-60s stayed the same. Today they still account for over half the leaders (56%). The under-61s thus remained in a minority in 1985 (44%) despite a distinct rise compared to 1983 (29%). Nevertheless, the figures vary depending on the area of activity. After 1980, as in 1965, economic leaders (of sector 12 in particular) were relatively younger than those in the political area (notably sectors 01.0 and 07) in which recruitment to high positions of responsibility seemed to take much longer and be more arduous when the activity of the party was normalized and focused on the economic development of the country. However, note that the opposite was true in the other two governments. In 1975, the personnel in the political domain, largely renewed following the Cultural Revolution, were slightly younger than the personnel in the economy made up partly of leaders who had come through that ordeal unscathed, partly of military people and partly of those who had been rehabilitated. The share of these latter increased in 1978 in the economic domain, then, in 1980, in the political domain (after the Third Plenum) where the proportion of septuagenarians was twice as large as in the economy.

For their part, the military leaders in the State Council were already older in 1975, as they continued to be drawn from the age groups of the historic leaders of the Communist Party, who had taken part in the Long March. However, the National Defence Scientific, Technological and Industrial Commission has shifted, as we have seen, to the control of younger civilian cadres.

If the results of the policy of rejuvenating leading groups at the central state level were so modest, is this not because the Cultural Revolution, unlike the Stalinist purges, was for many leaders no more than a hiccup in their career?

### The Ordeal of the Cultural Revolution: the Hidden and the Survivors

The Cultural Revolution, launched by Mao Zedong in 1966 with the support of Lin Biao and Zhou Enlai, was aimed at renewing leading groups too loyal to Liu Shaoqi and Deng Xiaoping, who controlled the secretariat of the Central Committee of the CP. These two were considered not loyal enough to the 'great helmsman'; they had indeed been moved to the 'second line' after the fiasco of the Great Leap Forward (1958). The structure and personnel of the state administration were thus profoundly transformed by the Cultural Revolution.

For cadres the issue of participation in this inquisitorial movement within the CCP remained, in 1983 as in the early 1970s but in the opposite sense, an important factor in promotion and hence in career. That is why the victims of the Cultural Revolution still dominated leadership positions in the central state departments in 1985 (72%), particularly in the political domain (81%).

The percentage of unknowns remained relatively unchanged until 1980 (about 10%). But it increased after 1983 (46% in 1985) mainly because new leaders, either too young or not occupying sufficiently important positions to be publicly criticized during the Cultural Revolution, held a larger number of posts in the central government.

It is for the same reason that, after reaching a peak in 1980 – over three-quarters of the leaders – the proportion of victims of the Cultural Revolution is tending to diminish compared to the percentage of those who retained their posts during the period (28%).

After 1980, the arrival in power of young economic leaders reduced the proportion of victims of the Cultural Revolution in this area. And only two leaders (Fang Yi in 04.2 and Ji Pengfei in 01.3) who had retained their post in the State Council during that period remained in the 1985 central government.

In total, while the ordeal of the Cultural Revolution still today constitutes a criterion of promotion, gradually those who occupied top posts before and during that period of turmoil are giving way to younger leaders whose memory of that dramatic period in the recent history of China is rather of the disorder that it led to in the economy than of personal sufferings of the kind endured by their elders.

## The Educational Level of Leaders

Although since 1979 the level of education has once again become a criterion of promotion, in 1985 the proportion of leaders of the central state administration who had university degrees remained small (52 out of 113, or one in two) and appeared to be lower than that of the 1965 government (at least 46 out of 87).

In 1985, two-thirds of ministers (38 out of 57) had university degrees and almost as many in the political sectors as in the economic and particularly industrial sectors. At the time of the reshuffle in 1982, if one is to believe the figures published by the Chinese authorities, 52% of the 167 ministers and vice-ministers had university degrees as against 37% of the 505 ministers and vice-ministers in office before the reform.[10] However, it is possible but unverifiable in the present state of our knowledge that more of the vice-ministers promoted at that time, most of whom were in their fifties and hence educated in the 1950s, might be university educated than the ministers.

The fact remains that 17 of the 19 ministers who entered the government between June 1983 and September 1985 had university degrees. Other factors, whether of a more personal nature (as in the case of Ding Henggao, for example) or deemed to be more important by the authorities, may have facilitated the promotion of new leaders without a university education. But the proclaimed goal of the CP was to give itself a government all of whose members had a higher education and this appears partially to have been put into effect.

## Knowledge of the Outside World

From the late 19th century, many young Chinese from the highest classes of society went abroad or learned foreign languages in order to assimilate scientific and technical knowledge which would promote the economic development of their country. Among them were many future leaders of the nationalist and communist parties. This criterion is all the more important because it helps to tell us about the attitude of the leaders of the Chinese government towards the outside world and thus about the type of relations that any country may expect of the People's Republic of China.

Knowledge of these periods of study abroad is reasonably complete for the leaders of the older generation. For the new cadres, it is highly likely that we do not have all the information.

In 1965, more than one leader in four had studied (at least in part) abroad: one in five in the economic and social domain, two in five in the political domain. One in six of these had studied in the USSR. Many were swept aside by the xenophobic torment of the Cultural Revolution, notably those who spent time in the former brother country (Deng Xiaoping, Luo Ruiqing, Xue Muqiao, Ulanfu, Lu Dingyi, Tan Zhenlin, etc.).

However, the trend was reversed in 1985 as cadres in their fifties, trained in the USSR and the countries of Eastern Europe during the 1950s, began to reach senior positions. The appointment of Li Peng to the post of vice-premier, followed by the arrival, at the head of major portfolios, of Ruan Chongwu (Public Security), Song Jian (Scientific and Technical Committee), all trained in the Soviet Union, and Li Tieying (Electronic Industry), a graduate of the University of Prague, were all signs of this new development. Knowledge of the outside world – including the USSR – is thus once again a positive factor in promotion rather than a handicap in the Chinese administration.

### Provincial Origin: a Strong Numerical Predominance of Coastal China

The provincial origin of the leaders of the central state administration has changed since 1965. Whereas then people from the coastal areas of China were in a minority (47%), today they are in a distinct majority (65%) although the population of the coastal provinces accounts for barely more than a third (37.5%) of the population of People's China (see *JJNJ*, 1983). This is the direct consequence of the progressive disappearance of the old generation of communists, many of whom came from the interior provinces where they had joined the guerrillas. Mao Zedong, born in Hunan (which has 5.4% of the population) had undeniably favoured the rise of people from his home area, twelve of whom (16.5% of the leaders) occupied leadership positions in the central state apparatus in 1965.[11]

The majority of leaders in the economic and social domain have always been from coastal China. Certainly, in 1965, this superiority was slight but in all subsequent governments it increased and in 1983 reached 70.5% of leaders. In 1985 it flattened out at 68%.

It is however in the political domain that the turnabout has been most striking; this underlines the arrival in power of a new generation of more skilled cadres whose careers had been held up during the Maoist period. In 1975 and 1978, two-thirds of the leaders in this domain were from the interior provinces, where only a slight majority came from in 1965. The Cultural Revolution first struck leaders from coastal China, more open to the outside world, and promoted the rise of cadres from the interior, except of course for the Shanghai group represented solely by Zhang Chunqiao in the State Council. It was in 1980 that a change appeared, which was confirmed in 1983 and 1985. Most of the leaders in the political domain – almost two-thirds in 1983 – came from the coastal provinces. The desire to promote cadres with a university education contributed, partly at least, to favouring leaders from that part of the country, who generally had a higher level of education than their colleagues from the interior.[12]

Finally, the leaders in the military sector, former leaders of the communist guerrillas were, until 1983, all from inner China except Ye Jianying, who was Cantonese. However, in 1985, while Zhang Aiping was from the interior province of Sichuan, Ding Henggao was born in the coastal province of Jiangsu.

Two regions have remained constantly under represented among the leaders of the central government: the north-east and the south-west. Since 1953, when Gao Gang, accused of wanting to establish an independent kingdom in Manchuria, was eliminated in circumstances that have remained obscure, the centre has long been suspicious of cadres from this region.[13] The north-east, unrepresented in 1975, remained under represented in the State Council in 1985 despite a slight increase (5% of leaders; 9% of the population). The south-west is in the same situation because of the high percentage of national minorities in that region, only a small number of whom succeeded in climbing up through the ranks of the CP. Only Sichuan (10% of the population), Deng Xiaoping's province, is represented (5%).

On the other hand, two regions have seen a significant shift in their representation: the east and the centre south. Slightly over represented in 1965, the east became heavily so after the Cultural Revolution. In 1985, more than one leader in two (52%), and almost two in three (61%) in the economic and social domain, were from this region.

Some provinces, such as Jiangsu, have recovered the high level of representation that they enjoyed before 1966 but, since 1980, others have provided far more leaders than before (for instance Zhejiang). This is the case in particular with Shandong province, from which over one leader in six in the central administration came in 1983 and one in seven in 1985.

This striking increase in the representation of Shandong is also the manifestation of the arrival in power of a new generation of younger leaders who joined the Communist movement during the Sino–Japanese war during which this province was one of the main centres of resistance.

Conversely, the death of Mao Zedong and the disappearance of the old generation of revolutionaries have clearly led to a considerable fall in the proportion of government leaders from the centre south region (34% in 1965, 18% in 1985). Only Henan, where the prime minister, Zhao Ziyang, was born, has maintained its position. Generally speaking, these provinces have provided political and military leaders rather than economic specialists.

Few leaders (3% in 1985) were born in the north-west whose population is relatively small and largely composed of national minorities. Finally, since 1978 the northern provinces, notably Shanxi and Hebei, have been over represented in the government (15% in 1985, as against 12% in 1965). For the new generation proximity to the capital has become an advantage in acceding to a high post in the central state administration, especially in the political sector (31%). It is as if the CP was seeking to maintain a certain presence of Chinese from the north, thought to be more disciplined and cool, in the most sensitive political positions.[14]

### Social Origin, the Great Unknown

As the old generation of Chinese Communists disappears, the information available on the social origin of the leaders of People's China shrinks dramatically. In the official biographies of the new cadres, nothing is said about their class origin, which used to be cited at great length – when it was right – during the Cultural Revolution. Thus the results obtained are too incomplete (maximum: 1965, 25%

known; minimum: 1983, 8.5% known) to be significant. However, the top leaders in the State Council, most of whom joined the Communist Party before 1938, come from better off classes. How could it have been otherwise in a country where the proportion of illiterates was so large and political power – perhaps more than in other countries – was closely linked to the mastery of writing (and calligraphy)?

Among the 21 government leaders in 1965 whose social origin we know, five were from ordinary backgrounds and 15 from well off families. The leaders of poor origin promoted thanks to the Cultural Revolution were gradually removed from government [15] which since 1980 has been headed by the son of a landlord.[16]

### The Virtual Absence of Women

There were no women at all in 1965 in the leadership of the state administration. They came for the first time into the State Council thanks to the Cultural Revolution. Indeed, the only government in which two women (Wu Guixian and Deng Gang) held posts of responsibility in the political domain was that of 1975, still made up of many Maoists. Since 1978, there have been fewer women, and they have occupied leading positions only in the economic and social domain, particularly Health and the Textile Industry.[17]

### Under Representation of the National Minorities

Very few members of the national minorities – Chinese citizens who do not belong to the Han majority of the country – have joined the Communist Party. Among those who have, most have risen to largely ceremonial positions (deputy to the National People's Congress or to the Chinese People's Political Consultative Conference). Only a handful of them has succeeded in entering the Central Committee of the CCP.

The State Nationalities Affairs Commission is the only organ to have been continuously headed by a member of a minority: Ulanfu (Mongol) in 1965 and Yang Jingren (Hui) since 1978. Apart from this latter, the 1985 government included another Hui, Mu Qing, from Henan, director since August 1982 of the Xinhua News Agency where, apparently, he has spent most of his career.

In all, the national minorities, 6% of the population of the PRC, accounted in 1983 for only 2% of the members of the central government. However, Mu Qing's appointment certainly indicates a breakthrough and shows a willingness on the part of the Chinese leadership to increase access.

## Mobility and Career of Leaders

### A Relative Immobility between Sectors of Activity

Most leaders of the central state administration have spent most of their career within the same department. This trend towards professionalization has become more marked since 1983, particularly in the economic and social domain.[18] Leaders who change sectors often use the same channels and the frequency of moves from one sector to another is undeniably a positive factor in promotion.

*Generalists versus Specialists*: Generalist ministers, i.e. leaders whose main experience was acquired outside the sector or sub-sector of activity in which they were at the time the government was formed, were in a minority in 1965 (35%), especially in the economic and social domain (31.5%). The transfer of soldiers to head many ministries during the Cultural Revolution, then the assignment of a good number of rehabilitated leaders to posts in sectors in which they were not specialists, i.e. where they had not spent most of their career, reversed the trend. In 1980, 61.5% of ministers were generalists.

After 1983 there was a return to a situation similar to that of 1965. In 1985, two-thirds of the ministers in the economic and social domain (68%) and one-third of those in the political domain (33%) were specialists in their sector (or sub-sector). In addition, 9 of the 25 generalist ministers did not change domain: for example, Zhu Muzhi, who had spent his whole career in propaganda and information (07.4), moved to culture in 1982 (07.1).

As for bureau directors, the same shift, although less intense, can be observed. In 1985, most of these were specialists in the political domain (60%) and half were generalists in the economic and social domain within which they had a greater tendency to move from one sector to another.[19]

Finally, virtually all leaders in the military domain had no experience in another sector of activity. Nevertheless, although Chen Bin, a career diplomat and specialist in security, was an exception, his successor, Ding Henggao, a civilian and a specialist in the national defence industry, had worked in a department of sector 12 closely linked to domain 02.

*The Most Commonly Used Channels between Sectors and Sub-sectors*: Few leaders in the economic and social domain moved into the political domain in the period before 1980.[20] Since 1982, the trend has been reversed. For example, sub-sector 01.0 (premier and vice-premiers without portfolio) is now dominated by economic specialists (Wan Li, Fang Yi, Zhang Jingfu, Gu Mu and Kang Shi'en). Among the typical channels within the political domain, it should be noted that the majority of leaders in sector 03 (public order and security) are former provincial first secretaries or governors (two in 1965, 1975 and 1978, three in 1980 and 1983, four in 1985). This type of recruitment is all the more interesting because it transcends the upheavals that China has suffered in the past twenty years: someone who can maintain security at the local level can do so at the national level; this is the basic idea that seems to govern the choice of leaders in this sector. However, while until 1983 the other leaders in this sector were specialists in it, in 1985, Jia Chunwang, Minister of State Security, close to Hu Yaobang, had spent most of his career in propaganda and Ruan Chongwu, Minister of Public Security, was a research engineer. This latter type of promotion is altogether something new.

Previously, it was relatively easy to move from the army to management of the economy and particularly of industry. But since 1982 the opposite trend has been evident. The military, who already before 1966 controlled three of the seven Ministries of Machine Building in sub-sector 12.2, increased their presence during the Cultural Revolution (five out of six in 1975) but were quickly sent back to their barracks after the death of Mao Zedong. In 1978, only one soldier, Song Renqiong, remained; he controlled the important Seventh Ministry of Machine Building (Space Industry). This ministry, headed for three years by a specialist in security, Zhang Jun, was entrusted for the first time in the history of the PRC to a civil engineer, Li Xu'e, a specialist in the space industry, in June 1985.

Another sign of this new trend is that the National Defence Scientific, Technological and Industrial Commission came under the chairmanship of a civilian, Ding Henggao, who had worked for a long time in the Seventh Ministry of Machine Building.[21]

The leaders in agriculture have not usually been specialists: a large majority of them had for a long time filled leadership positions of a political nature at the local level: Tan Zhenlin and Liu Wenhui in 1965, Luo Yuchuan in 1978, Wan Li, Huo Shilian, Gao Yang and Yong Wentao in 1980, Yang Zhong and Lin Hujia in 1983 and 1985. Now the soldiers present before (Wang Zhen and Qi Yong) and just after the Cultural Revolution (Sha Feng) have totally disappeared from this sector and specialists have been increasing since 1983 (for instance He Kang and Du Runsheng).

*The Frequency of Sectoral Mobility:* The majority of leaders who have changed (sub-)sectors or domain have done so only once in their career. It might have been thought, once again, that the time factor would increase the frequency of sectoral mobility. Certainly in 1978 and above all in 1980, ministers who had worked in two or three (sub-)sectors and two or even three different domains were more numerous than before, but since 1983, the situation has returned to proportions only slightly higher than those of 1965: in 1985, half – as opposed to two-thirds before the Cultural Revolution – of the leaders who had changed type of function had done so only once.

Until 1980, leaders in the economic and social domain exhibited a higher rate of sectoral mobility: half of them had had professional experience in at least three (sub-)sectors as against one political leader in six in 1980 and one in eight in 1978.

The opposite trend, begun in 1983, was confirmed in 1985: 46% of political leaders as against 30% of economic leaders had experience in three sectors or had changed domain. It is thus now easier for leaders of the central state administration to move from the economic to the political than from the political to the economic.

The frequency of sectoral mobility is one factor of promotion: Deng Xiaoping, Song Renqiong and Wang Zhen, all members of the Political Bureau of the CCP, have had economic, political and military responsibilities in turn. While no leader in the present government has been through all three areas of activity, the first two vice-premiers, Wan Li and Yao Yilin, are among those ministers who have a relatively rich professional experience: the former spent a long period in the capital construction sector, as well as in transport and agriculture and the latter's career was initially in commerce, then in external economic relations and finally in planning (01.1). On the other hand, the former (who acts for Zhao Ziyang when he is away) also held leadership positions in the provinces whereas the latter has worked at the centre since 1949. Might the scale of provincial experience also be a positive factor in promotion?[22]

**Greater Geographical Mobility**
Since 1983, more leaders of the central state administration, in particular those of ministerial rank and in the economic domain, than before the Cultural Revolution have held posts in the provinces. Moreover they were often sent there again to pursue their careers. While east China remains one of the main regions where these leaders acquired provincial experience, Manchuria and the north have become new nurseries of future ministers. More than was the case formerly, the wealth of provincial experience is a positive factor in promotion.

*The Intensity of Geographical Mobility:* Before the Cultural Revolution, few provincial leaders moved to the centre to become ministers in the State Council, which, since its formation in 1954, had been continuously headed by the same people or by former vice-ministers who had belonged to the central government since the early 1950s.

On the other hand, in 1975, a number of civilian and military provincial leaders (40% of ministers) came to Beijing to take over portfolios left vacant by the victims of Maoism. Then, in 1978 and 1980, this percentage was reduced by the return of the latter, who, after a break of ten to fifteen years, resumed their careers at the centre. After being rehabilitated, several of them were, initially, appointed to provincial posts. The increase after 1978 in the proportion of leaders who had begun their careers at the centre and then continued them at the local level before being called back into the centre (24% of ministers in 1980, 11% in 1985) is also due to the despatch of senior leaders to some provinces to settle urgent problems there.[23]

Until 1980, two-thirds of ministers had some provincial experience, many of them between 1949 and 1954, before being called to the central government. In 1983, this proportion rose to three-quarters in the economic domain and four-fifths in the political domain. Almost half the ministers (48%) spent the first part of their career at the local level. This is a new phenomenon. It is reminiscent of what we saw in the Cultural Revolution, but the great difference lies in the fact that the majority of ministers in 1985 are specialists in their sector who first showed their mettle in the provinces and not Maoist activists and soldiers with no specialized knowledge of their portfolios.

Finally, virtually all the military leaders in the State Council have pursued their careers at the centre since 1954. The only exception was Chen Bin who held posts abroad, like leaders in other fields of central government (11% in 1985 as against 2% in 1965).

Cadres who have pursued their careers in the central state administration since 1954 or even 1949 thus have less of a tendency to prevent provincial leaders acceding to ministerial posts. The desire for renewal and rejuvenation on the part of the leading group in 1982 undeniably contributed to this evolution. It is likely that ministers will be initially recruited among leaders who began their careers in the provinces and who, called to the capital, often with the rank of vice-minister, continue in the same line in central government before perhaps being sent to the local level to resolve particularly delicate problems without this move being considered as a demotion.

*The Localization of Provincial Experiences: the Return of Leaders from the North-east*: Until 1983, the constancy of the percentages is altogether surprising: 55% of the provincial experiences of leaders had been acquired in the coastal regions as against 45% in inner China. This proportion is virtually identical to that of the value of the industrial and agricultural output of the two parts of the country in 1981: 56% as against 44%. However, in 1985, this balance was no longer so perfect: coastal China had become the part of the country where leaders from the provinces had mostly worked (66%).

If in 1965 and 1980 two-thirds of the provincial experiences of leaders in the political domain had been acquired in the coastal provinces, this was in part because numerous government leaders had, particularly before 1954 and in east China (Shanghai), held administrative posts.

Conversely, in 1985, there were slightly fewer leaders who had held posts in east China (29% as against 34% in 1965), especially in the political domain, whereas former leaders of north-east China had begun after 1978, in the economic and social domain, to be more represented in the central government (22% in 1985 as against 9% in 1965). Since the elimination of Gao Gang, the centre has continued to be suspicious of cadres both born and working in Manchuria and has rarely called them into givernment. This shift thus constituted a major change in the carefully maintained balance between provinces in which leaders have worked, built up links, formed networks of clients and sometimes formed cliques. The marked return of the north-east – seven of the fifteen ministers in the industrial sectors have worked there – is symbolized by the rise of Ma Hong, a former member of the Gao Gang clique, who reappeared in 1979, president of the Academy of Social Sciences until September 1985 and director of the Technical–Economic Research Centre.

Apart from this, since 1978 proximity to the capital appears to have become a positive factor in promotion to the government: the number of leaders who have held posts in the north tripled between 1965 and 1985 (20 as against 7) and 10 of the 14 economic leaders in the State Council who have worked in this region have occupied senior posts in the municipality of Beijing. The most typical case is probably that of Li Peng, a rising star in the government, who, during the Cultural Revolution, according to his official biography, maintained the electricity supply in the Beijing-Tianjin region 'with the backing of Zhou Enlai'.

*Provincial Experience, a Positive Factor in Promotion*: Wealth of provincial experience certainly constitutes a positive factor in promotion within the upper echelons of the Chinese administration. The most typical example is that of Zhao Ziyang himself, who held responsible positions in four different provinces (Henan, Guangdong, Inner Mongolia and Sichuan). This vital aspect of his career probably influenced Deng Xiaoping's choice of him. The case of Li Peng, who held posts in Jilin and Liaoning and then Beijing, is similar.

### Vertical Mobility: the Continued Predominance of the Mode of Promotion Vice-Minister/Minister

Promotion within the State Council has been the constant pattern – three-quarters of ministers and eight out of ten bureau directors in 1985 – and has even somewhat increased since 1983. The fact is that among ministers, apart from the 1975 government in which eight regional military leaders were promoted, the proportion of those who had already held central government posts was virtually identical before (66%) and after the Cultural Revolution (61% in 1978 and 64% in 1980).

Today, more provincial leaders, who rather tended to become ministers directly between 1978 and 1980, are going through the required route of the post of vice-minister in the same department. This channel, in all previous governments but to a greater degree since 1983 (42% in 1985 as against 25% in 1965 and 31% in 1978), constitutes the chief mode of recruitment to the post of minister. On the other hand, the percentages of ministers who change portfolios (one in eight), who come from a provincial administration (one in eight) and who come from the central apparatus of the CCP (7%) are falling.

The recruitment of bureau directors was even more in 1985 (80%) than in 1965 (70%) from inside the State Council. However, while until 1978 these had mostly occupied posts of deputy in the same department, usually for many years, since 1980, vice-ministers more easily became bureau directors (25% in 1985).

However, the vice-minister/minister mode of promotion within the same department is predominant only in the economic and social domain (83%). The rise of ministers in the political domain is more varied: while slightly more than half of them in 1985 (57%), as before the Cultural Revolution, became ministers by climbing the echelons within the State Council, the other half was made up of local political leaders (29%) or, to a lesser extent, of cadres in the central apparatus of the CP (14%).

Since 1982, leaders in the military domain have been promoted from within the state administration which was rather the case in 1965, whereas following the Cultural Revolution the two ministers of defence (Ye Jianying and Xu Xiangqian) did not previously occupy any post in the State Council and were chosen from among the members of the Military Commission of the Central Committee of the Communist Party.

Although in general provincial leaders who become ministers were of a higher rank than those reaching the post of bureau director, no precise rule of promotion between the local echelon and the centre can be identified: all were provincial first secretaries, governors, secretaries or assistant secretaries. Nevertheless, in the economic and social domain, the promotion of vice-ministers who have been able to become specialists 'on the job' has been gradually combined with direct appointment to the top of ministries of heads of factories (Wu Wenying to the Textile Industry) or industrial companies (Wang Tao to the Petroleum Industry) or research institutes (Lie Tieying to the Electronic Industry). That is why, while the modes of promotion of government leaders have been regularized, greater account has been taken of the technical skills of candidates, especially in the economic and social domain.

## Mobility between the Administration of the Communist Party and that of the State at the Central Level

This mobility has diminished sharply in the economic domain, since the economic departments of the Central Committee of the CCP have not been re-established. It has been maintained in the political domain where, however, multiple office holding has virtually disappeared since 1982, whereas in the military domain it has remained common.

The number of departments of the Central Committee has not remained unchanged. Before the Cultural Revolution, there not only existed the political departments (General Affairs, Organization, Propaganda, United Front Work and International Liaison) and the Military Commission (identified in 1958) which remained constantly active but also three economic departments (Industry and Communications, Finance and Trade and Agriculture) which were not re-established after the Cultural Revolution. On the other hand, the Central Party Control Commission was reconstituted at the time of the Third Plenum of the Eleventh Central Committee in December 1978 with the name of Central Commission for Discipline Inspection.

In 1965, most of the leaders of the State Council who had come directly from departments of the Central Committee of the CP (seven out of eight) continued to occupy their posts in these organs. To these were added nine other leaders who had begun their career in the state administration and had subsequently added posts in the organs of the Central Committee to their posts in the government. One leader of the State Council in five was also working in the central administration of the CP. At the time, the mobility of leaders between the organs of the Central Committee and those of the government occurred rather in the direction party/state in the political and military domains and in the direction state/party in the economic and social domain.[24]

After the Cultural Revolution, the suppression of the three economic departments of the Central Committee naturally caused a fall in the number of moves from party organs to state ones in the economic and social domain. The desire of the present leadership of the CP to distribute work better and limit the amount of multiple office holding between these two administrations probably ruled out any re-establishment of these departments. In the 1985 government, there were only two cases of multiple office holding: first, Du Runsheng, in charge of both the Rural Policy Research Centre (*nongcun zhengce*) of the Central Committee and the Rural Development Research Centre (*nongcun kaifa*) of the State Council. While Du's role in the working out of rural policy has certainly been vital, this type of appointment limits the impact of the reform of the Chinese administration. The second case, which was also the only move observed between the political and economic domains, is that of Hu Sheng, President of the Academy of Social Sciences since September 1985, who spent all his career in propaganda and who was transferred directly from the central Party History Research Centre of the Central Committee of the CP which he continued to head.[25]

In the political sectors and sub-sectors, some of which (07.1 and 07.4) were directly controlled until 1982 by the heads of the equivalent organs of the Central Committee, particularly the Propaganda Department, the results of the reform cannot be denied. Nevertheless, mobility between these organs remains. Moreover, while since 1982 not a single member of the Central Commission for Discipline Inspection of the CP has belonged to the government,[26] the persistence of multiple office holding in the public order and security sector (03) as well as in nationalities affairs is indicative of the concern of the communist government to police the population closely and keep tight control of activities it considers to be illegal or to have centrifugal tendencies. In fact, Liu Fuzhi, Minister of Public Security from 1983 to 1985, and previously Minister of Justice, had, since 1982, been secretary-general of the Politics and Law Commission of the Central Committee. This Commission was chaired by Peng Zhen, then Chen Pixian and since 1985 by Qiao Shi, three men with decisive influence in this domain.[27] Similarly, Yang Jingren, director for United Front Work of the Central Committee, has been responsible since 1982 for the Nationalities Affairs Commission: it is the only 'functional system', to use Doak Barnett's (1967, pp. 69, 456–7) terminology, which is still today headed by a single person.

Finally, the military leaders on the State Council were consistently chosen from among the members of the Military Commission of the Central Committee of which they usually became members before entering central government. Today that rule is no longer so rigid.[28]

In all, for leaders in the economic and social domain a period in the administrative organs of the Central Committee seems no longer to be a positive factor in promotion whereas such experience remains so for some leaders in the political domain and for virtually all in the military domain. In the other direction, however, there is significant state economic leadership representation in the Central Committee of the CCP.

### The Position of Leaders of the Central State Administration in the Central Political Organs of the Communist Party

Two shifts – apparently contradictory but in reality proceeding from the same political will – in the representation of leaders of the central state administration in the central political organs of the Communist Party have been a reduced representation in the Political Bureau and the Secretariat but a distinctly greater presence, in particular of ministers in the economic domain, in the Central Committee.

*The Political Bureau*: The number of members of the Standing Committee of the Political Bureau belonging to the government has plummeted since 1980. Now, only the premier (Zhao Ziyang) belongs to it whereas previously two vice-premiers without portfolio (Deng Xiaoping and Chen Yun in 1965, Deng Xiaoping and Zhang Chunqiao in 1975, Deng Xiaoping and Li Xiannian in 1978) were members of it.[29] The tendency was not, in 1985, so marked for the Political Bureau itself.

In 1985, 14% of ministers were members or alternate members of the Political Bureau, as against 11% in 1965, 16.5% in 1975, 15.5% in 1978, 7.5% in 1980 and 9% in 1983. While the most important vice-premiers, ministers and state councillors continued to belong to this ruling organ of the CP (Wan Li, Yao Yilin, Tian Jiyun, Li Peng and Fang Yi), there were virtually no leaders of the other political (sub-) sectors and the economic domain in the Political Bureau. Nevertheless, for the first time since the 1960s, the Minister of Foreign Affairs, Wu Xueqian, was identified as a member of the Political Bureau of which Chen Muhua, President of the People's Bank of China, remained an alternate member.[30]

Finally, Zhang Aiping, appointed in 1982, was the first Minister of Defence since

1949 not to belong to the Political Bureau. This shift signifies the determination of the government to limit the place of the army in the party leadership. It also shows that the military in the government are no longer the most powerful leaders of the PLA.

*The Party Secretariat*: Before the Cultural Revolution, five members of the secretariat out of 16 (8% of ministers) occupied posts in the three domains of activity of the State Council. In 1980, this organ was re-established but assigned six of its twelve members solely to the economic and social domain of the state administration (11% of ministers). At that time, it looked as if the former economic departments of the Central Committee had been moved to the State Council and directly headed by officials of the Secretariat, who were in charge of the main government commissions.[31]

Although since September 1985, among the three members of the Secretariat who belong to the government – Wan Li, Tian Jiyun and Li Peng – (5% of ministers) only the last named has held a ministerial portfolio, these remain the most influential persons in the Standing Committee of the State Council and the only secretaries of the Central Committee who are specialists in economics. That is why, in the absence of specialized departments of the Central Committee, the leading core of the government constitutes a centre of decision-making and economic management. They are comparable to the Secretariat in 1965, not because the State Council's Standing Committee is autonomous in relation to the leadership of the CP but, on the contrary, because the highest bodies of the CP are represented in it by their principal leaders competent in this domain.[32] Was the transfer of Qiao Shi to the State Council in March 1986 not to enhance the influence of political leaders at the head of central state administrations and thus limit the power of the economists?

*The Central Committee of the CCP*: While most bureau directors (89%) now do not have membership of the Central Committee, in contrast to the years before the Cultural Revolution, the proportion of ministers belonging to it has risen from 54% in 1965 to 80.5% in 1983, then to 84% in 1985 (including alternates).

Until the Twelfth Congress of the Communist Party (1982), half as many leaders of the economic and social domain as of the political domain were members of the Central Committee. But in the 1985 government, nine ministers out of ten in the economic and social domain and three-quarters in the political domain were members of the Central Committee.

The industrial sectors (08, 09, 11, 12) were previously very poorly represented in the Central Committee: in 1965 three of the 20 ministers in these sectors belonged to it (including alternate members) as against six out of 13 in 1975, eight out of 15 in 1978, nine out of 20 in 1980 and 13 out of 15 in 1983. Since September 1985, all the ministers in these sectors have belonged to it. This shift is doubtless the reflection of the new political line of the Communist Party which is aimed at increasing the power and prestige of officials in the economic departments of state (Lee, 1983, pp. 686–7).

Conversely, until 1983, nine out of ten ministries in the political domain were controlled by a member of the Central Committee. If since then the opposite trend has been underway, today as formerly the judicial organs are poorly represented in the 'parliament of the CP': no minister of justice since 1949 has belonged to it.

Finally, all the ministers in the military domain have always been members of the Central Committee.[33] Since 1983, however, in both the economic and the political domain, it is not entry into the Central Committee that favours the promotion of leaders of the central state administration but, on the contrary, their accession to the post of minister that opens up for them the door to the Central Committee, which for a minority is a step towards the Political Bureau or the Secretariat. Membership of these two latter highest bodies of the party seldom eases the way into the State Council; in addition, the vice-premiers and ministers who are members of it tend to be relieved of their portfolios, which are then given to younger leaders, and they retain solely a role of coordination in the Standing Committee of Government.[34]

Are the present Chinese leaders better equipped than their elders to carry out the economic development of the country?

1) The change of generation and the evolution of the political regime have helped to alter the profile of leaders of the state administration. The present leaders, mostly from coastal China, joined the CP during the Sino-Japanese war and have a greater wealth of provincial experience. Partly due to the upheavals of the Cultural Revolution, this greater interaction between the central and local administrations has undoubtedly improved the professional quality of senior cadres who probably tend, because of their provincial origin, to be more open to the outside world.

Since 1982, ministers, now often younger, have been much less obliged to unload their responsibilities on to their deputies but have been themselves able to carry on the work of their department. Studies at university level, especially abroad, are once again undeniably a positive factor in promotion whereas social origin no longer seems to be taken into account.

The present leaders, for the most part direct or indirect victims of the Cultural Revolution, might be thought to form a more homogeneous team. Specialization, professionalization and new patterns of promotion, in particular in the economic and social domain, are undeniably improving the quality of the leadership of the Chinese administration.

Finally, at the central level there is no longer any dual administration of the economy. Since the Cultural Revolution the State Council has been managing the economy under the sole control of the Political Bureau and above all its Standing Committee to which the premier has always belonged. Moreover, ministers are also generally the secretaries of the CP committees of the department they are running. Of course the re-establishment of the Secretariat in 1980 relieved the Political Bureau of some of its prerogatives, notably political and ideological ones. But with the Secretariat apparently deprived of major departments which used to be directly subordinate to it, and where, as we have seen, economic specialists are in a minority, can it play an exclusive role in this domain? Are not some if its members who do not belong to the central government – for example Deng Liqun, in charge of propaganda from 1982 to 1985[35] – trying to limit the application of decisions to which they were not party or which they opposed, by using the only powers they possess, in particular propaganda, to distort or amplify the campaigns launched by the leadership of the CP? The campaign against spiritual pollution in the winter of 1983–4 was a good example of this.

Conversely, most of the secretaries of the Central Committee who sit on the Standing Committee of the State Council are economic specialists and it is as members of this body that they head, like the heads of the staff offices of the government before the Cultural Revolution, one or several sectors of activity of the central state administration. That is why the Standing Committee of the State Council seems to be a more autonomous and efficient centre of decision-making and economic management than before.

2) There are, however, limits to these improvements. The over representation of leaders from east and north China, the virtual absence of women and the under representation of the national minorities may engender a number of tensions within the administration and between the administration and society.

Nor is the rejuvenation – which in any case is quite modest – of leaders a panacea, the more so as often still the old retired leaders continue to influence decision-making, thanks to their prestige or their network of ties (*guanxi*) with serving senior officials. Moreover, the promotion of new cadres is slowed down by the persistent priority given to veteran officials, in particular for the control of key economic and political portfolios. In addition, in the medium term (ten years), the rejuvenation of the leadership will probably be hindered by the arrival of cadres in their 50s whose career was disturbed by the Maoist period and by the potential rivalry between leaders in their 60s trained in the USSR during the 1950s and leaders in their 40s sent to the West, especially the United States, since the death of Mao.

On the other hand, as Barnett showed already in 1965, ministers, who of course in socialist countries are more like senior officials than politicians, have a tendency to spend all their career within a single functional system or to a lesser degree within a single sector of activity. This pattern of promotion limits the professional experience and breadth of vision of leaders and increases departmentalism (*benweizhuyi*) and conflicts between departments.

In the political domain, the action of the government remains closely controlled by the departments of the Central Committee of the CP and in the economy the creation of a Rural Research Centre may mark the beginning of another shift which might lead to the re-establishment of true economic departments of the Central Committee in the guise – so as not to go against the present reform – of the multiplication of research centres placed under the control of this body.[36]

Finally, the 'sacred union' of the victims of the Cultural Revolution is in large part artificial. The Liuists and the Dengists of yesterday were at one on questions that are today outdated. The wide opening to the outside world and the partial decollectivization of the economy have created new fracture lines which also run through the ruling teams of the central state administration whose appointment is the result of a trade-off between the leaders of the main opinion groups (Deng Xiaoping, Chen Yun and Hu Yaobang).

Permanence or change? The leaders of the central state administration are better equipped to confront the challenges of economic development but their career remains determined by a politico-administrative system whose functioning has been only partly modified.

# Appendix

## The Three Domains

### Economic and Social Domain

| | | |
|---|---|---|
| Sectors | 01.1 | Economy |
| and | 01.2 | External economic affairs |
| sub-sectors | 04.1 | Education |
| | 04.2 | Research |
| | 05 | Labour, training, social affairs |
| | 06 | Health, medicine |
| | 08 | Construction, public works |
| | 09 | Fuel, energy, raw materials |
| | 10 | Agriculture, sylviculture, hunting, fishing, agricultural technology, environment |
| | 11 | Extractive industries, mineral resources, raw material industries |
| | 12.1 | Processing industries and light industries |
| | 12.2 | Machine construction and defence industries |
| | 13 | Transport and communications |
| | 14 | Trade and distribution |

### Political Domain

| | | |
|---|---|---|
| Sectors and sub-sectors | 01.0 | Premier, vice-premiers and state councillors without portfolios at the central level; first secretaries and secretaries, governors and assistant governors at the local level |
| | 01.3 | Foreign affairs |
| | 01.4 | General services |
| | 03 | Public order and security |
| | 07 | Recreation, cultural and religious affairs and services, information |

### Military Domain

| | | |
|---|---|---|
| Sector | 02 | National defence |

Some sectors have not been easy to allocate to domains. For example, education and research possess an obvious political content. But we felt that the need to train a skilled labour force and develop science and technology were the principal – and economic – missions of this sector. Similarly, we felt that the social sectors (05, 06) are closer to the economic sectors, which they assist on an everyday basis, than to the political sectors in which the ideological control of the party is much closer. Sector 01.0 was created because in each government a number of vice-premiers and state councillors (since 1982) hold no particular portfolio that might indicate their principal assignment. As members of the Standing Committee of the State Council, they are entitled to be heard on every item and are the expression of a subtle political balance. That is why, like the premier, who coordinates the activities of the various sectors, they play a role that is more political than economic.

# Notes

1. For studies of the Central Committee of the Chinese CP, see particularly: Donald W. Klein, 1962b, pp. 57–64; Robert A. Scalapino, 1962, pp. 67–148; William De B. Mills, 1983, pp. 16–35; and Wolfgang Bartke and Peter Schler, 1985. On provincial personnel, see: Frederick C. Teiwes, 1967; Michael Oksenberg, 1971; Kau Ying-Mao, 1971; D. Goodman, 1980 and 1986; W. De B. Mills, 1985. See also the articles on subnational and functional elites in the above mentioned work by Scalapino. There are analyses of the personnel of a ministry in *China Quarterly*, no. 14, October–December 1960, pp. 28–39; Daniel Tretiak, 1980, pp. 943–63. Finally, there have been some studies of the highest bodies of the CP and the state: Paul Wong, 1976. More recently, Lee Hong-Yong has published an interesting study of the reform of administrative personnel (ministers and vice-ministers, provincial secretaries, members of the Central Committee and directors and assistant directors of departments of the Central Committee) (1984, pp. 34–47).
2. In the known chart of the departments of the Central Committee, only the Rural Policy Research Centre of the Secretariat and to a lesser degree the Investigation Department and the Research Centre of the Secretariat seem to play an economic role.
3. We have preferred recent and official sources since they give more detail and sometimes correct the information gathered by old and foreign sources. The sources used are: *Gendai*, 1972; *Who's Who in Communist China, 1969*; Donald W. Klein and Anne B. Clark, 1971; Wolfgang Bartke, 1981; *Zhonggong renminlu*, March 1982. See also Donald W. Klein, 1962a.
4. For 1965, we have used the list of organs of the State Council published in the *Renmin Shouce*, 1965, pp. 125–7 as a basis. For 1975, to the list published by the NCNA on 17 January 1975, we have added the bureaux functioning that year according to the *China Directory*, 1977. For 1978, *Beijing Information*, no. 10, 13 March 1978, pp. 45–6, published the list of ministers to which we have added the list of functioning bureaux that year according to Bartke, 1981, pp. 648–52. For 1980 we have used as a basis the list published in *China Aktuell*, September 1980, pp. 800–804, the list supplied by *BKNJ*, August 1980, p. 46 and the *China Directory*, 1982, pp. 35–6. For 1983, we have used the list published by *Beijing Information*, no. 26, 27

June 1983, and for the bureaux the *China Directory*, 1984, pp. 174–80. Finally, for 1985, we have updated the list in *China Directory*, 1985, pp. 46–8 and 100–113.

5. In 1985 there were ten of them: the Construction Bank, the Bank of China, the Supreme People's Court, the Supreme People's Procuracy, the Chinese Academy of Sciences, the Chinese Academy of the Social Sciences, the Federation of Supply and Marketing Cooperatives, the Investment Bank, the Agricultural Bank and the Bank for Commerce and Industry.

6. 'Rising cadres' (*qiyi ganbu*) only began to collaborate with the CCP in 1949 and are thus not considered as veterans. See Barnett, 1967, p. 45.

7. In June 1985 he became the vice-chairman of the State Education Commission headed by Li Peng; Hu Yizhou, who succeeded Shen Tu in March 1985 at the head of the CAAC, is also one of those who 'came over'.

8. The number of unknown birthdates is quite high and varies between 17% in 1965 and 43% in 1975, which limits the significance of the results. However, we have calculated the average age of leaders whose year of birth is known, then we have distinguished three age groups: septuagenarians, sexagenarians, and the under-61s. We have used the age of leaders at the time the government is formed as the base.

9. Report by Zhao Ziyang on the restructuring of the State Council to the Twenty-second session of the Third National People's Congress, 2 March 1982, (*SWB/FE*/6974, C 3/3, 10 March 1982); report by Zhao Ziyang to the Twenty-third session of the Fifth National People's Congress, 26 April 1982 (*SWB/FE*/7014/C/2-4). In 1985, the average age of the principal leaders of the 81 departments of the State Council was 56.6, *Beijing Information*, no. 38, 23 September 1985, p. 4.

10. *Beijing Information*, no. 19, 10 May 1982, p. 3. In 1985, 71% of the principal leaders of the State Council had a university level education (*Beijing Information*, no. 38, 23 September 1985, p. 4).

11. Taking as a base the present administrative provinces, two ways of classifying provinces have been used. The first is to group on the one hand the coastal provinces (Liaoning, Hebei, Beijing, Tianjin, Shandong, Jiangsu, Shanghai, Zhejiang, Fujian, Taiwan, Guangdong and Guangxi) and, on the other hand, the interior provinces, that is the other eighteen. The contrast between coastal China, turned towards the outside world since the 19th Century, and inner China, more traditional and more resistant to modernization, is a classic one. The second way of classifying them is to group the provinces into six large regions; these are the ones the Communist authorities used in the 1950s and 60s and are still the geographical and economic groupings that Chinese usually refer to.

12. According to the results of the 1982 census, the proportion of university graduates per 100,000 inhabitants was 562 in the coastal provinces and 366 in the interior. The national average is 440 graduates per 100,000 inhabitants (*Beijing Information*, no. 16, 16 April 1984, p. 29).

13. This phenomenon was observed in the 1950s by Klein (1962b) who highlighted the under representation of the north-east in the Central Committee.

14. In particular in sector 03: in fact Ruan Chongwu, Minister of Public Security, Jia Chunwang, Minister of State Security, and Cui Naifu, Minister of Civil Affairs, are from Beijing.

15. Three vice-premiers without portfolio (Wu Guixian, Chen Yonggui and Chen Xilian) and the Minister of Public Safety who in 1976 became Premier (Hua Guofeng).

16. The Minister of Defence also belongs to this social class, as does Kang Shi'en: Yao Yilin is the son of an official and Ji Pengfei is from a middle peasant family. Belonging to the communist ruling class by birth or marriage is undoubtedly a

factor in promotion but one that is rarely known. Thus Li Peng was adopted by Zhou Enlai at the age of 11, Liao Hui, director of the state bureau responsible for Overseas Chinese, is the son of Liao Chengzhi, Ding Henggao and Zou Jiahua, Minister of Ordnance Industry, are sons-in-law of two old marshals – respectively Nie Rongzhen and Ye Jianying – who officially retired in September 1985.

17. The leading female ministers are Chen Muhua, president of the People's Bank of China and Qian Zhengying, Minister of Water Conservancy and Power.

18. Our information on the career of leaders of ministerial rank is almost complete (2% of unknowns in 1975 and 1978). Conversely, as regards leaders of the rank of bureau director the percentages of unknowns vary between 4% in 1965 and 36% in 1985.

19. For example, Wang Lin was vice-minister of several economic departments (09, 12) before being appointed director of the Office for Building the Economic Zone in the Yangzi Delta.

20. We have treated as original (sub-)sector the one in which a leader spent most of his career. The (sub-)sector in which he was posted in the government being studied when it was formed is called the arrival (sub-)sector.

21. This ministry has moreover become a veritable nursery of ministers. In fact, in addition to the two above-mentioned leaders, Song Jian (State Scientific and Technological Commission) and Rui Xingwen (Urban and Rural Construction and Environment) are both former vice-ministers of the space industry.

22. Li Peng, Vice-premier and chairman of the State Education Committee since June 1985, an energy expert, and Ruan Chongwu, Minister of Public Security, former director of a research institute under the Ministry of Nuclear Industry, then scientific attaché in West Germany and finally chairman of the Shanghai Planning Commission, have acquired a rich professional experience which probably helped their rise to the highest echelons of the politico-administrative hierarchy.

23. The best known examples are those of Wan Li, appointed first secretary of the Anhui CP committee in 1977, and Zhang Jingfu who succeeded him in that post (1979–82). Both left relatively minor portfolios (respectively railways and finance) to try out in an economically backward region an agricultural reform that was later applied in the whole country. However, these appointments were also tests. The positive results of the experiments as well as the political evolution of the CCP after the Third Plenum enabled the former to become head of the State Agricultural Commission in February 1979 and the latter to become chairman of the State Economic Commission in May 1982.

24. While Lu Dingyi, director of the Propaganda Department of the CP, became Minister of Culture, Yao Yilin, Vice-minister of Trade, was promoted assistant director and then director of the Department of Finance and Trade of the CP; it was the same for Gu Mu, Vice-chairman then Chairman of the State Capital Construction Commission, who was subsequently appointed director of the political Department of Industry and Communications of the CP.

25. Some members of the government participate in the activities of *ad hoc* groups or commissions placed under the control of the Central Committee probably because the leadership of the CP wants to give them a particular importance. Thus, Cue Yueli, Minister of Public Health, and He Kang, Minister of Agriculture, are members of the Central Patriotic Public Health Campaign Committee of the CP.

26. This has become a rule: for example, Qi Yuanjing left this commission in September 1985 shortly after being appointed Minister of the Metallurgical Industry.

27. Although Liu Fuzhi's successor in 1985, Ruan Chongwu, has not yet been

identified as a member of this Commission, it is likely that he sits on it *ex officio*. The promotion of Qiao Shi to vice-premier in March 1986 is the latest and not the least example of the persistence of multiple office-holding in sector 03.

28. Ding Henggao, chairman of the Science, Technology and Industry National Defence Commission, has not yet been identified as a member of the Military Commission of the CP.

29. In 1965, Lin Biao, Minister of Defence and Vice-premier, was also a member of this supreme organ of the CCP.

30. Another exception, although a more marginal one, Hu Qiaomu, a member of the Political Bureau, took over the leadership in March 1983 of the National Academic Degrees Committee of the State Council.

31. Yao Yilin at Planning, Fang Yi at Science and Technology and the Academy of Sciences, Hu Qiaomu at the Academy of Social Sciences, Gu Mu at Capital Construction, Yu Qiuli at Energy and Wan Li at Agriculture.

32. The other members of the Secretariat (11 members) are responsible for ideological questions (Deng Liqun), political questions (Hu Yaobang, Chen Pixian, Wang Zhaoguo, Hu Qili, Qiao Shi, Hao Jianxiu) and military affairs (Yu Qiuli).

33. For the first time in the history of the PRC, Zhang Aiping, the Minister of Defence, left the Central Committee before being relieved of his government posts. But he was old and would soon have been replaced.

34. The replacement in September 1984 of Fang Yi, a member of the Political Bureau since August 1977 and of the secretariat from February 1980 to September 1982, and his replacement by Song Jian as chairman of the State Scientific and Technological Commission points in the same direction.

35. See especially the articles by Luo Ping in the *Zhengming* of April and May 1984.

36. It is very possible that some organs of the Central Committee do not appear in the publicly available organizational charts. The identification in September 1985 of a leading group in the Central Committee responsible for financial and economic affairs whose assistant general secretary, Yuan Mu, turns out to be an assistant of Tian Jiyun, in the secretariat general of the central government, underlines the close inter-relationship of party and state organs and limits the significance of the formal distinctions between these two administrations (*SWB/FE*/8057/BII/2); *XH*, 12 September 1985. See also Barnett, 1985.

# 5 Regional Disparities since 1978

## P. Aguignier

The purpose of this chapter is to examine the effects of the recent economic reforms on regional disparities. The evolution of these disparities since 1978 is briefly described and some explanations (mainly arising out of the study of changes in the financial flows between central and local governments) are suggested. Finally, the way in which the Chinese leaders today view the problem of regional disparities is examined.

## The Evolution of Disparities

### Long-Term Trends 1949–83

In 1949, the key feature of the economic geography of China was its imbalances: the few industrial establishments were concentrated in areas close to the coast (Liaoning, Shanghai and southern Jiangsu, Canton). The rest of the country was virtually devoid of infrastructure and remained to be developed.

Correcting these imbalances has been a constant concern of the Chinese government, both for economic reasons (to bring industrial activities closer to sources of raw materials, most of which are situated well inside the country) and for strategic reasons (so long as it was concentrated, industry was vulnerable in the event of war) or social reasons (promoting the reduction of inequalities in living standards).

For thirty years, then, considerable resources, in people and capital, were drained from the rich coastal regions to be invested in the interior of the country. We shall return below to the way in which these transfers were made.

An examination of the figures in Table 5.1 (see Appendix for Tables) makes it possible to assess the effects of these efforts. The first lesson to be drawn from these figures is that the growth rates of the various provinces have been quite close to one another: only the most glaring imbalances (Shanghai) have been attenuated to any significant degree. But what can also be observed is the relative decline of the three provinces in the north-east (formerly Manchuria), as well as the persistence, even the aggravation in some cases, of the gap separating the provinces in the north-west and south-west from those in the rest of the country.

This persistence is only partly a failure of the policy of developing the interior regions: without the deliberate policy carried out for nearly thirty years, the gaps would have widened further.

**Recent Trends**

We shall now see that what was true for the long term is no longer true for the recent period: in fact, since 1978 China has experienced very sharp growth (in five years, industrial and agricultural output have increased by 46%), but the growth has varied enormously from region to region (see Table 5.2). The extreme values range from 7.2% for Qinghai to 84.7% for Zhejiang. Analysis of the figures in Table 5.2 reveals the following trends:

• The major differences observed are to be explained more by the evolution of industrial output than by that of agricultural output. The growth rates of the latter are clustered around the national average.

• For industrial output, on the other hand, some provinces have experienced exceptional growth since 1978; these are (in growth rate order): Zhejiang (over 100%), Hubei, Jiangsu, Fujian, Guangdong. With the exception of Hubei, these are coastal provinces. At the other extreme, the provinces in the north-west have been experiencing industrial stagnation (except for Xinjiang, thanks to the increase in petroleum output).

• Several of the poorest provinces (Yunnan, Hebei, Guangxi, Guizhou and the provinces in the north-west) have growth below that of the country as a whole. Among the provinces whose output index (see Table 5.1) is below 100, only Anhui, Guangdong and Fujian have growth much above the average: the others are stagnating or falling back.

The regional structure of growth is thus tending to strengthen disparities: this marks a profound break with previous trends. We shall attempt to explain this break and see in what way the reforms introduced since 1978 may have provoked it.

## Causes of the Recent Evolution of Disparities

**New Directions in Industrial Policy**

As is known, one of the first measures in the economic policy pursued by Deng Xiaoping and his associates was to promote the growth of light industry (consumer goods) at the expense of heavy industry. The reformers felt that the previous priority given to heavy industry had been harmful to the progress of other sectors of the economy. Consequently, between 1978 and 1981, the growth rate of light industry was distinctly higher than that of heavy industry. At the end of 1981, emphasis was somewhat shifted to heavy industry and in 1982 and 1983, there was some catching up. In 1984, the growth of the two sectors was in balance. The two years of catching up did not make up for the gap that had built up between 1978 and 1981, since in five years heavy industry grew by 66% as against 94% for light industry (see Table 5.3 and also Chapter 2, Appendix 3).

This sectoral aspect of industrial growth affected developments in the regions: the interior provinces, almost devoid of industry before 1949, acquired an industrial infrastructure based on heavy industry because of the priority given to it. The coastal provinces, which already had a light industrial base (notably textiles), have retained a more balanced structure.

Consequently, in the provinces in the north, north-west and south-west, developed since 1949, the share of heavy industry in industrial output was higher than the national average, and these provinces suffered more than the others from the new economic policy. In 1981, in particular, most of these provinces had a negative industrial growth rate.

Since 1982 there has been a return to more traditional sectoral priorities and this phenomenon no longer plays a preponderant role. We shall see that other factors, deeper and more permanent, have taken the place of sectoral imbalance.

## The Financial Crisis of the State

*The Chinese State Budget:*[1] The Chinese state budget is a sort of pyramid: naturally it includes the income and expenditure of the central administration, but it also includes those of the provinces;[2] in turn the provincial budgets include the budgets of lower levels of the administrative structure (municipalities, prefectures), and so on. The state fixes the procedures by which each unit draws up its budget, which is consolidated at the higher level.

Since 1949 the budget in China has had two major peculiar features: in the first place, the Communist government, contrary to its Guomindang (Nationalist) predecessor, has succeeded in centralizing a large part of the country's revenue in the national budget. Between 1950 and 1980, budgetary income (*caizheng shouru*) as a percentage of national income (*guomin shouru*)[3] fluctuated between 30% and 40% and settled at an average of 34%, figures lower than those encountered today in the USSR (60%), but higher than those in most developing countries.

In the second place, the budget occupies a dominant place in the financing of investment: between 1952 and 1980, 80% of investment financing was achieved through the budget. This proportion (higher than that experienced by most centrally planned countries) is to be explained by the fact that enterprises were obliged to hand over virtually all their profits to the state, and to turn to it to finance their fixed capital formation.

In China, as in the USSR, there are two broad categories of budgetary revenues: the profits of state enterprises, and fiscal receipts. The rules governing the formation of these revenues have always been defined by the central government: the central government has in fact always controlled the price structure – which determines the distribution of the profits of enterprises – as well as the nature and rates of the main taxes, which determine the distribution of fiscal revenues. The sole prerogative of local governments has been to fix the rates of a number of taxes of minor importance (whereas in India, for example, where the states enjoy extensive powers in matters fiscal, there are large differences in the tax revenues of local governments). The prerogatives of central government do not stop there: from the early 1950s procedures were introduced enabling the centre to fix independently of one another the total income and expenditure of each province, the sole constraint being that of the balance of the overall budget. The consequence of this is that there is no direct relationship, for a province, between the amount of income collected on its territory and the amount of expenditure that it can undertake. The centre has thus been able to cream off part of the financial resources of the rich provinces (obliged to present surplus budgets) to subsidize the deficits of the disadvantaged provinces. These mechanisms have been reformed many times, but the centre has always been in a position to redistribute a large part of the sums going through the budget as it sees fit. Even when in 1958 and 1970 significant planning responsibilities were devolved to the provinces, the budgetary reforms that accompanied the planning reforms remained very modest and had little effect (when they were not immediately abrogated, as was the case in 1959 with the 1958 reform).[4]

We shall now see that the whole functioning of the mechanisms that we have just described (virtually unchanged from 1950 to 1978) has been profoundly altered by the reforms carried out since 1978.

*The Impact of the Reforms on the Financial Balances*: The finances of the Chinese state are in the throes of a profound crisis under the impact mainly of two factors: the existence of very large budgetary deficits on the one hand (see Table 5.4), and the uncontrolled growth of the amount of financial resources not going through the budget (Extra-budgetary Funds or EBF), on the other.

a) *The budget deficits.* The 'silent revolution' (see Aubert, 1982) that the Chinese countryside has undergone since 1979 with the *de facto* decollectivization of a large part of agricultural activities has undeniably succeeded in stimulating output and raising the standard of living of a section of the peasantry.

One of the main components of the new agricultural policy was the raising of producer prices (which had been frozen since 1964): between March 1979 (date of the first increases) and the end of 1981, the average state procurement price of agricultural products (including above quota purchases) increased by 28.5% (*SYB*, 1981, p. 403). But because of the spectacular rise in output (above all for cash crops), the sums disbursed by the state for the procurement of agricultural products rose by 71.2% (*SYB*, 1981, p. 431).

While the first rises were partly passed on (in November 1979) to the retail prices of goods of agricultural origin (food products, clothing), it was not the same with subsequent ones, the state fearing the social consequences of too high an inflation of consumer prices. The difference in the evolution of producer prices and consumer prices thus resulted in the appearance of deficits in the accounts of commercial enterprises, deficits which had to be covered by state subsidies: 'thus there has emerged in recent years an inverse relationship between the evolution of agricultural prices and the evolution of budget deficits' (Lemoine, 1984, p. 34).

It is technically difficult to determine the amount of these deficits and subsidies, because Chinese accounting does not show them directly (i.e. by increasing expenditures), but rather by deducting them from income (the figure for the category 'income from enterprises' is net of the losses of deficit enterprises). But there are several indirect methods of estimating them.

The first involves examining the evolution of income transmitted to the budget by enterprises since 1978 (see Table 5.5). It fell from 57 billion to a little under 30 billion in 1982. Industrial enterprises played only a small part in this fall: their income fell by only 5 billion, partly because of the industrial reform (see below). It was the income of other enterprises (construction, transport, but above all commerce) that was affected, falling from +13 billion to –10 billion in four years, a fall of 23 billion.

This 10 billion deficit in 1982 represents only the difference between the income and losses of the enterprises concerned and the total losses must be much higher. This is in fact confirmed by another source (Qiao, 1983, p. 17) which informs us that the amount of price subsidies rose from 8.4 billion in 1978 to 34.8 billion in 1981 (see Table 5.6). We may note in passing that this increase (+26.4 billion) is indeed of the same order as the decline in the income transferred to the budget by commercial enterprises. Account must also be taken of the fact that in some regions the state agreed to lighten the burden of the agricultural tax in order to stimulate production there and to grant advantageous fiscal conditions to enterprises managed by communes and brigades. In 1979, the cost of these measures was 2.2 billion, and in 1980, 2.9 billion (Xu Yi and Chen Baosen, 1982, p. 24).

The enterprise management reforms also contributed to the appearance of deficits. The Chinese industrial reform (see especially Aubert and Chevrier, 1982, and Chevrier, 1983) envisaged enterprises being able to retain part of their profits (calculated on bases that were to be fixed for several years). Drawing on an experiment carried out by Zhao Ziyang in Sichuan in 1977–8, the reform began to be generalized in 1979, but was frozen at the level reached in 1981. The total amount of profits retained by enterprises rose, if Chinese statistics are to be believed, from 4 to 17 billion yuan between 1979 and 1982 (Xu Yi and Chen Baosen, 1982, p. 26, for 1979, and *JJNJ*, 1983, p. II–138, for 1982). The absolute value of this growth is higher than the diminution in the profits turned over by industrial enterprises to the budget, which indicates that total profits have increased.

The effects of the industrial reform thus explain both part of the deficits (through the dimunution of profits turned over to the budget) and part of the increase in extra-budgetary funds (whereas the funds diverted from the budget by the agricultural reform went to swell the incomes of peasants more than the EBF).

Lastly we should mention that other measures than those we have just described contributed to aggravating the financial problems of the state: the wage increases granted in several stages since 1976 have eaten away at the profits of enterprises and increased administrative expenses; in 1979, 49 large towns were authorized to deduct 5% of their industrial and commercial profits to finance urban development expenditure, and part of the profits of enterprises managed by the counties (*xian*) were granted to these as extra-budgetary income: these latter two measures are said to have increased the financial resources available to the localities by 2 billion yuan (Xu Yi and Chen Baosen, 1982, pp. 25–6).

The burden of the various subsidies (and the resulting budget deficits) limit the centre's room for manoeuvre: the surpluses of the rich provinces are not sufficiently available to be spent or invested in the disadvantaged provinces. We shall now see that, at the same time, the extra-budgetary resources of the rich provinces have increased considerably.

b) *The growth of EBF*. Extra-budgetary funds come from many sources: part of profits, that the reforms allow state sector enterprises to retain; profits of collective sector enterprises; part of the depreciation funds built up by enterprises; the yield of some local taxes and surtaxes, etc.

These funds share the common characteristic of being controlled by the local authorities, and, since they do not appear in the budget, of not being subject to any mechanism of inter-provincial redistribution. Between the early 1950s and the late 1960s they came to between 10% and 20% of the amount of budgetary income. They began to grow slowly and regularly in the early 1970s, and reached 38% of budgetary income in 1978. The EBF then took off, and reached almost 70% of budgetary income in 1983 (see Table 5.7). Their role is particularly important in the financing of investment, since the share of investment financed outside the budget in total investment is today about 60%, whereas since 1950 it had been under 20% (see below).

Unfortunately there are no statistics on the regional distribution of the EBF: however it seems reasonable to think that their distribution is at least as imbalanced as that of budgetary income: in fact, budgetary income and EBF for a given province depend on the same two variables, which are the level of industrial output (which determines the amount of fiscal receipts), and the average rate of profit of enterprises. The figures in Table 5.8 illustrate the imbalance in the distribution of budgetary income (it will be noted in particular that the three municipalities produced 30% of revenue). Since EBF are today of the same order as budgetary income, and are wholly retained by the provinces, the redistribution of resources carried out by the budget is becoming less and less significant.[5] The centre has thus lost the ability to control the geographical distribution of investment. To mention only one example, in 1983, the total amount of investment in the collective sector (financed entirely outside the budget) for the whole of the north-west and south-west regions was 3.80 billion RMB. For the province of Jiangsu alone, this amount was 5.87 billion RMB (*SYB*, 1984, p. 300).

The crisis of finances at the centre is thus harmful to the backward provinces in two respects: on the one hand, larger and larger amounts no longer pass through the budget and are thus not redistributed. On the other, the amounts that continue to pass through the budget are declining and above all are not available to be invested in the interior because of the burden of subsidies.

This phenomenon is already having its effects today, but what is even more serious is that it is self-sustaining (more income in the rich provinces makes possible more investment which generates new income) and mortgages the future.

We shall examine more closely one of these consequences, by studying the recent evolution of the collective sector.

*The Explosion of the Collective Sector*: A look at Table 5.9 will show that one of the characteristics of the growth that China has experienced since 1978 is that it has been sharper in the collective sector than in the state sector (see chapter 7 for definitions and further discussion).

The collective sector, although growing rapidly, still provides only 30% of Chinese industrial output (but this statistic underestimates the real weight of collectives enterprises, since many of them operate in the areas of transport and services, for which no precise figures are available). It has two components: one, urban, made up of a myriad of light industrial enterprises, the other, rural, made up either of enterprises that work on sub-contracts from urban enterprises, or of enterprises specializing in the primary processing of agricultural products or in activities such as cattle raising or pisciculture, or again in construction enterprises.

Several factors contribute to the dynamism of the collective sector: in the urban areas, the inflation of the EBF has led to a sharp rise in investment by local authorities in this sector; thus, in five years to 1984, the stock of fixed capital of collective industrial enterprises rose from 28.4 billion RMB to 61.1 billion. In the rural areas, the return to a mode of exploitation close to tenanting, the liberalization of rural markets, and the considerable progress of cash crops, have led to the growth of a multitude of small peri-agricultural enterprises.

The collective sector makes a not insignificant contribution to the evolution of disparities: developing without any financing by the centre, the collective sector is concentrated in the rich regions. Five provinces are way ahead: Liaoning, Jiangsu, Zhejiang, Shandong and Guangdong, all coastal provinces. Table 5.10 shows the extreme concentration of the collective sector in these five provinces; they provide 47.8% of its output as against 2.3% for the north-west and 6.5% for the south-west. Jiangsu alone provides twice as much as the south-west and north-west combined in collective sector industry, whereas it provides half as much in state sector industry. This is a good illustration of the differences of distribution between the two sectors.

In Zhejiang, the province that has experienced the fastest growth in all China in the last five years, the growth rate of collectively owned industry since 1979 has always been markedly higher than that of the state sector. In five years, the output of the collective sector grew by 250% as against only 115% for that of the state sector. The collective sector in provinces like Zhejiang or Jiangsu is thus experiencing a veritable explosion. So long as the financial constraints operating on the interior provinces are not removed (see the previous paragraph on the state financial crisis), it is difficult to see how this explosion might spread to the rest of China and thus make possible a more favourable evolution of regional disparities.

## Inadequate Remedies

Chinese leaders are certainly concerned about the regional imbalances in growth. But it seems that today growth is a more urgent imperative than equality. In addition, at present, they do not have the financial means to pursue a vigorous policy of developing the backward regions.

The specific solutions that have been advanced so far are few: a special fund, intended to finance projects in regions inhabited by minorities or in disadvantaged regions, was set up in 1981 but its amount (a few hundred million yuan a year), while not negligible, is quite inadequate to solve the problem.

For some years the government has also been encouraging the coastal industrial provinces to make compensation agreements with raw material producing provinces, investment and technical assistance then being repaid in kind. There appear to be more and more of these agreements, but unfortunately there are no precise statistics. It is known for example that there are several agreements linking Shanxi, a big coal producer, with various provinces (including Jiangsu) and contracting to supply some two million tonnes of coal a year. In 1981 and 1982,

6,000 compensation contracts were made between provinces, for amounts totalling some three billion RMB.

It must finally be noted that the recent reforms of the price system may have beneficial effects on the economy of the interior provinces. Raw materials in China have been supplied at very low prices, which leads to frequent deficits in the enterprises producing them. By improving the situation of these enterprises, the recent increases may thus lead to an indirect transfer of resources between the coast which consumes more raw materials than it produces and the interior which is in the opposite situation.

All these measures will still not be adequate to deflect the forces that are currently aggravating the disparities. There is no doubt that these forces are in part the outcome of the recent reforms. But, aware of the urgency of their country's breaking out of its underdevelopment, the leaders are probably prepared to pay a high price for the success of their reforms, ready even to accept that only a part of the country fully benefits from them.

## Notes

1. In this paragraph we shall set out a few facts that are necessary for the understanding of what follows.

2. By province we mean the basic unit of the territorial organization of China. There are 29 of these units: 21 provinces strictly so called, 5 autonomous regions, and 3 special municipalities with the rank of province because of their importance: Beijing, Tianjin and Shanghai.

3. The concept of national income (*guomin shouru*) in Chinese accounting is the one that comes closest to the notion of gross national product. However it is narrower, since it excludes services not directly linked to the production of material goods. National income takes account of the net output of the following sectors: industry, agriculture, construction, transport, commerce.

4. For a detailed study of these issues, see Lardy, 1978 and Aguignier, 1984.

5. All these features have in addition been amplified by a reform of the budget machinery, promulgated in 1980, which aimed to fix for a period of five years the amount of central levies on provincial resources (whereas these amounts were formerly renegotiated each year). The centre had to reverse this decision in 1981, by introducing exceptional levies, so as to meet the budget deficits.

# Appendix

**Table 5.1**
**Output per head, by province, as a percentage of the national average[a]**

| Provinces | Population 1983 (millions) | Geographical region | Industrial & agricultural output 1952 | Industrial & agricultural output 1983 | Industrial output 1983 | Agricultural output 1983 |
|---|---|---|---|---|---|---|
| Beijing | 9.3 | | 187 | 337 | 446 | 103 |
| Tianjin | 7.9 | | 479 | 362 | 483 | 103 |
| Hebei | 54.2 | North | 95 | 86 | 78 | 104 |
| Shanxi | 25.7 | | 81 | 96 | 98 | 92 |
| Inner Mongolia | 19.6 | | 126 | 74 | 64 | 94 |
| Liaoning | 36.3 | | 222 | 106 | 237 | 108 |
| Jilin | 22.7 | North-east | 164 | 121 | 121 | 121 |
| Heilongjiang | 33.1 | | 238 | 137 | 145 | 120 |
| Shanghai | 11.9 | | 771 | 683 | 945 | 121 |
| Jiangsu | 61.4 | | 95 | 152 | 154 | 148 |
| Zhejiang | 39.6 | | 98 | 117 | 112 | 127 |
| Anhui | 50.6 | East | 56 | 65 | 53 | 90 |
| Fujian | 26.4 | | 72 | 70 | 60 | 90 |
| Jiangxi | 33.8 | | 93 | 65 | 52 | 94 |
| Shandong | 75.6 | | 72 | 100 | 89 | 123 |
| Henan | 75.9 | | 65 | 66 | 52 | 91 |
| Hubei | 48.3 | | 101 | 106 | 108 | 103 |
| Hunan | 55.1 | Centre south | 76 | 75 | 62 | 100 |
| Guangdong | 60.7 | | 89 | 85 | 84 | 87 |
| Guangxi | 37.3 | | 69 | 55 | 42 | 82 |
| Sichuan | 100.8 | | 65 | 67 | 56 | 89 |
| Guizhou | 29.0 | South-west | 66 | 45 | 36 | 64 |
| Yunnan | 33.2 | | 60 | 54 | 45 | 74 |
| Shaanxi | 29.3 | | 75 | 74 | 73 | 77 |
| Gansu | 19.9 | | 65 | 71 | 74 | 65 |
| Qinghai | 3.9 | North-west | 109 | 67 | 60 | 82 |
| Ningxia | 4.0 | | 109 | 71 | 67 | 79 |
| Xinjiang | 13.2 | | 110 | 81 | 67 | 109 |
| *China* | *1024.95* | | *100* | *100* | *100* | *100* |

[a] These figures give the value of gross output per capita for each province (for agriculture and industry only, as statistics are not available for transport, commerce and services), expressed as a percentage of the national average: thus an index of 200 means that output per capita in the province concerned is double that of output per capita for the whole of China.

*Source: Statistical Yearbook of China, 1984.*

**Table 5.2**
**Growth rate in 1983 compared to 1979, by province (in %)**

| Provinces | Industrial and agricultural output | Agricultural output | Industrial output |
|---|---|---|---|
| Beijing | 46.7[a] | 77.7 | 43.8 |
| Tianjin | 49.6 | 71.8 | 47.8 |
| Hebei | 27.3 | 36.4 | 22.2 |
| Shanxi | 40.2 | 44.6 | 38.4 |
| Inner Mongolia | 39.7 | 37.5 | 41.1 |
| Liaoning | 35.4 | 46.5 | 33.1 |
| Jilin | 44.3 | 48.3 | 42.1 |
| Heilongjiang | 32.7 | 36.5 | 31.4 |
| Shanghai | 33.7 | 61.6 | 32.5 |
| Jiangsu | 69.8 | 54.2 | 77.9 |
| Zhejiang | 84.7 | 47.2 | 112.0 |
| Anhui | 50.8 | 47.4 | 53.6 |
| Fujian | 51.2 | 43.8 | 57.0 |
| Jiangxi | 46.4 | 62.5 | 33.6 |
| Shandong | 46.1 | 59.6 | 39.3 |
| Henan | 7 | 7 | 44.3 |
| Hubei | 65.1 | 26.0 | 91.8 |
| Hunan | 41.2 | 30.4 | 47.8 |
| Guangdong | 50.3 | 43.0 | 54.0 |
| Guangxi | 34.9 | 34.6 | 35.2 |
| Sichuan | 47.6 | 45.8 | 49.1 |
| Guizhou | 42.9 | 38.0 | 47.3 |
| Yunnan | 33.1 | 30.0 | 50.0 |
| Shaanxi | 31.1 | 28.4 | 32.5 |
| Gansu | 12.5 | 20.0 | 9.7 |
| Qinghai | 7.2 | 11.6 | 6.0 |
| Ningxia | 19.1 | 36.0 | 5.1 |
| Xinjiang | 57.2 | 52.8 | 60.8 |
| *China* | *46* | *46* | *46* |

[a] All the figures in this table are positive.

NB: All the provincial figures for 1984 were not yet available. Therefore only the year 1983 has been used.

*Source: Statistical Yearbook of China, 1984.*

**Table 5.3**
**Sectoral distribution of industrial growth (in %)**

|            | Total industrial output | Heavy industry | Light industry |
|------------|------------------------|----------------|----------------|
| 1979/1978  | + 8.5                  | + 7.7          | + 9.6          |
| 1980/1979  | + 8.7                  | + 1.4          | +18.4          |
| 1981/1980  | + 4.1                  | - 4.7          | +14.1          |
| 1982/1981  | + 7.7                  | + 9.8          | + 5.7          |
| 1983/1982  | +10.5                  | +12.4          | + 8.7          |
| 1984/1983  | +14.0                  | +14.2          | +13.9          |
| 1984/1978  | +66.0                  | +46.6          | +93.7          |

*Source: Statistical Yearbook of China, 1984.*

**Table 5.4**
**Budgetary deficits since 1978 (in billions of yuan)**

|              | 1978   | 1979    | 1980    | 1981    | 1982    | 1983    |
|--------------|--------|---------|---------|---------|---------|---------|
| Income       | 112.11 | 110.33  | 108.52  | 108.95  | 112.40  | 124.90  |
| Loans        | 0.15   | 3.64    | 4.30    | 7.31    | 8.39    | 7.94    |
| Income – Loans | 111.96 | 106.69 | 104.22  | 101.64  | 104.01  | 116.96  |
| Expenditure  | 111.10 | 127.39  | 121.27  | 111.50  | 115.33  | 129.25  |
| Deficit      | +0.86  | –20.70  | –17.05  | –9.86   | –11.33  | –12.29  |

*Source: Statistical Yearbook, 1984, pp. 417, 418, 419.*

**Table 5.5**
**Evolution of enterprise income from 1978 to 1982 (in billion yuan)**

| Year | Total | Industrial | Other   |
|------|-------|------------|---------|
| 1978 | 57.20 | 44.04      | 13.16   |
| 1979 | 49.29 | 45.12      | 4.17    |
| 1980 | 43.52 | 44.82      | – 1.30  |
| 1981 | 33.57 | 41.59      | – 6.22  |
| 1982 | 29.65 | 39.71      | –10.66  |
| 1983 | 24.05 | 39.81      | –15.76  |

*Source: Statistical Yearbook, 1984 p. 418.*

**Table 5.6**
**Price subsidies**

|       | In billions of yuan | As a % of budgetary expenditure |
|-------|---------------------|---------------------------------|
| 1965  | 0.5                 | 1.1                             |
| 1978  | 8.4                 | 7.6                             |
| 1979  | 14.6                | 11.5                            |
| 1980  | 21.3                | 17.6                            |
| 1981  | 34.8                | 31.2                            |

*Source:* Qiao Rongzhong, 1983, p. 17.


**Table 5.7**
**Evolution of EBF since 1978**

|                              | 1978  | 1979  | 1980  | 1981  | 1982  | 1983  |
|------------------------------|-------|-------|-------|-------|-------|-------|
| In billions of yuan          | 34.75 | 45.34 | 55.78 | 64.61 | 65.0  | 87.4  |
| As a % of budgetary expenditure | 31.0 | 41.1 | 51.4 | 59.3 | 57.9 | 70.0 |

*Sources:* 1978–81, Li Fuyu, 1983, p. 24; 1982, Rong Zihe, 1983, p. 5; 1983, *Economic Yearbook* 1984, p. IV–32.

**Table 5.8**
**Provincial budgets, 1981**

| Provinces | Income | Expenditure | Balance | % Income | % Industrial output | Sources |
|---|---|---|---|---|---|---|
| | *In billions of yuan* | | | | | |
| Beijing | 4.91 | 1.48 | + 3.43 | 5.75 | 4.18 | *SYB* 81, 29 |
| Tianjin | 4.09 | 1.45 | + 2.64 | 4.79 | 3.85 | 83, V-9[1] |
| Hebei | 3.41 | 2.33 | + 1.08 | 3.99 | 4.20 | 83, V-12 |
| Shanxi | 1.97 | 1.74 | + 0.23 | 2.31 | 2.29 | 82, VI-26 |
| Mongolia | 0.42 | 1.64 | − 1.22 | 0.49 | 1.15 | 83, V-29 |
| Liaoning | 7.77 | 2.67 | + 5.10 | 9.10 | 8.71 | 83, V-34 |
| Jilin | 1.12 | 1.59 | − 0.47 | 1.31 | 2.59 | 82, VI-50 |
| Heilongjiang | 1.56 | 2.58 | − 1.02 | 1.83 | 4.84 | 83, V-54 |
| Shanghai | 17.15 | 1.60 | +15.55 | 20.09 | 11.76 | 82, VI-62 |
| Jiangsu | 6.30 | 2.38 | + 3.92 | 7.38 | 8.99 | 83, V-65 |
| Zhejiang | 3.40 | 1.71 | + 1.69 | 3.98 | 4.13 | 83, V-74 |
| Anhui | 2.07 | 1.55 | + 0.52 | 2.42 | 2.51 | 83, V-84 |
| Fujian | 1.45 | 1.43 | + 0.02 | 1.70 | 1.58 | 83, V-89 |
| Jiangxi | 1.28 | 1.40 | − 0.12 | 1.50 | 1.77 | 83, V-97 |
| Shandong | 5.10 | 2.56 | + 2.54 | 5.97 | 6.64 | 82, VI-109 |
| Henan | 3.42 | 2.61 | + 0.81 | 4.01 | 3.93 | 82, VI-114 |
| Hubei | 3.69 | 2.36 | + 1.33 | 4.32 | 4.76 | 83, V-113 |
| Hunan | 2.82 | 2.14 | + 0.68 | 3.30 | 3.40 | 83, V-122 |
| Guangdong | 4.10 | 2.96 | + 1.14 | 4.80 | 4.83 | 83, V-126 |
| Guangxi | 1.30 | 1.60 | − 0.30 | 1.52 | 1.58 | 83, V-141 |
| Sichuan | 3.15 | 3.15 | + 0 | 3.69 | 5.32 | *CREA* 238:31 |
| Guizhou | 0.56 | 1.26 | − 0.70 | 0.66 | 0.85 | 83, V-152 |
| Yunnan | 1.27 | 1.57 | − 0.30 | 1.49 | 1.37 | 83, V-157 |
| Xizang | 0 | 0.49 | − 0.49 | — | — | 83, V-165 |
| Shaanxi | 1.35 | 1.64 | − 0.29 | 1.58 | 2.03 | 83, V-169 |
| Gansu | 1.30 | 1.12 | + 0.18 | 1.52 | 1.44 | 83, V-175 |
| Qinghai | 0.11 | 0.55 | − 0.44 | 0.13 | 0.23 | 83, V-179 |
| Ningxia | 0.14 | 0.47 | − 0.33 | 0.16 | 0.24 | 83, V-183 |
| Xinjiang | 0.17 | 1.48 | − 1.31 | 0.20 | 0.79 | 83, V-189 |
| *Total* | *85.38* | *51.51* | | *100.00* | *100.00* | |

Note (1) This and all following references (except for Sichuan) are to JJNJ.

**Table 5.9**
**Industrial growth in the state sector and the collective sector (in %)[a]**

|  | State sector | Collective sector | Of which: rural enterprises |
|---|---|---|---|
| 1979/1978 | + 8.9 | + 6.9 | +10.3 |
| 1980/1979 | + 5.6 | +18.8 | +20.0 |
| 1981/1980 | + 2.5 | + 9.4 | +10.4 |
| 1982/1981 | + 7.1 | + 9.5 | + 9.6 |
| 1983/1982 | + 9.4 | +13.5 | +16.7 |
| 1984/1983 | +11.0 | +21.9 | ? |
| 1984/1978 | +53.3 | +110.4 | >100 |

[a] The state sector is wholly planned whereas the collective sector, in the provinces, municipalities and districts is outside the plan.

*Source: Statistical Yearbook*, 1981, 1983, 1984.

**Table 5.10**
**The collective sector in five coastal provinces, 1983**

|  | % of total population | % of total industrial output | % of total industrial output of state sector | % of total industrial output of collective sector |
|---|---|---|---|---|
| Jiangsu | 6.1 | 9.2 | 7.1 | 16.4 |
| Zhejiang | 3.9 | 4.3 | 3.2 | 8.4 |
| Shandong | 7.5 | 6.6 | 6.1 | 8.4 |
| Guangdong | 6.0 | 5.0 | 4.3 | 7.1 |
| Liaoning | 3.5 | 8.4 | 8.5 | 7.5 |
| *Total of 5 provinces* | *27.0* | *33.5* | *29.2* | *47.8* |
| *Whole of north-west* | *7.1* | *4.9* | *5.6* | *2.3* |
| *Whole of south-west* | *16.1* | *8.0* | *8.4* | *6.5* |

*Source: Statistical Yearbook*, 1983, p. 213.

# 6 Industrial Restructuring and Autonomy of Enterprises in China: Is Reform Possible?

**François Gipouloux**

A complex set of political and economic reasons lay behind the profound changes in China's development strategy at the end of 1978: poor economic results during the years following the death of Mao, the inertia of the middle bureaucracy, divergences among the leadership. At the time of the Third Plenum of the Eleventh Committee (late 1978) and even more at the Second Session of the Fifth National People's Congress (1979), the Chinese leadership stressed the need for an overall readjustment of the economic system. It marked the end of a long period of extensive development of the productive forces and the return to a better use of existing resources. Following impressive successes achieved in agriculture, the reformers turned their efforts towards revitalizing the urban economy. From 1979 to 1984 a series of reforms marked industrial development. Seven years after Deng Xiaoping's return to power and the affirmation of his economic strategy we shall attempt a preliminary assessment of the reform policy in industry and assess the degree of autonomy of enterprises.

## The Difficult Reorganization of Industry

Despite a remarkable growth rate for several years[1] industry is facing serious difficulties which growth has made even more apparent. They are as much due to the combination of external constraints (low level of the productive apparatus, energy shortage, transport bottlenecks) as to the dysfunctions of an excessively rigid planning system. The centralized allocation of investment, human resources and raw materials has led to massive waste in structural overproduction, and has often sacrificed domestic consumption. Low productivity, and poor quality of output are endemic shortcomings in many industrial sectors.

### Imbalances between Heavy and Light Industry

The imbalances affecting the industrial structure proved to be greater in the late 1970s than they had been during the First Five Year Plan (1953–57). The imbalance was felt all the more deeply because energy production had suffered several setbacks. The shortage of consumer goods and the stagnation in housing construction worsened the social malaise. Finally, the employment situation was becoming more and more worrying. While in 1981 there were over 100 million wage-earners, the estimated number of unemployed was 26 million.

Social as well as economic factors militated in favour of the reversal of priorities in industry. A survey by the Ministry of Light Industry, published in 1981, revealed that an investment of 10,000 yuan created 94 jobs in heavy industry, 257 in light industry and 800 in handicrafts (the making of everyday articles and shoes). The same advantages were noticeable at the level of energy consumption. According to the same report, for an output valued at 10,000 yuan, heavy industry consumed 17 tonnes of coal and 5,000 kWh, whereas light industry used only 3.5 tonnes of coal and 1,780 kWh to create goods to the same value.

The readjustment affected not only the relative shares of light industry and heavy industry, but also the internal structure of heavy industry. The output of crude steel fell slightly between 1979 and 1982 compared to special steels, while in chemicals, the sectors servicing agriculture and light industry received a lot of new funds. The economic results for 1981 clearly revealed the new priorities. Whereas steel and machine tools were hit hard by the readjustment (−10% for the output of pig iron and −25% for the number of machine tools), light industry recorded striking results: +34% for bicycles (17.45 million), +32.8% for sewing machines (10.19 million), +94.3% for TV sets (4.84 million) and +60% for cameras (596,000) (*Economic Reporter* (Hong Kong), February 1982).

This trend continued in the following years, but light industry no longer appeared as the panacea. The long lead period of projects, their often high costs, the waste and low rate of profitability were, according to an official spokesman, the four evils burdening the development of light industry. In the bicycle industry, for example, it is recognized today that while the state invested 240 million yuan, it was above all small projects that benefited from it, and economies of scale were impossible.[2] While a bicycle produced in an enterprise making a million units a year costs 66 yuan, factories with a production capacity lower than 100,000 units a year can scarcely hope to make a profit.[3] Despite this statistical evidence, 80 small factories were started up between 1979 and 1982, and supplementary investments have had to be borne each year by the state, as output (and losses) grew (*China Daily*, 23 May 1984).

**The Enlargement of the Market Economy**

Since 1978, a sector governed by the mechanisms of supply and demand has developed outside the plan. Rather than signifying the true development of a market economy, this has to do with making up for the shortcomings of planned distribution, either in the sphere of consumption, or in that of the allocation of industrial equipment or some raw materials. Increasing the number of channels of circulation, suppressing some bureaucratic impediments, making possible a relaxation of price control – these were the declared objectives.

Since the introduction of the new policy, the market economy, whose articulations had been systematically destroyed during the 1950s, has come to be seen as indispensable for reducing the discontinuities and waste that used to mark the bureaucratic management of the productive apparatus. In recent years, this necessity has received the official stamp of approval: 'In the historical period of socialism', wrote Jiang Yiwei, the editor of the journal *Economic Management*, commodity economy cannot be done away with. On the contrary, it has to be developed to a high level as the only means to build a powerful material base for socialism. Development of commodity production requires full application of the law of value and adherence to the principle of 'to each according to his work' in the distribution of goods for personal consumption. If these principles are valid, an enterprise, as a basic unit in commodity production, must act as a commodity producer and enjoy its independent interests as a commodity producer (1980, pp. 61–2).

Unfortunately, the overwhelming majority of leaders at the intermediate or local level do not seem prepared for the changes of economic policy. Those for whom centralized planning and allegiance to political bodies constituted the alpha and the omega, refuse to give up the reductive equations that for years took the place of economic thought for them: plan = socialism; market = capitalism. This is because a long tradition of economic attitudes dominated by Soviet influence has always contrasted plan and market. From this dichotomy problems arose that are far from being peculiar to China, but which are felt with painful acuteness at a time when the country is seeking to integrate itself into the world economy: separation of production and social demand, disjunction between price and value, extra financial burdens for the state, and tendencies of enterprises to autarky.

## The Autonomy of Enterprises and its Limits

The theme is not new. It was mentioned for the first time in 1979, but the shift of the cutting edge of reforms, from the rural areas to the urban economy, in the autumn of 1984, gave it a particular prominence.

### The Relaxation of Management Procedures

The goals these reform policies set at the level of the enterprise were to make possible a better use of human resources and capital, fight against irresponsibility and waste, raise productivity and improve the quality of output. This sudden agreement on management disciplines arose first of all from the observation, 'We have for a long time accorded much more attention to basic construction than to production and management', made by Vice-premier Yao Yilin in 1981, who added, 'we must put an end to this situation where no one is responsible for many production lines, and for management where waste remains massive' (*BR* 11, 1981).

The explanation for these defects lies in the dual origin of the Chinese system of industrial management. It bears the imprint of both a long mandarin tradition of state control over the economy, and the Soviet model such as it was introduced to China in the 1950s. But whereas in the USSR a series of reforms, short-lived it is true, radically transformed industrial practices in the early 1960s, mandarin-style management has continued in China without any major changes despite the political upheavals that have occurred over the last two decades. Today, expanding the autonomy of enterprises seems to be one of the main instruments to reform management procedures.

The experiment began in 1979, in Sichuan, the home province of Premier Zhao

Ziyang. The system of retaining part of the profits made possible the establishment of a first link between the economic interests of the enterprise and its performance. In 1979, the State Council issued five decrees on: expanding the autonomy of enterprises, profit retention, removal of a tax on investment, raising the depreciation funds, recourse to credit. By 1980, the experiment had affected more than 6,000 industrial units scattered throughout the country.

The next decisive step was taken in 1984 when the State Council issued provisional regulations on expanding the autonomy of enterprises (*JJRB*, 12 May 1984). This mainly involved reducing constraints in the areas to which the rest of this section will be devoted.

*Production and marketing*: Under the new provisions, enterprises are authorized to produce according to market needs, once basic plan targets have been achieved, and contracts with the state fulfilled. Enterprises are also free to sell the products they make on their own initiative as well as articles above the quota to be supplied. Prices can then be 20% higher than prices fixed by the state.

*Supply*: The purchase of raw materials was formerly subject to approval by central bureaux. Endless meetings and mountains of paperwork burdened the procedure. In addition, enterprises were not certain of seeing their requests met, and it was often impossible for them to avoid producing poor quality materials. Now contracts link enterprises to suppliers. A timid form of competition has even developed between them, aimed at ensuring a better quality of raw materials supplied to the user. Nevertheless many legal problems remain unanswered. Commercial law is very little developed, and there is practically no recourse in the event of incomplete or delayed deliveries.

*Personnel Policy*: It is in this area that the greatest rigidity can be observed, despite the innovations introduced. Factory managers now have the possibility of appointing their assistants (assistant managers, chief engineers, chief accountants, etc.) and to hire or fire middle-level administrative staff. To some extent, they may even promote, reward or dismiss some of the workers. It remains the case, however, that an industrial unit is not free to hire or fire in terms of its economic objectives, but must submit, in the recruitment of staff, to the decisions of the labour bureaux. The two crucial problems remaining in this area are overmanning and the poor qualifications of the staff assigned. An accepted palliative lies in the screening carried out by the affected enterprise, in the form of an aptitude test. The economist Xue Muqiao (1980, pp. 139–145) proposed, rather tongue in cheek, that, between industrial units and labour there should be a move from 'shotgun marriage' which was the rule, to 'romantic marriage'. However, a reform of the centralized labour allocation system has little chance of success, so long as enterprises are not relieved of some of their social responsibilities: production units are required to look after housing, medical assistance, payment of pensions and in many cases to take responsibility for the education of the children of staff and provide for their employment.

*Pay*: Although the system of wages remains unchanged (the so-called eight-grade wage system, introduced in 1954), factory managers are now allowed to make more flexible use of an incentive fund for the payment of bonuses, and thus reward workers who have made particular contributions. The objective is of course to link pay to economic results and to fight egalitarianism and sinecures.

*Profit Retention*: The changes introduced in this area aim to make enterprises more responsible and reduce waste. Units are now authorized to retain a share of the profits, which rises in proportion to the overfulfilment of the plan. But enterprises are far from being completely free in the use of these funds. They are to be used to contribute to self-financing, to be allocated to the factory's social services (housing, canteen, hospitals) and distributed as bonuses, in proportions laid down by the central authorities.

*Allocation of materials and depreciation*: Until recently, allocation of materials was the responsibility of central departments, and was done in a unified way. The major problem was the lack of coordination between the planning departments and those responsible for the distribution of materials. Today enterprises demand that the materials needed be allocated to them at the time plan targets are assigned. Additionally, equipment that is short can be borrowed or purchased from other units, without going through the central departments. This relaxation must be seen as the end of a central dogma in Stalinist political economy. Although China is a long way from the formation of a market in capital goods, the means of production can, in certain conditions, be seen as commodities, and as such be the object of commercial transactions. Finally, depreciation rates were raised from 50% (in 1978) to 70% (in 1985).

It is too soon to assess the full impact of these reforms, which will be extended or affirmed in the coming years. But it can already be noted that their implementation runs up against two problems: the persistence of the Soviet organizational model in industry and the resistance of the politico-administrative bureaucracy.

## The Conservatism of Industrial Organization

The low degree of cooperation and the lack of specialization among industrial branches is often denounced in the economic press. Many, if not most, factories have remained at the 'big and all-embracing' (*da er quan*) stage ever since they were first set up. These are units where all the manufacturing processes necessary to produce a given item are performed in a single place. This autarkic stage, which coincided with the First Five Year Plan, could be justified in the 1950s when there was no real industrial network. At a later stage such a situation constituted an obstacle to technical progress and increased productivity. But things change slowly in this area. In 1978, 80% of the 6,100 state enterprises placed under the First Ministry of Machine Building were still all-embracing factories (*wan meng chang*) (Li Zongwei and Wu Wenzao, 1980, p. 3).

The lack of coordination that characterizes this arrangement of the industrial structure retards measures of standardization and sometimes contributes to the disruption of a whole branch of production. One instance was agricultural machinery. Of the 173 factories making tractors, two-thirds in 1978 were of the 'small but all-embracing' type, and were far from satisfactory. Peasants frequently complained that the 'iron buffalo is dead', i.e., that the tractor was fit only for the rubbish dump. Conversely, production costs were high. In 1978, 102 factories in the branch (almost two-thirds) had suffered losses totalling 102 million yuan (Li Zongwei, Wu Wenzao, 1980, p. 4). Everywhere stress is now being put on the need to achieve greater integration of a branch of industry: product specialization, standardization of parts, and also development of after sales service networks.

However, these efforts run up against the inertia of the administrative system. The big economic departments that were set up in the 1950s encouraged the appearance of autarkic units, coming under separate industrial ministries and tending to behave like independent fiefdoms. In such a context, management sought to depend as little as possible on raw materials, energy or parts supplied by other units. To counteract the unwieldiness resulting from this old administrative structure the authorities now seek to maintain a degree of competition between the various factories in the same branch; to oppose privileges and monopolies; to abandon purely administrative management methods; and to prevent raw materials, spare parts or energy bottlenecks.

In order to be effective, these changes of course imply a radical change in mentalities and behaviour on the part of the staff responsible for the running of factories.

## The Question of Cadres: towards a Decline of Political Appointees

The average Chinese factory is organized into twenty or so departments, heading the production lines of workshops and sections. Figure 6.1 is an example taken from one of my visits.

Including both production workers and non-productive workers, the breakdown of the various categories of staff is as follows:

**Table 6.1**
**Staff of a Chinese Factory**

| Professional category | Totals | % of total staff |
|---|---|---|
| Production workers | 780 | 45.88 |
| Ancillary workers (cleaning, checking) | 520 | 30.58 |
| Supervisory staff | 150 | 8.82 |
| Engineers and technicians | 50 | 2.94 |
| Administrative and political cadres | 200 | 11.76 |
| Total staff | 1700 | 100 |

**Figure 6.1**

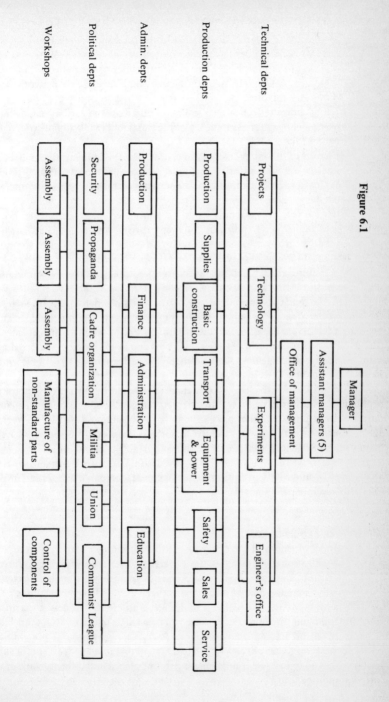

The figure and table invite several comments. In the first place, the plethora of cadres comes out very clearly: almost 25% of the total staff. The large number of unproductive workers has been a structural problem in Chinese industry since the implementation of the First Five Year Plan. It testifies to the nature of authority within the enterprise, which rests, as in the past, on a surveillance network rather than a technically qualified managerial staff. In the second place, the uneven distribution of cadres reflects a clear imbalance between the various management functions: few technicians (less than 3% of the staff), but many administrative and political cadres (almost 12%).

The retraining of this latter category of cadres, whose administrative skill level is generally pretty low, is a priority objective. Nationally, the educational level of cadres remains low: 70% of administrative staff has, in the best of cases, completed junior secondary school.[4]

The First Ministry of Machine Building conducted a survey in 1980 on the education of higher level cadres in 2,400 enterprises, and found that 64.3% of managers had primary or junior secondary education, 21.4% upper secondary education and 14.3% university education (Huan Xiang, 1980).

Starting in June 1983, 5,000 managers were required to take an examination. Afterwards, those who had passed were given a diploma, those who failed were allowed to resit, and those who were found to be incompetent had to leave their jobs (*Beijing Information*, 26 December 1983). It now seems almost impossible to carry on being a factory manager for life. From January 1985, a factory manager can only stay at his post for one term of four years. This can be extended only once if he is within the prescribed age limit, depending on his performance (XH, 15 December 1984, State Council Directive).

Another problem is the ageing of managers. Alerted by the seriousness of the problem, the authorities began introducing younger blood into management in industry. In Beijing, this policy has had some success: at the end of 1983, the average age of executives in the city's 17 industrial bureaux dropped from 56.5 to 48.3, and from 49.6 to 45.9 in its 190 large and medium sized industrial enterprises. University educated executives made up 64.3% of the industrial bureaux's leadership, up from 35.5% in 1982, and 37.8% of enterprise management, compared with 21.6% in 1982 (XH, 30 December 1983).

## Administrative Organization

The economic reforms and the extension of the autonomy of enterprises tend to disrupt organizational hierarchies. It is perhaps this that explains a current confusion in the management system. Supreme responsibility in the Chinese factory is vested in the 'manager placed under the authority of the Party Committee'. The formula is ambiguous, and reality equally so. Until 1956, Chinese enterprises, faithfully following Soviet methods, were run by a single manager. Ten years later, under the Cultural Revolution, the role of Party Secretary became pre-eminent Today there seems to have been a return to a system that prevailed (except for short periods) from 1956 to 1966: a single manager, but placed under the tutelage of the Party Committee.

Three formal powers now exist in the factory: the decision-making power (*juece quan*), which falls on the manager; the power of direction (*zhihui quan*), assumed by the Party Committee; and the power of supervision (*jiandu quan*), which falls to the Assembly of Workers and Employees.[5]

But the limits and powers of these three types of authority are not always clearly defined. What we find in the exercise of power is the overlapping of the functions of administrator (in the most mandarin sense of the term) and manager. At the higher level, there are a lot of people who 'command' (*zhihui*) in the sense the Chinese give this term, that is, give orders, set objectives, assign tasks. These directives are usually issued on the basis of political criteria, and only indirectly have an economic purpose. Managers, on the other hand, are thinner on the ground; these are the people who, in terms of the definition of it given in China today, organize production in terms of an economic target.

The dominance of mandarins over economic leaders is not something new in China. It can even be suggested that this phenomenon has been a constant feature in all the attempts at industrialization since the late 19th Century. Today, the imperative of industrial modernization makes the gap between the degree of sophistication of production procedures and the slowness of joint administrative procedures acute. Just as the former is concentrated and exercised only through a single person (*yi ge ren shuole suan*), so the latter is diluted and gets lost in the labyrinth of countless departments and sections. In any case, democracy is reduced to its most formal expression.[6]

The excessive number of non-productive departments, the diffuse lack of responsibility, the low level of skills of political cadres, are all factors that are causing a crisis of bureaucratic management. The general trend is towards simplification and compression of grades into six or eight broad divisions in which technical and management functions would be clearly favoured. But it is proving extremely difficult to establish more efficient structures, based on a different rationality, and the attempt is provoking a series of running conflicts. Let us simply note here the conflict between technical cadres and political cadres, whose influence is declining.

## Making Enterprises Responsible towards the End of the Big Pot?

Whereas, on average, 20% to 25% of Chinese enterprises are running at a loss, leading to worrying shortfalls for the budget, a system of taxation of the profits of enterprises has gradually replaced that of the 'big pot', the aim being to inspire enterprises to greater profitability.

The first stage in this process occurred in June 1983. Small state enterprises (those with capital below 1.5 million RMB and profits below 200,000 RMB a year) simply came under the new income tax code. Medium sized or large state enterprises whose fixed capital exceeded the above mentioned category became liable to an income tax (55% of profits) in addition to handing over part of their profits.

During the second stage, which began in October 1984, medium sized and large enterprises were relieved of the obligation to hand over part of their profits and were simply liable to income tax. This stage was also marked by an increase in the number of taxes, an adjustment of their rates, and a more flexible definition of the notion of small enterprises (*JJRB*, 24 June 1984). The old industrial and commercial levy, in particular, was broken down into an output tax, a value added tax and a turnover tax (*SHKX* 7, 1984, p. 26).

However, tax evasion and various abuses by local authorities toward enterprises soon began to appear: in some regions, 50% of collective and state enterprises, and 70% to 80% of individual traders were not paying tax. In 1984, tax evasion in Hebei was estimated at 100 million RMB, and more than half this amount was due from state enterprises (*JJRB*, 22 May 1985, *RMRB*, 24 May 1985). But local authorities sometimes allow some enterprises to keep the full amount of their taxes thus building up for themselves powerful regional clientage networks. Finally it is not uncommon that rural enterprises are over-taxed. Thus 5.28 million yuan were returned to rural industries by the Treasury authorities in Xinxiang district (Henan) (*China Daily*, 3 August 1985).

In fact, Ma Hong, the President of the Chinese Academy of Social Sciences, had already warned against the slowness with which the profitability of enterprises was increasing. The rate of increase of profits and taxes was markedly lower than that of output value. Thus, in 1983, the output value of the largest state run industrial enterprises had registered a 9.3% increase over 1982 while profits and taxes turned over to the state went up by only 6.3% (*RMRB*, 7 May 1984). There again, the explanation is simple: underutilization of output capacities, lengthening of the turnover period of circulating capital (75 days in 1965, 112 days in 1982), poor use of labour.

Despite the efforts made over the last six years, in industry the capacity of the system to reform itself runs up against the constraints that are inherent in excessive centralization.

1) The borders between state functions and those of enterprises are still fluid. 'The state', writes Huan Xing,

> intervenes directly in the management of enterprises, which are administered by the various departments of the central government or by the various local departments that come under them, and which formulate development strategies in the light of their own needs. The relations inherent in economic development are thus disrupted (*Beijing Information* 20, 20 May 1985).

2) The control exercised by government bodies over enterprises is still, as we have seen, excessive: in the area of planning, supply of raw materials, and allocation of labour particularly.

3) So long as price reform is not completed, the market will only play a marginal role. Major distortions still exist between supply and demand, price and value, and the plan seems incapable of responding to market signals.

4) Egalitarianism still remains dominant in the distribution of incomes because of the absence of a real wage reform.

But we should not forget the conjunctural constraints: the very high growth recorded in industry (+21.1% over the first nine months of 1985) has led to a loss of control over the main macro-economic levers.

Is China moving towards a two level economic system, in which centralization would coexist with decentralization and strong regional and social disparities would appear? It is too early to say.

In this context, reform of the urban economy seems condemned to progress in fits and starts. The very logic of reform implies that a whole category of political cadres should lose power as a new stratum of technicians emerges, and as the fragile consensus that for thirty years had been formed between the Communist Party and the working world of labour based on a double compromise is called into question. The compromise was between low productivity and full employment, shortage of consumer goods and relative egalitarianism in income distribution. By upsetting this compromise, reform threatens the whole system of bureaucratic management, as well as the ways in which conflicts are arbitrated. The breaks put on reforms in industry since 1979 are evidence of the resistance at the intermediate level. Relations between economic departments and enterprises are once again caught up in the vicious circle which is described with fatalism or exasperation: 'Control by the tutelary authorities over the enterprise, Stifling, Liberalization to avoid complete asphyxiation, Disorder, Control again.'

## Notes

1. These figures must be used with the greatest caution because of the well known lack of precision of Chinese statistical presentations, the varied ways added value is calculated, and countless biases.

2. Of the 5,769 projects completed in light industry between 1979 and 1982, only 92 were large or medium-sized (*China Daily*, 23 May 1984).

3. In Beijing, in 1985, a bicycle cost 170–185 yuan.

4. According to a statement by Yuan Baohua, Vice-chairman of the State Economic Commission (*China Daily*, 19 November 1983).

5. The Assembly of Workers and Employees is a structure representing the whole staff. It is elected for two to three years and meets about every six months. Its remit extends from social questions to purely technical problems (discussion of the production plan). In some cases, it is empowered to elect the management.

6. The specialist literature unambiguously reveals the shortcomings of administration: vivid accounts describe 'the travels of official documents' (*wengong luxing*), 'the art of contacts', whole departments paralysed by the absence of a head, etc. On the first experiments in industrial organization, see A. Feuerwerker, 1970.

# 7  The Urban Collective Economy[1]

## Martin Lockett

State enterprises dominate China's urban economy. They employ about three-quarters of the workforce, produce seven-eighths of industrial output and use nine-tenths of fixed assets. Such a dominant role is typical of socialist economies. State enterprises, too, tend to be relatively large in terms of employment: averaging perhaps 400 in industrial units. Until recently policies have emphasized the importance of state sector dominance and the advantages of large-scale production units.

But while this state dominance of the urban economy is clear, the role of other sectors is also significant. The most important of these has been the urban collective sector. In theory these enterprises are owned and controlled by their workforce, as well as being relatively independent of state planning (a form which will be referred to as cooperative ownership). Such cooperative ownership is similar to the situation of producer cooperatives (also known as workers' cooperatives) in capitalist economies, though of course their economic and political environment is different. China's collective sector was formed in three main phases: the first through the socialist transformation of handicraft industry in the 1950s, a second through the growth of neighbourhood industry, especially following the Great Leap Forward of the late 1950s, and a third through the drive to employ young people in the late 1970s and early 1980s.[2] However, as will be shown below, in most cases the theory of cooperative ownership has not been put into practice and instead there has been effective collective ownership in which control is in the hands of urban local government and related bodies at various levels. Further, there has been a strong tendency until recently for successful collective enterprises to be converted into state ones, thus reinforcing concentration of ownership in the state sector.

While in advanced capitalist economies trends towards concentration of ownership have continued, there has been if anything a trend towards reduced scale (measured in terms of employment per establishment). In terms of ownership, the privatization of state enterprises has become a political goal of many Western governments. The positive role of small enterprises in product innovation has been emphasized, as have other features of small business such as flexibility to changing market conditions (Rothwell and Zegveld, 1982). It has been estimated by Birch (1979) that over 80% of net new employment in the USA between 1969 and 1976 was in establishments of under 100 employees, with 56% in independent firms. Japan has been taken as an example of the role of small and medium enterprises in economic development.

In this respect the contrast between Japan and China is clear. In 1983, in Japan almost three-quarters of the manufacturing workforce was in small and medium enterprises, each averaging 17 to 53 workers (depending on the lower limit of size taken). In contrast, only one-third of the urban Chinese workforce are in the roughly comparable categories of collective and individual enterprises.[3]

This chapter will examine the reasons for this state of affairs, and the basis for recent changes in policy towards the collective sector and smaller enterprises in general. It will first examine the theoretical basis for the relative neglect of the collective sector. Then it will examine the structure of this sector and its role in the economy. Finally the impact of recent policy changes will be evaluated and their implications discussed.

## The Collective Sector in Socialist Economic Theory

In looking at the collective sector, it is important to be aware of the distinction between (1) ownership in the sense of formal property relations, (2) control in the sense of the actual management of economic activities, and (3) scale in the sense of the size of production (or service) units. Marxist analyses of capitalism have in general asserted that increasing concentration of ownership, centralization of control and increasing scales of production are more or less inevitable features of capitalism (e.g. Mandel, 1968, p. 163), as well as being progressive in developing both productive forces (Marx, 1976, p. 1078) and increasing the potential for revolutionary change as workers are brought together in large-scale units. The contradiction between the effective socialization of production on the one hand and private ownership on the other is seen as the most general and fundamental contradiction of the capitalist mode of production (Engels, 1947, p. 321; Mandel, 1968, p. 170). Thus small-scale production is seen as backward in terms of both production and social relations. For example, Lenin argued that in pre-revolutionary Russia,

> In the small industries . . . we always find survivals of patriarchal relations and of diverse forms of personal dependence, which, in the general conditions of capitalist economy, exceedingly worsen the condition of the working people, and degrade and corrupt them (1960, p. 546).

Such theoretical arguments can be seen to underlie both the theory and the policy towards small and medium sized enterprises in post-revolutionary society. Most notably in the USSR but also elsewhere the general tendency has been for large and increasing levels of ownership, control and scale to be seen as both inevitable and desirable, reflecting Lenin's belief that 'large scale machine industry is precisely . . . the foundation of socialism' (1918, pp. 126–7) while small-scale production engendered capitalism. Stalin too argued that the superiority of socialism rested not only on its planned economy but also on the USSR being 'a land of the most concentrated industry' (1931, p. 362).

The role of the collective sector and individual businesses was therefore transitional, with the assumption that they would necessarily be backward in terms of productivity, innovation and social relations. However it was seen as necessary for smaller buinesses to remain in certain sectors as a transitional form, moving from individual to collective and finally to state ownership. In the USSR, this has applied essentially to agriculture rather than to the urban economy, in which nationalization was virtually complete during the period of war communism (Nove, 1972). This transitional nature of collective ownership was emphasized by Stalin (1952, p. 68) who argued that a major precondition for communism was 'by means of gradual transitions . . . to raise collective farm property to the level of public property' as well as to replace commodity circulation by planning by which 'the central government, or some other socio-economic centre, might control the whole product of social production' (p. 69).

Theoretically such an approach is justified by Bettelheim (1975, p. 50) who argues that because some units are less closely integrated into the overall economy or serve only local needs, lower levels of ownership, including cooperatives, are desirable as in such circumstances the decisions made would be 'socially more efficient' (p. 71) when compared with those of a central body. However, in the longer term, socialization of the means of production is seen by Bettelheim as an 'objective necessity' (p. 122), while cooperatives in particular may become opposed to 'overall social interests', especially when they are large and mainly economic in character (p. 53).

While the arguments of Bettelheim are more often associated with those of the Gang of Four in China, many of the basic assumptions on the transitional nature of the collective sector are shared with their political opponents. Such a theoretical perspective was behind Chinese views of the role of the collective and individual sectors from the 1950s through to the 1980s. Concentration of ownership in the form of state ownership (also known as 'ownership by the whole people'), centralized control through the economic planning system and large-scale production were seen as important goals. There was, however, debate on the speed with which these goals could and should be reached. Thus for example, Xue Muqiao (1981) strongly criticized past moves towards state ownership as premature yet still asserted that, 'Socialist collective ownership is a form of transition from individual ownership to ownership by the whole people' (p. 56) and that, 'The gradual transition of collective ownership to ownership by the whole people is inevitable' (p. 62). Similarly Deng Jie, a leading figure in the handicrafts cooperative movement, argued (1958, p. 100), 'Socialist collective ownership is good, but whole people [i.e. state] ownership is even better'.

Thus while state ownership and control (combined with increasing scale) was the goal, in practice it was accepted that, because of certain diseconomies of scale, various forms of individual and collective ownership would remain for smaller scale production as a transitional measure. Even in China where policies since the late 1950s have often stressed the need for a combination of large and small enterprises (expressed in the slogan of 'walking on two legs': Thomas and Lockett, 1983), small enterprises were seen as essentially transitional and an aspect of China's lack of economic development.

Despite the arguments in the West about the role of small businesses in promoting flexibility and innovation, relatively little attention has been paid to the potential role of small and medium enterprises in socialist economies, even by reform economists.[4] For example, Brus, who has argued for a decentralization of many economic decisions (e.g. in 1973 a and b), suggests as an 'economic law' that the development of productive forces results in socialization, without considering issues of scale in any depth (1975, p. 209). The one theorist who has emphasized these issues is Nove (1983) who sees diseconomies of scale behind many of the problems of the Soviet and other socialist economies, stressing not only the complexity of large-scale planning but also the political power of larger units in the allocation of resources (1983, pp. 77–9). Nove's view calls into question the assumptions of increasing scale and concentration of ownership, as well as arguing that many of the problems in this area seen by Bettelheim are permanent rather than transitional (p. 233).

Such a view finds echoes in some of the more applied studies and policy measures in socialist economies. There have also been significant differences between socialist economies, with Hungary and Poland maintaining relatively large collectively owned sectors; but even these tended to have large units by the standards of capitalist economies. The clearest case of recent change is that of Hungary where specific measures have been implemented since 1982 in order to promote cooperatives and partnerships though their impact has so far been limited (Laky, 1984; Hare, 1983a). However, relatively little research has been undertaken on the role of urban cooperatives in socialist economies to assess its actual and potential contribution to economic development.[5]

## The Structure of China's Urban Collective Sector

China's collective sector has developed on the basis of the three sources mentioned above: handicraft cooperatives, neighbourhood industry and job creation for urban youth. However, many of these, especially what were handicraft enterprises, have developed substantially beyond their initial basis in terms of their size and technical level. For example, in 1981 gross labour productivity in the larger urban collectives was almost four times the figure for handicraft cooperatives in 1956. The collective sector has grown substantially from 6.5 million in 1957 to 27.4 million in 1983 (*SYB*, 1984, p. 110), implying a total job creation of the same order as total employment in the UK, not counting enterprises transferred to the state sector. The most striking feature, however, of the development of the collective sector is the divergence between the theory of collective enterprises and the way in which they are run in practice.

### The Theory of Collective Ownership
In theory the main differences between state and collective ownership are:

1) *Ownership:* by the workforce in the collective sector, rather than by the 'whole people' via the state. The workforce therefore has the formal right to decide on such issues as mergers, changes in status, asset transfers etc.

2) *Independent accounting:* collective sector enterprises are ultimately theoretically responsible for their own profits and losses, and account for these independently as enterprises or groups of them.

3) *Planning:* officially the collective sector is guided by state plans rather than being bound by them. Products are commodities sold in some form of market rather than being allocated by state planning.

4) *Democracy:* the rules governing the operation of the enterprise, as well as major decisions and appointments of top managers, should be determined democratically by a workers' general meeting or equivalent.

5) *Financing:* rather than handing over all profits to the state and applying for allocations of funds for investment etc., collective enterprises retain the profit made (after payment of taxes) to be used for reinvestment, bonuses and other purposes.

6) *Voluntary participation:* joining a collective enterprise is in theory voluntary, with decisions over who to employ being in the hands of the enterprise rather than an external body.

### The Divergence of Theory and Reality
Formally we can see that collectively owned enterprises are supposed to be significantly different in operation from state ones. But the divergence between the theory and the reality has been substantial – although it has been reduced somewhat since 1978. The first main area of difference is in the division of the collective sector into big and small collectives, with the former being groups of enterprises in a particular municipality or area, a form which arose during the Great Leap Forward as handicraft cooperatives were amalgamated (Lockett, 1986). Table 7.1 summarizes the differences between these types of enterprise.

From Table 7.1 it is possible to see that the big collectives are a form rather similar to state enterprises as they are subject to the planning of a state ministry and in many other respects are managed in a similar way. Some recent Chinese analyses have emphasized this: for example Xiao Liang et al. (1980, p. 221) argued that from the point of view of (1) assets, (2) control of production, and (3) labour management, 'from the individual viewpoint of workers and staff, working in these units is exactly the same as working in state enterprises'. However there is one significant difference in the area of (4) provision and accumulation of capital. Although much of the rest of the formal framework governing the collective sector has been ignored in practice, big collective enterprises have retained a significant proportion of their profits, though at the level of the group of enterprises rather than individual ones. Thus there is the possibility of rapid local development of such big collectives with a town or city's Second Light Industry Bureau acting rather like a holding company with individual collectives as subsidiaries. While each plant is small or medium scale, the effective level of ownership is municipal. Widely quoted cases of such a form of development are Changzhou in Jiangsu

**Table 7.1**
**Forms of Industrial Ownership in Urban China**

|  | *Formal ownership* | *Administrative superior body* | *Theoretical level of profit/loss responsibility*[a] |
|---|---|---|---|
| State | Whole people | Specialized municipal bureau (or central ministry) | All state enterprises |
| Big collective | Members of group of enterprises | Municipal Second Bureau of Light Industry (or specialized municipal bureau) | Group of enterprises |
| Small collective | Members of individual enterprise | District or neighbourhood management bureau (under local government) | Individual enterprise |

[a] before post-1978 economic reforms.

*Source:* Lockett (1986).

Province (Wu Jiapei and Li Wenrui, 1979) and in Weihai in Shandong (Xiao Liang et al., 1980).

It is, however, more difficult to generalize about the small collective enterprises which are still formally organized as individual, independent small-scale units of ownership. Some do take this form but it seems that many are effectively controlled more or less directly by the lower levels of the state in a town or city. In fact some may be more closely controlled than big collectives, although the local bureaux running them will have some autonomy over products and other issues. Also, as will be shown below, even in cases where some independence remained, until recently the resources which should have been allocated to these small collectives were appropriated by other bodies. In short, the theory of the urban collective sector is broadly that of cooperative ownership whereas the practice has been of collective and local government ownership, though with certain significant differences between the big and small collective forms.

So in analysing the role of the urban collective sector and the extent to which the state restricts or promotes their development, it is necessary (1) to distinguish the theory of the collective sector from what has actually happened, particularly in relation to the degree of local state control; (2) to analyse the differences between big and small collectives as in practice the former are fairly similar to state enterprises; and (3) to be aware of the potentially different interests which national and local state organizations may have.

## The Role of the Collective Sector

This section considers two aspects of the urban collective sector: first, the situation of enterprises in relation to the state sector and the overall economy, and second the situation of workers in the sector relative to other groups. Table 7.2 gives a picture of the relative importance of the state and urban collective sectors in the economy as well as other relevant figures. It shows that about a quarter of the workforce not in rural communes is employed by the urban collective sector. This is concentrated in light industry within which the collective sector plays a major role. But labour productivity (using gross output value) is only about half that of state enterprises on average. As a result, about a sixth of gross industrial output comes from the urban collective sector.[6] It is not possible to break down these statistics between big and small collectives. However, most urban collective output is from the big collectives, particularly those under the Second Ministry of Light Industry which in 1980 had an output value of 49.3 billion yuan from 58,000 enterprises with 6.85 million workers (*China Daily*, 30 January 1982). The productivity level of these big collectives is therefore about 60% of the state sector average while small collectives' labour productivity is probably of the order of a half (or less) of this figure.[7]

Thus the evidence from official statistics indicates that in terms of levels of output and productivity, big collectives are somewhat lower than state enterprises whereas small collectives are much lower. As a result the small contribute proportionately more to employment than to output. However, such figures do not reveal the structure of the relationships between the urban collective sector and other parts of the economy.

### Urban Collective Enterprises in the Economy

The role of collective enterprises will be examined in four areas: (1) industrial structure, (2) relations with the state, (3) financial factors and (4) personnel.

In the area of industrial structure, the role of the collective sector is rather similar to that of small firms in capitalist economies. In general the urban collective sector does work which state sector enterprises for various reasons do not wish to do. This is partly a question of producing small everyday consumer goods which are in demand but which have not been given priority in state planning. But also many urban collectives, especially small ones, are involved in sub-contract work for larger state enterprises or use the waste products from them. Larger state enterprises may sub-contract simpler work out to small urban collectives either to avoid managerial problems or to cut costs where wages are lower (see below). In fact, Chinese planners have made favourable references to the Japanese system of a

> pyramid-structure of contracts, subcontracts and sub-subcontracts. At the top of the pyramid are a few modernized big enterprises while the bottom is made up of a great number of small enterprises with simple equipment (Zhuang Qidong et al., 1980, p. 43).

Thus the collective sector plays a role which is complementary to the larger scale state sector as a result of its greater flexibility. In this respect its structure is similar to that in capitalist economies. However, the role of capitalist small enterprises in

**Table 7.2**
**Employment and Industrial Sectors in China (1983)**

| | State | Urban collective | Urban individual | Rural commune/ township | Total |
|---|---|---|---|---|---|
| Total workforce (m) of which: | 87.71 (19%) | 27.44 (6%) | 2.31 (0.5%) | 342.58 (74%) | 460.04 |
| industrial[a] workforce | 35.52 (59%) | 15.74 (26%) | 0.24 (0.4%) | 8.73 (14%) | 60.23 |
| Number of industrial enterprises | 87,100 (22%) | 118,500 (30%) | n.a.[c] | 186,100 (47%) | 391,700[c] |
| Industrial output value[b] (gross, bn yuan) | 475 (77%) | 94 (15%) | 1 (0.1%) | 41 (7%) | 611 |
| Fixed assets[d] (bn yuan) | 477 (89%) | 37 (7%) | n.a. | 24 (4%) | 538 |
| Profits (bn yuan) | 64 (84%) | 8 (10%) | n.a. | 5 (6%) | 77 |
| Taxes paid (bn yuan) | 39 (85%) | 4 (10%) | n.a. | 2 (5%) | 46 |
| Workforce in heavy industry (m) | 24.12 (80%) | 6.05 (20%) | n.a. | n.a. | n.a. |
| Workforce in light industry (m) | 11.4 (54%) | 9.68 (46%) | n.a. | n.a. | n.a. |
| Employment growth rate (annual, %) 1966–78 | 5.6 | 3.9 | n.a. | n.a. | n.a. |
| 1978–83 | 3.4 | 6.2 | n.a. | n.a. | n.a. |
| Average earnings per year (yuan) | 865 | 698 (81%) | n.a. | n.a. | n.a. |
| Number of women workers (m) of which: | 28.15 (32%) | 13.84 (50%) | n.a. | n.a. | n.a. |
| industrial women workers | 11.79 (33%) | 8.89 (56%) | n.a. | n.a. | n.a. |

[a] Industrial excludes construction, energy, transport, commerce, distribution, scientific, educational, social service and administrative units and workers, in order to arrive at a category close to Western 'manufacturing' categories.
[b] Industrial output gross value is at 1980 fixed prices.
[c] N.a. indicates not available or not applicable.
[d] Figures for fixed assets, profits and taxes are for independent accounting collective enterprises only.
*Source:* Lockett, 1986, derived from *SYB*, 1984.

technical innovation and related activities such as consultancy does not appear to the same extent in Chinese urban collectives. While it is true that the flexibility of collectives has meant that they have been able to move fairly rapidly into expanding sectors of the market (for example, electrical consumer goods such as fans and electronics assembly), they have not played the same role in high technology areas as a result of state restriction and personnel problems, factors which are outlined below.

In the second area, of relations with the state, the methods of economic management adopted in China differ substantially from those in capitalist economies. Planning is obviously the key difference, and in China this has both promoted and restricted the urban collective sector. For a start the creation of the sector has been to a large degree the result of state policies – initially through state control of commerce and then more directly in such areas as changes in ownership status and materials allocation. State planning on the one hand means that the autonomy of collective enterprises in choosing product lines and determining prices is reduced. However the local groupings of enterprises in which both big and small collectives have typically been organized have had some autonomy and flexibility, as well as being able to accumulate and redistribute funds from individual enterprises.

State policies have tended to restrict urban collectives in the allocation of materials for use in production. Until recently major materials were allocated almost entirely by planning bodies. Big collectives tended to be included in these plans, either under a Second Light Industry Bureau or another specialist one. As a result, materials are made available for most but not all of their planned production.[8] However, they did to some degree get second-class treatment compared to state enterprises, for example not getting their share of materials when there were supply problems. Small collectives not undertaking sub-contract work for large enterprises have been in a much less favourable position as their allocations of materials cover less of their needs and are given much lower priority. In fact their position in this respect is worse than in a market system of allocation, as a result of both the planning system and the incentives for larger state enterprises to keep high stocks. In the north-eastern province of Liaoning it was claimed that this resulted in small collectives paying 10-15% more than other enterprises for materials of lower quality (Liu Wenzhu, 1979). And it was admitted by a provincial party leader that 'for many years . . . [collective enterprises] have run their business by relying on personal channels and behind the scenes deals' rather than official methods (Zhu Chuan, 1980, p. 33). Similar problems exist in the area of marketing. It is possible for the burden of adjustment to changes in state plans to be passed on to collectives by state enterprises.

But while such practices have restricted the development of the urban collective sector, other state policies have played a key role in promoting it. Here the price system has been very important, as has lack of competition until recently. The profits of industrial enterprises have been a major source of state revenue as prices for many products have been maintained well above production costs. This has meant that the less efficient collective sector enterprises have been able to be competitive even with higher production costs. The greater flexibility of collectives and their greater freedom from rigid direct control via the planning system has also meant that they can move into relatively profitable market gaps more easily than state enterprises. Thus the relationship between collective enterprises and the state has been an ambiguous one, involving both restriction and promotion.

The third area to be considered is that of the financial aspects of collective enterprises. Parts of this have been touched on above, including price discrimination against collective enterprises in supplies and marketing. One way out of this is to undertake sub-contract work, but this does not eliminate such problems altogether. Chinese analysts have pointed to the exploitative nature of sub-contract work. For example, Li Shuren and Huang Yinzhu (1979, pp. 7–8) argue that in Shanghai 'a considerable part of the value created by collective enterprises is transferred to large industrial enterprises' which as a result 'get credit for achievement and enjoy more bonus and welfare benefits', while Zhuang Qidong et al. (1980) quote examples of very low processing fees which are reduced when productivity increases as a result of the lack of power of collective enterprises within the planning system.

There have been a number of mechanisms by which collective enterprises' profits have been taken out of their control. Initially, of course, there are state taxes based both on turnover ('industrial and commercial tax') and profits ('income tax'). The former is at a fixed rate and applies to both state and collective sectors while the latter is a progressive tax of up to 55% which has been applied primarily to collectives. However, collectives have also been subject to a range of further levies which have reduced the amount retained within the collective sector, sometimes to very low levels. The clearest is the collection of 'collective undertaking fees' by the bodies responsible for managing the collective sector. While these have been reduced somewhat in recent years, in 1981 in Shanghai big collectives gave 30–40% of their post-tax profits to the city's Handicrafts Bureau, and a similar amount to their superior body; while in small collectives 60% of post-tax profit went to local district and/or neighbourhood bodies. Some of these were used to develop the collective sector as a whole in a particular area, but in other cases they are used as general subsidy to local government. On top of these have come more or less arbitrary levies by local state bodies which have included ones for civil defence, 'cash awards for the staff of neighbourhood offices', urban construction work, target practice for the armed forces, pensions for traffic accident victims and even levies for chrysanthemum shows! Zhong Zhang and Dong Yan (1983) calculate that a collective enterprise was likely to retain only 4–5% of its profit. Given the control of collective enterprises by the local state, they have not been able to resist this transfer of resources over and above official limits.

Thus in a number of ways the collective sector has been used by the local state as a source of revenue. While in some cases these financial transfers have been used to develop the local economy in ways which would be beyond the capacity of individual enterprises, in others this has not been the case – and collectives have not been able effectively to resist these pressures. However it should be emphasized that there have also been transfers in the other direction, both in terms of investment and in the transfer of old machinery and technical knowledge from state enterprises to the collective sector.

On the fourth area, of personnel, several points should be noted. The first is that, despite the legal idea that collectives should be able to choose their own workers, in practice they have been allocated workers through the state system of labour allocation. This has meant that they are more or less forced to take the workers which the local labour bureau wants them to have. In the past this has led to collective enterprises tending to be given less healthy and well trained recruits, particularly in the case of small collectives. In particular, collectives have not been allocated graduate level personnel (Zhuang Qidong et al., 1980, p. 46), and cannot expect to be able to recruit skilled workers or managers from state enterprises (except when they have retired). This lack of mobility and skilled personnel has tended to restrict the potential for technical innovation in the urban collective sector.

The collective sector has also been used as a source of labour for state enterprises. Partly this is a result of the upgrading of collective plants to state ownership, which tends to benefit the workforce. But in addition, given the worse wages and prospects, especially in small collectives, young workers have seen collective sector jobs as a way of gaining work experience in order to obtain jobs in state factories. The collective sector has been used to some extent as a pool of labour by larger state enterprises.

So, to sum up the discussion of the role of the urban collective sector from the viewpoint of the enterprise, it is clear that in a number of ways the collective sector has been 'exploited' by the state and state enterprises and that it performs a role similar to that of small firms in a capitalist economy. In some respects it is more restricted than equivalent capitalist small firms, e.g. in recruitment, as a result of the concentration of both economic and political power in the state in a socialist economy, while in others it has been promoted and supported much more than would be possible in a capitalist economy, e.g. by the price system. Present reforms in the economic planning system are likely to reduce some of the past administrative restrictions on the collective sector as well as increasing the ability of enterprises to accumulate through profit retention; however they also have the implication that efficiency and profitability will increase in importance, particularly if there is any systematic price reform.

### The Position of Workers

Moving on to the question of the position of workers in the collective sector, three areas will be discussed: (1) wages, (2) other conditions and the status of workers, and (3) sexual inequalities. Table 7.2 above showed that in 1983, the average annual earnings in the collective sector were 698 yuan and were 81% of the average in the state sector. However, this aggregation of big and small collective workers masks a major inequality between workers in the different types of collective.

In both big and small collectives workers have generally been paid a fixed wage on scales decided by the local government. The big collective wages are slightly below the equivalent in a state factory, following a system similar to the national eight wage grades for state sector manual workers. For example, in the engineering industry in Beijing a grade 3 worker would get 40.5 yuan in a big collective and 43.0 yuan in a state one. For higher grades the differential was higher – at grade 5 the respective wages were 54.0 yuan and 64.5 yuan (Jiang Nan, 1980, p. 7). In fact, until recently there was a regulation in many places that workers in a big collective could not earn more than in an equivalent state enterprise, although some areas treated collective sector workers more favourably, for example Weihai Municipality in Shandong Province which is now held up as a model (Xiao Liang *et al.*, 1980, pp. 219–20). So, broadly, wages in big collectives are similar if a little lower than in the state sector.

The picture in small collectives is of much lower pay. It seems that pay levels are on scales set by municipal governments, and are much lower than in big collectives. For example, in Shanghai in September 1981, the municipal scale for small collective workers was from 33 yuan to 42 yuan plus a typical bonus of 3 yuan, compared to a range up to 100 yuan in a state factory, plus a bonus averaging 7 yuan. The highest wage in a small collective was only 57 yuan for the top grade of technical staff, perhaps half of the top wage in a state factory. There are probably more regional and other variation in small collective wages than in the state and big collective sectors – for example, in Tianjin in 1980, Zhao Yang (1980, p. 39) stated that many small collectives had an average wage of under 30 yuan, a maximum of 35 yuan and no bonuses. So in terms of earnings those in small collectives earn much less than in other factories. When compared with household expenditure data, the average wage of a small collective worker is about the national average used to support one person (38 yuan – *SYB*, 1982, p. 429).[9] Relative to average living standards, small collective workers are paid little more than a subsistence wage (though it should be remembered that workers in many Third World countries may not even get this).

As well as lower wages, collective sector workers have had lower welfare and other benefits. Again there are considerable differences between big and small collectives, with the former having pension, sick pay, maternity and other benefits similar to those provided under the state labour insurance scheme. These benefits form an impressive package, particularly for a low income developing country, and are comparable with those in advanced capitalist societies (in relation to overall wage levels). State enterprises also provide childcare facilities, canteens, recreation facilities etc., in many cases. They play in addition an important role in providing housing, as most workers in state plants will tend to live in accommodation provided by their unit.

In contrast, small collectives have provided hardly any of these benefits. Labour insurance – where it exists – is much worse than in the state sector. Many workers will get no retirement pay or similar benefits. Housing will seldom be provided by a small collective enterprise. A further question is that of job security. Workers in state plants have an exceptionally high degree of job security and are very unlikely to be made redundant or sacked for other reasons, though recent moves towards a contract system for new workers are intended to reduce this level of job security. It is likely that small collective workers are more vulnerable to losing their jobs, though the risk is still probably not very high.[10]

Another question is that of the status of workers in the collective sector. Given the importance of the political sphere in China, this does have some significance. During the Cultural Revolution, it was alleged that urban collectives were only 'semi-socialist' and the 'tail of capitalism'. As a result there was less likelihood of advancement for those in the collective sector. Examples are quoted of cadres in collective enterprises not being circulated with documents which went to those in the state sector and being excluded from relevant meetings. Further, any cadres who moved from the state sector to the collective lost their status, as well as reducing other benefits such as pension rights (Korzec and Whyte, 1981, p. 268). Some of this systematic discrimination against those working in the collective sector has now been removed, but in practice many of the same attitudes and disincentives to working in the collective sector remain. So in the areas of workers' wages and other benefits, as well as of status, the general picture is that big collective workers are in a similar though slightly inferior position to state sector workers, while that of small collective workers is significantly lower than either of these.

One further important aspect of the collective sector needs to be discussed: that of sexual inequalities and the collective sector's role in relation to these. Table 7.2 showed that the proportion of women working in collective sector industry is much higher than that in the state sector – 57% as opposed to 33%. This implies that women tend to be in jobs which have lower pay, welfare and other benefits and status, despite the existence for many years of equal pay legislation. If the figures could be broken down further into big and small collective sectors it is probable that this pattern of inequality would be even more marked. Although no figures appear to have been published on the difference between men's and women's pay within enterprises, analysis of the relationship between average pay in ten broad areas of employment in both state and collective sectors shows that there was a negative correlation between the proportion of women employed and average pay, even when the difference between state and collective ownership is taken into account.[11]

Thus the collective sector plays a role in maintaining inequalities between men and women in urban areas. Partly this is a result of the origin of neighbourhood industry in creating jobs for women without work outside the home. While in Marxist theory entry into the labour force and working outside the home is often seen as the key to women's equality, it is clear that in many cases in China women's work is in less productive sectors, lower paid and with worse conditions than men's – and that the structural division between state and collective sectors, as well as that between big and small collectives, plays a role in perpetuating the inequalities associated with this sexual division of labour.

It is difficult to obtain a clear picture, but within these structural constraints it is likely that there has been some narrowing of the differences on average but that differences between enterprises and areas have grown. This is the result of a number of factors. Inequalities are likely to have risen with the growth of bonuses in both state and collective sectors, though until 1982 bonus payments were a much more significant element in state sector pay. The increasing importance of bonuses is likely to increase differences between successful and less successful enterprises, though again the extent of this differentiation is hard to judge. In Hunan for example (Ji Long, 1984, p. 84), policy in light industrial collective enterprises is to have 'Eight Possibles' of:

| Cadres: | promoted & demoted |
|---|---|
| Workers: | employed & dismissed |
| Wages: | rising & falling |
| Bonuses & Welfare: | increasing & decreasing |

Previous restrictions on earnings levels in the collective sector have been relaxed so that earnings can now be higher than in the state sector. In some youth cooperatives and other small collectives (as well as in individual self-employment) there have been systems of piecework or a direct relationship between enterprise performance and pay. In some cases this has meant that significantly higher earnings are possible than in the state sector. However even when such high earnings are possible, it appears that most young people prefer to take jobs in the state sector or, failing that, in big collectives as these give greater security in both wages and welfare as well as better access to scarce resources such as housing.

In these non-wage areas, there have been moves to improve the position of small collective workers in at least some areas. The growth of insurance business in China has given an institutional channel for collective enterprises to maintain welfare funds without having to bear all the risks involved. In more developed urban areas there are signs of a trend towards the use of such schemes with either individuals and/or enterprises making contributions (*SWB*, 19 February 1982, 6958/B11/16 and 3 March 1982, W1174/A/2-3). One recent report claimed that contributory retirement pension schemes have 'become almost a standard practice in many collective enterprises' (*BR* 11, 23, 19 August 1985), though Xiao Weixiang (1984, p. 54) states that these 'operate within the limits permitted by actual capability'.

So the effect of reforms and associated policies has been to improve the relative position of collective sector workers to some degree, with those in more successful enterprises gaining more. Overall the average earnings of collective sector workers rose from 77% of the state sector average in 1979 to 81% in 1983, with bonus payments rising from 59% to 81% of state sector averages over the same period (calculated from *SYB*, 1984, p. 455). The relaxation of controls on pay levels has also opened up a trade-off between wage levels and security for at least some workers, enabling in principle greater choice for workers. There has also been relaxation of past constraints on labour allocation. In Shanghai at least, policy has changed to allow national cadres and other state employees to retain their status if they work in collective enterprises, and for the enterprises to have a greater say in recruitment. In particular they can recruit retired skilled workers and technical staff, as well as being 'loaned' staff by state enterprises, including 'those who have been placed in unsuitable work' in state enterprises (Wenhui Bao, 4 July 1984, in *CREA*, 85–003, pp. 36-8).

**Institutional Reform**

The major trend in policy has been to attempt to reintroduce elements of cooperative ownership in place of collective ownership. So far this has happened in a limited way despite apparent major policy changes and has run in parallel with reforms in the state sector. By June 1984 it was reckoned that 70% of light industrial collective enterprises were using some form of contractual responsibility systems for sharing profits between enterprises and higher level bodies (Ji Long, 1984, p. 79; Xiao Weixiang, 1984, p. 53). This method used for big collectives is similar to that in use in the state sector, and the issues raised by Ji Long (1984) are little different from those in the state sector, including internal responsibility systems and management control.

Other policy changes have involved more emphasis on other aspects of cooperative ownership, including self-responsibility for profit and loss; greater enterprise autonomy and reduced administrative control; more democratic management with a workers' assembly or elected workers' congress appointing senior managers and taking major decisions; and an end to forced transfers of collective enterprises' assets and personnel to the state sector. However, most of these are also similar to changes in the state sector implemented in the early and mid-1980s. The limits are also similar as typically state bodies would have veto rights over elected managers, as in the state sector. Thus in many ways we can see a convergence of state and large collective sectors towards a hybrid of state and cooperative ownership.

In the area of taxation new provisional regulations were introduced in April 1985 which reduced the tax burden on collective enterprises with below 100,000 yuan profits by about 7% through a readjustment of tax bands (*SWB*, 1 May 1985, W1336/C2/p. 3). Again there are parallels with the state sector, which has officially begun to implement a similar form of tax system.[12] In the case of commerce it has been argued that the tax burden of collective shops is significantly less than for state ones in contrast to the past. Much attention was paid in the new tax regulations to procedures regarding tax evasion, including substantial surcharges and the possibility of criminal prosecution. Informants exposing tax evasion could also be rewarded confidentially (Article 18). This concern reflects the growth of corruption and tax evasion more generally in China, as well as the weakness of the auditing and tax inspection infrastructure.[13]

The extent to which these policies have been implemented on the ground is uncertain. Certainly self-responsibility for profit and loss has not resulted in formal bankruptcy, though in July 1985 three collective enterprises in Shenyang were given a one-year warning that they could be declared bankrupt in what XH described as 'a move believed to be the first in the 36 years of the People's Republic' (*SWB*, 7 August 1985, 8023/B11/10).

Another development is that state enterprises have created collective ones, particularly for children of the existing workforce, which are more or less tied to the parent enterprise – the collective status being a method of entering new areas of activity and avoiding constraints on expanding their own workforce. However, the general trends are clearly towards increasing elements of cooperative ownership in place of those of collective ownership.

## Role of the Collective Sector

The status of the collective sector and smaller units as a transitional form on the way to large-scale and state ownership has been significantly changed in recent years. First there has been the partial shift from collective to cooperative forms of ownership discussed above, which have reduced the extent of state control over collective sector enterprises. Second has been the shift in emphasis away from heavy industry towards light industry and services in which historically the collective sector has been more important. It has been recognized that the flexibility associated with smaller scale enterprises is valuable and that state management has been unable to meet local needs in the past.

Third has been the desire to create jobs while minimizing central state expenditure. The collective sector has been seen as a major source of job creation, especially for young people, as the growth of youth cooperatives from the late 1970s indicates. But also the growth of the collective sector is a way of giving greater flexibility to the state sector through sub-contracting and similar relationships. Further, growth in the collective sector is a way of speeding changes in labour policy such as reduced job security, which the contract system is expected to achieve in state enterprises.

The results of these policies have been that, in 1984, half of new employment was in the collective sector, with a further 11% in the private sector. In terms of job creation this claimed to be successful with the official unemployment rate reduced from 6% in 1979 to under 2% in 1984 (Xin Ling, 1985, p. 4). The clearest changes have, however, been in particular sectors, notably commerce. During the 1980s the dominant position of the state sector in retailing has been significantly eroded by the collective and individual sectors, while the structure of the sector has changed significantly. Between 1978 and 1983 the number of urban retail and service outlets increased by a factor of over five from 0.4 million to 2.1 million, with employment up from 3.6 to 8.9 million (*SYB*, 1984, p. 377). Of this increase, probably over a third was in the collective sector and a similar amount in the individual private sector which had grown to 2 million by the end of 1983.[14] The state sector's share of retail sales (urban and rural) had decreased from over 90% in 1978 to 72% in 1983 (Peng Baoquan, 1985, p. 26) and by 1985 was further reduced, with the growth of both collective and individual commerce. This growth of commercial outlets was one of the clearest visual contrasts in Chinese urban areas between the early and mid-1980s. In short, current policies have reinforced the importance of the collective sector as well as giving rise to the rapid growth of a private sector.

## Privatization?

Particularly in the service sector and commerce, there have been limited moves towards 'lowering' the level of ownership of some units from state to collective or even individual – a policy confirmed in the October 1984 Central Committee decision on economic reform (Communist Party, 1984, p. 26). By early 1985, 58,000 service businesses and 11,000 industrial ones had been converted to collective or individual management. In these, rents are paid to the state on contracts of up to five years, but the collectives or individuals have significant autonomy (*SWB*, 20 February 1985, 1326/A/2; also 16 January 1985, W1321/A/2-3). The Sihui County Ceramic Plant was taken by Guangdong Province as a model: planned to be shut down, it was then managed on a three year contract by a collective of ten former workers with much better results (*SWB*, 18 February 1983, 7261/B11/11; *CREA*, 1983, 83-018, p. 2). Another case is that of Ling Fangyou in Shenyang who won a public bidding to operate a 147 worker pump factory in Shenyang and who 'gets

30% of the factory's annual profit after paying rent and taxes' (*SWB*, 20 February 1985, W1326/A/2).

Another change has been the growth of individual capital stakes in collective enterprises. For example in Shanghai, 'As a means of encouraging the gathering of funds . . . collective enterprises may draw up their own prospectuses when soliciting share subscriptions from their employees or the public' (Wenhui Bao, 4 July 1984, in *CREA*, 85-003, p. 37), while part of what Ji Long (1984, p. 84) sees as the good experience of Hunan light industry is 'the system of buying shares with eligibility for receiving dividends'. The objective behind these is both to raise funds and to develop worker commitment to the enterprise (Xiao Weixiang, 1984, p. 54). An example given by He Jianzhang and Zhang Weimin (1982, p. 197) is of a Harbin furniture factory raising finance through 100 yuan shares sold to its workers, with dividends dependent on profits.

Alongside this has been the growth of a regulated private sector of individual and family businesses which legally can only hire very limited amounts of labour – initially one or two assistants and up to five apprentices according to 1981 regulations but relaxed in 1983 to ten apprentices (*Issues and Studies*, vol. 20, no. 4, April 1984, p. 7). By 1984, there were almost three million individuals working in the private sector (*SYB*, 1985, p. VIII), mostly in commerce. The age composition had changed too, as initially older and retired workers formed the basis of the sector but since then many more young people have joined (Liang Chuanyun, 1984; Peters and Schädler, 1983). However there are still fears of insecurity and poor marriage prospects for individual workers (see Fang Sheng, 1982, p. 172).

So, with these forms of 'privatization' in urban areas, are we witnessing the growth of a capitalist sector? Four forms can be seen: the first is the conversion of state ownership to cooperative ownership, the reverse of previous trends towards state ownership – the main form of change in state enterprises. The second is the individually owned private sector which is limited to very small individual or family businesses with very limited hiring of labour and so is in general individual or family labour, not involving capitalist relations of production. However, in the future there is the question of whether successful businesses can expand, and whether this will be on the basis of private or cooperative ownership. The third is the growth of individually invested capital in collective enterprises, which can be seen as cooperative if owned by workers on an equitable basis but may have capitalist elements if by outside investors. The fourth is that of individual contracts to run small enterprises, for even though formal ownership remains in the hands of the state, the relations of production within the enterprise are in many ways capitalist. The numbers involved are small, with 5,917 state service sector enterprises in the whole country converted to individual management on contract (State Statistical Bureau, 1985, p. VI) with a significant proportion of these probably not using hired labour. Thus in urban areas we can see some of these changes reinforcing certain forms of cooperative ownership, some creating an individual private sector which is not capitalist and some giving rise to elements of capitalism through private control of state assets using hired labour in China's urban areas.

**Theory of the Collective Economy**

The theoretical views of the role of collective and cooperative ownership have undergone considerable change in China over the last five years. As summarized by Xiao Liang (1982, p. 159),

> Previously downplayed as a transitional form for changing individual economy, the collective enterprises, owned and managed by the labouring people with state support, are now seen as an ideal method to respond to some of China's real social and economic problems, both at present and for a long time to come.

This change has led to a reappraisal by some economists of the traditional Marxist–Leninist view of the gradual move from individual ownership through collective ownership to state (whole people) ownership. Yu Guangyuan (1980), for example, adopted a cautious approach to the future arguing that collective and state ownership might both evolve into a new third type. This view is taken by Xiao Liang (1982) who sees a future in which

> collective ownership will most likely fuse with ownership by the whole people to find a kind of socialist public ownership that is more perfect, more advanced, and more advantageous to the development of the productive forces (p. 171).

There has also been greater recognition of the potential of small enterprises in specialized fields and in technical innovation. For example, Li Yue and Chen Shengchang (1981) argue this, though they argue too that in general China has too many small and medium sized enterprises.

Thus in China today one can see the start of a significant reappraisal of previous views on the collective sector which goes beyond previous critiques of too rapid transition to state enterprises. These point towards a future convergence of state and collective forms – a trend which can to some extent be seen in present reforms in which elements of cooperative ownership have been reintroduced to the urban collective sector and introduced into the state one. Thus present developments must be seen as a break with the past in both theory and policy.

# Conclusions

This chapter has shown how, in the past, Chinese thinking about the collective sector was similar to that in other socialist economies. Briefly, this meant that the existence of collectively owned enterprises was a transitional phase between individual private enterprises and state (whole people) ownership. The direction of policies from 1949 to 1978 was consistent with this approach. Since 1978, however, there has been a shift in thinking to the extent that many economists and policy-makers no longer see the urban collective sector as just transitional, but as an enduring form with distinct advantages in certain areas of the economy. There has also been some reappraisal of the ultimate benefits of scale of production and operations. The result has been an increasing role for the urban collective sector, notably in employment generation, currently providing around half of new job opportunities.

This chapter has also shown the substantial divergence between the official theory of how collective enterprises should be organized and how they have been managed in practice. It has characterized this as the difference between a theoretical cooperative ownership system and a practised collective system. This divergence has been reduced to some extent since 1978, through the reintroduction of elements of cooperative ownership. At the same time there has been some convergence of state and collective sectors in terms of the desired methods of managing their operations, for example responsibility for profit and loss. Alongside this there has been the rapid growth of an individual private but non-capitalist sector in urban areas, together with some elements of capitalism particularly through individual leasing of enterprises. It is important not to see the growth of the individual private sector as capitalist, although there may be pressures towards this in the future.

From the viewpoint of its workers, the collective sector – in particular small collectives – provides lower wages and welfare benefits. Though these have improved somewhat in the last few years, the difference is still significant. One particular effect of this is in reinforcing sexual inequalities as many collective sector workers are women. In this and other respects, the collective sector in urban China resembles the small business sector in capitalist economies.

Looking towards the future, the trend in Chinese policies towards the collective sector over the last few years does mark a distinct break with the past. It is argued that there will be substantial positive effects on the economy through expanding the collective sector relative to the state sector and emphasizing cooperative rather than collective ownership. The direction of these developments combined with reforms in the state sector is to decrease the administrative and other institutional divisions between the state and collective sectors. The effect will be to increase differentials between enterprises as well as to increase the importance of economic factors as opposed to administrative decisions. The pattern which may emerge is one even more similar to the small firm sector in capitalist economies such as Japan than is the case today, while retaining key aspects of a socialist ownership system.

# Notes

1. The research on which this article is based was supported by the UK Economic and Social Research Council. It was also assisted by a visit to China in 1981 under the British Academy/ESRC exchange scheme with the Chinese Academy of Social Sciences Institute of Industrial Economics. Particular assistance on various aspects was provided by the Shanghai and Sichuan Academies of Social Science, the Sichuan Second Bureau of Light Industry, Hongkou District (Shanghai), Liu Gang, Lu Guangmian and Rewi Alley. Parts of this chapter are based on Lockett (1986).

2. For more details see Lockett, 1983 and 1986.

3. Given the different basis of these statistics, an exact comparison is not possible. However the broad trend is clear and cannot be accounted for by differences in categories. The Japanese figures are taken from MITI (1985, p. 91) and the Chinese from Table 7.2. The Japanese definition is of establishments employing fewer than

300 workers. The lower limits taken in the figures quoted in the text were of 4 and 20 workers respectively.

4. Until recently this had been paralleled by a neglect by Western Marxists of the changes taking place in advanced capitalist economies in terms of both scale and location of enterprises.

5. There are exceptions to this, particularly on Poland, for example Balawdyer (1980), Campbell (1981 and n.d.), and Kowalak (1981).

6. The proportion of net industrial output is probably rather lower. According to the World Bank (1981, p. 91) in 1979 about 12% came from the urban collective sector.

7. Such a productivity structure is similar to that in Japanese industry where the productivity of medium sized manufacturing enterprises is about two-thirds that of large enterprises, with those under 100 employees averaging between a third and a half of the large firm average depending on size (MITI, 1985, p. 93).

8. Estimates of about half and two-thirds of materials required by big collectives under the Second Ministry of Light Industry are given by Zhuang Gidong et al. (1980, p. 46) and Li Shuren and Huang Yinzhu (1979, pp. 10–11).

9. A household of, say, four members with two wage-earners in small collectives would have been in the bottom 2% of urban households in terms of per capita consumption in 1981 (see *SYB*, 1982, p. 428).

10. This pattern of wage levels and welfare benefits is again similar to Japan, though wage differences are if anything less in China. In Japan (all industries) those in medium sized (100 to 300 employees) enterprises receive 83% of large enterprises' average pay, while those in small enterprises receive between 59% and 70% on average depending on size (MITI, 1985, p. 94).

11. The correlation between the proportion of women and average pay was –0.69 ($r^2 = 0.48$). The data used was from *SYB*, 1984, pp. 126–8, 456.

12. Equivalent 1983 state regulations are in *JJNJ*, 1984, pp. IX–84–6. These have the same top tax rate of 55% and a similar eight tax bands for smaller state enterprises, with rates the same as for collective enterprises at that time (see *Jingjixue Zhoubao*, 1983, for these).

13. From January to September 1985, the Chinese Auditing Administration (established in 1983) uncovered 'errors and violations of the law covering 5.3 billion yuan' (Zhu Ling, 1985).

14. These figures are based on analysis of the figures given in *SYB*, 1984, pp. 119, 122 and 377. As the areas considered urban may differ between tables, these figures cannot be exact.

# 8 A Brief Outline of China's Second Economy

**Wojtek Zafanolli**

The study of the second economy of a socialist country is of considerable interest since it enables the researcher to raise a number of questions on exactly how the economic system of that country really functions, and through it, the politico-administrative system as a whole. In the case of China where, since 1978 and particularly since 1982, a vigorous political campaign has been waged against 'economic crime' (*jingji fanzui*),[1] a great deal of information on the subject of the second economy has appeared in both the national press and that of Hong Kong. This information occasionally provides some answers to these questions, but more often than not it is too fragmentary and serves only to reveal the existence of a considerable discrepancy between the statutory 'official' aspect of the system and its real mode of functioning, without enabling the researcher to measure this discrepancy with any precision or determine how widespread are the illegal economic practices under attack. The following example illustrates this difficulty.

According to one Hong Kong trader, entire sectors responsible for China's export trade are controlled by veritable illegal 'holdings', managed by the sons and daughters of generals and high level cadres.[2] This businessman contacted the Department of Metals and Mining Products for Canton during the Canton Trade Fair in the fall of 1980 in order to buy large quantities of coal. After several days of fruitless discussion he began to despair of reaching an agreement when he was approached in his hotel by a young man who claimed to have good contacts with the Department's people in Beijing responsible for negotiating contracts with foreign partners, and who made him the following offer: he and his friends would be prepared to put in a good word for the businessman in return for a 'commission' of 2% on the deal. The latter accepted and was therefore able to buy 200,000 tons of coal in less than a year.

In this person's mind at least, there was no doubt that the enormous bureaucratic apparatus with which he was faced was little more than a facade, and that the real decision makers were these bands of children of high level cadres (*gaogan zidi*). With the information available at present, however, it is not possible to determine if the intervention of these new 'compradores'[3] is common procedure or exceptional, and if their existence is tacitly accepted by the authorities or if the latter are unaware of these practices, which may only be limited to small groups of corrupt officials. Let us simply say that the large number of legal cases, and particularly those concerning 'economic crimes', in which members of China's Golden Youth are implicated permit one to conclude that this phenomenon is far from negligible.[4]

It should be noted in this context that in a country like China, the aim of the official press is not to inform the public, but to illustrate and put into effect a given political line. Consequently the publication of a news item such as an economic 'scandal' is not merely determined by editorial choice, but is a political decision motivated, among other things, by the importance attached to the problem. If it is impossible to make generalizations about – and especially to quantify – the manifestations of a second economy, attentive reading of the press, taking this bias into account, may nevertheless reveal the main axes around which this second economy revolves. However, another difficulty arises from the sources themselves. The notion of 'economic crime' covers a variety of transgressions and generally no distinction is made between illegal acts resulting from straightforward corruption and those made on behalf of an enterprise, for example. The only differentiation is between the various crimes themselves, according to their gravity. This means that a greal deal of work is required to classify and interpret the sources themselves.

There exist, *a priori*, three different kinds of economic crime: institutional offences, committed by an institutional agent (enterprise, administrative organ, etc.); offences pertaining to corruption, which by definition are the prerogative of the cadres (*ganbu*); and lastly what could be termed the crimes of the poor, which cover the various machinations to which ordinary citizens, with no access to power whatsoever, are driven in their day-to-day existence (theft and appropriation of public property, absenteeism, etc.). For the purpose of this chapter we shall limit ourselves to the first category, institutional offences. Despite their apparent heterogeneous nature, all three types of 'economic crime' are clearly inseparable and may to some extent be brought down to a common denominator, but this will not be our concern here.

## Economic 'Lures'

Unlike corruption, which is characterized by individual abuse, institutional offences may be seen as a result of the contradictions rife within the system and which incite enterprises and economic institutions to adopt practices beyond the scope of official legality. A great number of these 'irregularities' are simply responses to economic motivation, committed in answer to what one might call the 'capitalist temptation'. This temptation has doubtless never ceased to exist, but it is significant to note that the timid measures taken to deconcentrate management and the few elements of a market economy that have been introduced in the past few years were immediately translated into a fantastic increase in these irregularities. It is as if the introduction of a private sector, essentially limited to services and the retail trade, and the partial rehabilitation of the notion of profit making, which followed the reform of 1979,[5] were enough to make enterprises and the organs of the economic bureaucracy understand that their funds could be invested for gain and that the goods they produce and for which they assume the centralized distribution could be transformed into the veritable props of a market economy and be exchanged on the basis of maximum profit. This may be illustrated by the case of a certain county (*xian*) in Guangdong province where, according to press reports in 1982, 80% of the non-commercial organizations had taken up some form of commercial activity in the past few years in violation of regulations, and the buying and selling departments (*bu*), whose function is supposed to be purely administrative, had taken up financial speculation and wholesale trade, buying up any bargain commodity for the purpose of reselling it several hundred miles away (*NFRB*, 15 May 1982).[6]

### The Black Market

The black market is simply a phenomenon resulting from the discrepancy between 'unified' prices (i.e. centrally fixed) and 'real' prices. The resale on the black market of goods which, in principle, may only be distributed according to the State Plan, occurs to a greater or lesser degree in all countries with a planned economy, and is particularly widespread in China today. It would not be an exaggeration to say that there is no point along the official distribution channel at which goods are not diverted to feed the black market. One case in particular, dealing with chemical fertilizer, illustrates this.

In 1981, because of the 'economic readjustment', the production of chemical fertilizer did not increase over that of previous years,[7] although demand had increased considerably because of the impetus given to agricultural production by the virtual decollectivization of the countryside (Aubert, 1982).[8] The 'shadow economy' (as it is called in the Soviet Union) reacted immediately to this change in the market by appropriating a portion of the fertilizer distributed on the official circuit, which of course resulted in a still greater shortage. Thus the urea used by a brigade in Jiangxi province, where the amount normally applied per *mu* is approximately 10 *jin*, was reduced to 2–3 *jin* in 1981 and was to be less than one *jin* in 1982 (*RMRB*, 3 June 1982). Indeed, nearly all the intermediaries between the producer and the final consumer (the peasant) temporarily became purveyors of chemical fertilizer on the 'parallel' market. According to a study made by a journalist in a region (*diqu*) of Anhui province, only 20% of the total production of the ten chemical fertilizer factories in that region actually reached the local distribution company for the means of production (*nongye shengchan ziliao gongsi*), despite the fact that this is the obligatory distribution channel. The remaining 80% was sold by the factories themselves (*RMRB*, 23 February 1982).

The provincial level buying and selling cooperatives and their regional subdivisions are also a link in the chain of official fertilizer distribution. At this level, too, an important quantity of fertilizer is sidetracked and sold at stalls on market days or by the roadside, at prices far above those guaranteed by the state. A standard procedure employed by these cooperatives is to barter the fertilizer they handle for other goods such as cars and trucks; and cooperative employees or cadres buy varying quantities of fertilizer directly from the cooperative for resale at 'market' price.[8] Before the fertilizer reaches its final destination, other 'obstacles' have to be overcome, with a quota of privileged clients at each step. These are, in order of importance: the people's commune, the administrative department (*guanli qu*), the brigade, and the production team. According to the complaint of one peasant, a first delivery of fertilizer received in his brigade in Hubei province was entirely taken over by its ten team leaders, the second one by the brigade accountants, and only at the third delivery were the real consumers, the farmers, able to get their share.[9]

### Real Estate

In China, as in other socialist countries, it would seem that the question of real estate is absolutely inviolable: the ground is either the property of the state or of the local collectives, its utilization is not free, and it may not be the object of any commercial transaction. However, it is interesting to note that here, too, economic logic wins over the statutory procedures of the system. We know that for the peasants the recently introduced production contracts are in fact equivalent to a redistribution of land. It is hardly surprising, therefore, that the peasants should have begun to buy and sell it, rent it out, and put it to other uses (such as building houses, digging graves, etc.) than those for which it had originally been contracted out.[10]

More surprising is the fact that the former people's communes, mainly those situated in the suburbs of cities, should also have launched into property speculation, sometimes on a very large scale. Their clients are on-the-level official organizations. In order to get around legislation, a land owning commune and an urban work unit (*danwei*) will sign a fake joint venture agreement under the terms of which the former provides the land and the latter the capital, the knowhow, and the equipment for a given project. Next, the urban work unit will buy out the commune's part of the contract, or else will rent it from the commune, which operation is equivalent to a real estate transaction. Other disguised forms of selling land have been perfected, such as long-term lets, with rent payments made every 10 to 15 years.[11] From the point of view of the commune, this kind of property speculation can be very lucrative. In a people's commune in the suburbs of Beijing, for example, a 15-square metre apartment built illegally by an urban enterprise on the commune's land brought the latter a monthly rent of 66 yuan in 1982, thirty times the official rent (*RMRB*, 12 April 1982). Under these conditions it is understandable that certain communes are neglecting agriculture to live off their rents, thereby creating shortages, of vegetables in particular, in the cities they are meant to supply.

### Market Production

A large number of these illegal practices by enterprises appear to be compensatory mechanisms for the discrepancy between cost and price. In a sector such as coal, for example, the profit rate in 1978 was 0.7% compared with the 24% average for state enterprises as a whole (Lin Zili, 1980). A coal mine will therefore have a spontaneous tendency to disguise its price increases by such tactics as fiddling on quality or weight. Numerous press accounts would confirm this.[12] Other procedures do exist, however, one of them being for the coal mine to lease out part of its Plan production quota to neighbouring communes. These communies would mine a portion of the coal for their own account and sell varying portions of their production back to the mine at a very low price, which the mine then would resell at state prices, passing it off as its own production. Thus in 1981 a coal mine in Yunnan used to buy coal at 7–8 yuan per ton from these peasant 'miners' and resell it at 16 yuan a ton to a thermal power station (*RMRB*, 28 July 1982). A subsidiary advantage to this manoeuvre is that it enables the coal mines to continue to benefit from the state subsidies they receive to cover their deficits.

Numerous other facts bear witness to the remarkable capacity of enterprises to adapt their behaviour to a micro-economic rationale which is in flagrant contradiction to the objectives officially set for them. This is the case with the tendency of enterprises to underestimate their production capacity in order to allow themselves a greater margin for the achievement of their Plan quota. Similarly, it is commonplace for an enterprise to exaggerate its input needs to insure against supply hazards, to build up stocks in anticipation of shortages, and to assure itself of a form of tender by hoarding goods which, if of no use to the enterprise itself, may be used as barter for the goods it does require.

Curiously, as a perverse result of recent measures of economic liberalization (the retention by the enterprise of part of its profit, etc.) and partial 'deplanification', these tendencies have become still more pronounced. Indeed, by underestimating its production capacity, exaggerating its consumption of raw materials, and building up stocks of goods for speculation, an enterprise can obtain the wherewithal for its own extra-Plan production, the only activity really of interest to it.[13] This is all the more serious in that 10% of the value of industrial production comes from what were commune and brigade enterprises, which are not included in the state Plan. To supply themselves with inputs, therefore, these enterprises have hardly any choice but to turn to the parallel market, and in particular to state enterprises, which illegally sell back to them part of their means of production. Conversely, the uncontrollable nature of these enterprises – in 1981 they numbered 1.3 million spread around the country and employed some 30 million people – places them in an ideal position for the role of intermediary for all kinds of trafficking and illicit agreements, enabling state enterprises to build up, among other things, illegal distribution networks under the cover of the sub-leasing contracts they sign.[14]

In fact, the most common abuses of which enterprises are guilty may be found in the distribution sector. At present goods may be divided into three categories: those which are 'unifiedly' bought and sold, i.e., under the state monopoly (*tonggou tongxiao*) and at fixed prices; those having a 'negotiable' price; and the remainder, which are freely distributed. Under these conditions there is a temptation for enterprises to try and pass off goods belonging to the first category as being from one of the other two. The practice appears to be so widespread that it even touches international trade. Two examples follow.

The first concerns coal, which in principle may only be exported by a certain company under the Ministry of Foreign Trade. After 1980, however, numerous coal producing regions began to sign export contracts for large quantities of humic acid, an organic byproduct of coal extraction used by the chemical industry. Because the export of this product is not under government control, it appears that the coal mines quite simply pack coal in 50 kg sacks used for transporting humic acid and sell it under this name. In April 1981 this meant that the ton of coal thus sold came to US$42–46 per ton including 'packaging', whereas the 'unified' selling price for coal, based on international market rates, was $56–57 per ton (*QSND*, April 1982).

The second example concerns tin, the export of which is also under state monopoly, but this is not the case with tin products, which come under the category of arts and crafts. Tin producing regions, therefore, recently threw themselves into the mass production of crudely made tin goods. These are exported through the normal channels and melted back into bars as soon as they leave China. At the end of 1981 the ton of tin thus 'transformed' was selling at US$11,000–12,000 as against the state price of US$15,000 (*QSND*, April 1982).

Joint ventures with foreign companies frequently give rise to abuses similar to those mentioned above concerning sub-contracting to commune and brigade enterprises. In a typical contract of this nature, a Hong Kong company will furnish, for example, denim for jeans which will be cut and made up by the Chinese associate for re-export. But both the Hong Kong company and the Chinese mainland partner may find it more advantageous to allow part (and sometimes the major part) of the production to be released on the domestic Chinese market.[15] Conversely, joint ventures with foreign companies may serve as a disguised means for exporting goods. This kind of cooperation might consist of making more or less fictitious transformations to local produce by means of 'equipment' provided by a foreign company. An example is rosin (colophony), an extract of pine resin used in the paper industry and in lacquer making. The production of rosin requires little investment and may be carried out by the peasants themselves, only they are not permitted to export without going through the State export organization. To circumvent commercial regulation, the communes make a deal with a foreign company and sign a contract whereby the latter provides them with 'production equipment', which in reality may consist of no more than dyes and a few buckets used for distilling the resin. Thanks to this, the communes are able to export blue-and red-tinted rosin quite legally under fanciful names. This traffic is easily explained by the pricing: one ton of tinted rosin would fetch as much as HK$2,000 in 1981, paid in foreign currency, which the communes are not obliged to hand over to the state, whereas the state would buy rosin for 800 yuan from the producers and resell it to Hong Kong at HK$5,000 a ton (*QSND*, April 1982).

**Parallel Finance**

The trend toward autonomy in production and distribution revealed in the various offences we have examined up to now is paralleled by a symmetrical trend toward financial autonomy. As a reaction against the 'big cauldron' (*daguofan*) from which all the enterprises 'eat their fill', these, and sometimes also the economic administration offices to which they are attached, are almost instinctively attracted to tampering with accounts and to tax evasion. In this way they obtain financial resources that may be used at the discretion of the enterprise, even for the fulfilment of the official Plan, and create a micro-economic breathing space for themselves without which they would suffocate.

One of the most current forms of this (fraudulent) concealment of financial assets by enterprises is the exaggeration of production costs by the insertion of expenses coming from other entries in the accounts, this being tantamount to a disguised withholding of profits from the state. A factory constructing housing for its workers will resort to this procedure quite spontaneously if it exceeds its budget for the project. Alternatively, a factory might reach an agreement with an enterprise providing it with materials by which the latter overcharges the factory and then the difference is split between the two.[16] To avoid paying taxes, a company might 'forget' to include in its accounts a number of sales for which it will have managed not to issue invoices, or a company might pay fictitious 'fees' to a commune or brigade enterprise which may itself also be more or less fictitious. The special characteristics of some branches of activity will also determine the corresponding form of fraud. This is the case with cereal buying organs which, since 1979, have had to pay the farmers more for their compulsory cereal quotas without this being reflected in the retail price. The resulting deficit is covered by state subsidies, so in order to receive even larger ones, the cereal organs frequently pass off cereal bought at the obligatory 'delivery' price for cereal bought at the freer and therefore higher 'negotiated' price (*yijia*).[17]

Since it is in the interest of an enterprise to conceal, by all possible means, its true profit making capacity in order to pay lower state taxes, it also has no real reason to resist worker pressure for wage increases and bonuses. Thus, despite government efforts to reduce these, the total amount paid out in bonuses during the first half of 1981 showed an increase of 38% compared to the same period in 1980, while wages rose by only 7.9%.[18] At the end of the financial year an enterprise will frequently prefer to distribute any surplus which it may have accumulated to the employees rather than hand it over to the state, and this is usually given in kind, that is, in consumer products. As protection from financial investigation, the expenses incurred by these 'bonuses' are entered in the books as purchases of equipment. Alternatively, these bonuses will appear in the accounts as 'loans' to the workers, which of course they are not expected to repay.[19]

The losses incurred by the state through non-payment of industrial and commercial taxes and the illegal retention of profit are considerable. Following a financial investigation carried out at the end of 1981, it was estimated that tax evasion alone represented 1.3 billion yuan for a tax revenue of 55 billion yuan for the same year (XH, 22 and 29 March 1982). As a result, the State Council (*Guowuyuan*) ordered a national tax investigation and the results, revealed at the end of July 1982, showed that 'the violation of economic and financial discipline' during the past two years had cost the state a total of 4.5 billion yuan.[20] It is not certain whether this sum includes the 1.3 billion yuan in tax evasion previously brought to light, but in either case the sum is still considerable, the more so since it certainly only represents the tip of the iceberg. In comparison, the budget deficit estimated for 1982 was three billion yuan (XH, 5 May 1982).

It is necessary to examine in passing the role of banks in relation to the second economy. Superficially, at least, they appear to be the ideal instrument for the economic and financial control of enterprises, which is precisely what the government intends them to be.[21] At present, however, their role seems to be diametrically opposed to this. On the one hand, when acting within a strictly legal framework, banks would seem to be hyper-bureaucratic organs. From what can be gleaned from the complaints of various enterprises, procedures for obtaining loans are extremely long and superfluous, lasting up to seven months for a simple request for a short-term loan.[22] On the other hand, banks are far from insensitive to the host of entreaties emanating from the second economy. Press reports over the past two or three years show that banks frequently respond to these by fulfilling all the regular banking functions, in the capitalist sense of the term, that might be required. That is to say that they agree to open accounts for all kinds of illegal but 'profitable' enterprises which are being set up throughout the country, although in China this is supposed to be a privilege granted only after prior agreement from the authorities. Banks also provide credit facilities for operations, the viability of which is assured but which from the point of view of economic legislation are considered illegal or even pure speculation.[23]

## Semi-legal Employment

Employment is without doubt the domain in which it is most difficult for an enterprise to resist the economic 'sirens'. This attraction is proportionate to the problems raised by the absence of a real labour market, splendidly summed up in the Chinese phrase, the 'iron rice-bowl' (*tiefanwan*). The problem exists in all socialist countries but is perhaps more serious in China than in, say, Eastern Europe. First, because of population pressure, disguised underemployment is extremely serious in China. Recently, the official discovery that a serious urban unemployment problem exists [24] and the priority it has received would seem to aggravate underemployment still further: every year enterprises are obliged to employ a quota of secondary school graduates, while children of retired workers 'inherit' their parents' jobs so that, as one company manager told the economist Lin Zili, 'We previously had five people doing the work of three, now we have seven' (1980). Second, rigidity in employment supply (which results at one and the same time in an inflated workforce and an incompetent one) is aggravated by rigidity in demand. In China, unlike in the Soviet Union, workers are usually attached to state enterprises for life and there is no labour mobility.[25] Consequently, to raise labour productivity or to get certain jobs done that are considered too 'dirty' by permanent employees, and, more frequently, in order to adapt themselves to production requirements and their inevitable fluctuations, enterprises have taken to surrounding themselves with a large fluctuating labour force from which they draw according to their needs. These workers, be they temporary (*linshigong*), seasonal (*jijiegong*), or under contract (*hetonggong*), all have an extremely precarious status and constitute a kind of lumpen proletariat compared to the permanent workers. Their existence is not a new phenomenon, and it is more or less tolerated by the authorities.[26]

Precarious and badly paid though these jobs may be, there has never been a shortage of candidates to fill them. Today, as before, these are largely recruited from rural areas. But their numbers have increased with the responsibility system (*zeren zhi*) recently introduced in the countryside, which leaves the peasants with more free time, since 'the cultivation of their contracted land requires only half their available time' (Aubert, 1982), thereby freeing a surplus labour force. Moreover, it is in the interest of enterprises today, far more than before, to improve labour productivity. In any case, the problem appears to be a very serious one at present. According to estimates, which cannot *per se* take an overall view of the phenomenon, in Guangdong province alone in August 1982 there were 340,000 workers from the countryside working outside of the State Plan and without legal authorization in urban state enterprises.[27] The magnitude of this 'unofficial' employment may indicate a possible qualitative change. Unable to increase the productivity of their permanent titular staff, companies may well find it more profitable to allocate most of their productive tasks to these semi-legal workers, while continuing to pay their permanent employees. This is undoubtedly the case of one enterprise in Guangdong province where over half the workforce is made up of temporary rural workers, despite the fact that the number of permanent workers is reportedly adequate for its production purposes. For this company, anyway, there is no doubt that its 'official' employees hold a kind of sinecure and are simply bleeding the company's budget.

## Economic 'Feudalism'

An economic rationale of sorts may be found for all the institutional offences we have considered up to now. But other kinds of institutional offences exist that are motivated by something else entirely, for they originate in rifts in the administrative apparatus. These rifts themselves vary, being either vertical (sectoral) or horizontal (territorial), giving rise in the former case to 'departmentalism' (*benwei zhuyi*) and in the latter to 'localism' (*difang zhuyi*). Their relative weight depends of course on the overall mode of organization of the economic administration. Although it will not be possible for the purpose of this Chapter to enlarge on this point, it would seem that by comparison with the Maoist period, 'departmentalism' has given way to economically motivated offences, whereas 'localism' appears to be at least as serious as it was before 1978, when it was openly encouraged because of the declared need for 'self-reliance'. Let us say, in justification, that the deconcentration (and not decentralization) of economic management power in favour of administrative districts set up after the Third Plenum (December 1978) by, among other things, regional organic law,[28] could only stimulate localism, and that economic reform is unthinkable if 'sectoral dictatorship' is not limited to some extent.

### Departmentalism

In a given sector of the administration, departmentalism represents the search for both autonomy and power. In economic terms this means that each vertical sector, and even each large production unit, will have a tendency to form itself into an all-purpose economic entity, with very little need to fall back on exchanges with the outside. As the saying goes in China, 'small or large, but complete' (*da er quan, xiao er quan*). A factory of a certain size, for example, will often have its own workshops for the production and repair of machine tools, its own schools, its own medical facilities, and all kinds of peripheral enterprises, even including mines on occasion. As for an administrative department, it will consider that it has the right to set up its own enterprises without authorization, even if this results in the proliferation of production units without any real economic use. This phenomenon gives rise to economic 'corridors', which start off in the ministries, and cover all activities subsidiary to their primary ones. This vertical integration enables enterprises to protect themselves from fluctuations in supplies and faulty deliveries. Above all, it transforms each branch and sub-branch of the administration into an economic 'feudality' with its own negotiating powers, capable of forcing the state to come to terms with it. Even the *gong'anju* (public security) is a veritable state within the state, with its own farms and factories employing 'slave labour' (the prisoners).[29]

China's present leaders wish to reintroduce production specialization and free enterprises from the hold the administration has over them where supplies and outlets are concerned. This directly undermines departmental interests, which explains why these transformations are stubbornly resisted at this level. A large number of departments refuse to grant the small amount of autonomy permitted to their enterprises and oblige them to receive their supplies from their own production sources, even if this necessitates transportation over long distances and the buying of inferior quality produce at greater expense than that which might be bought elsewhere. Retaliation measures are frequently taken by the concerned economic administration against enterprises that dare to supply themselves with raw materials without going through the commercial departments to which they are attached. These measures may include boycotting of the recalcitrant enterprise, or a refusal to pay the salaries of workers from a factory using its inactive machinery for the manufacture of some extra-plan product that falls outside of its normal domain.[30]

Nevertheless, relations between enterprises and their economic administration are not only characterized by antagonism. On the contrary, improvement in the economic situation of an enterprise may frequently be in perfect accord with the interests of the administrative 'feudalities' to which it is subordinated, and a chain of solidarity will be established all along the line of the official hierarchy. In this event, the administrative bureaux will cover up for, if not blatantly support, the illegal activities of their enterprises. A flagrant example of this is the case of the Shenzhen branch of the Electronic Techniques Import-Export Company. Although this company's official raison d'être was supposed to be the importation of production equipment for the electronics industry, it specialized in the buying of consumer goods such as television sets, radios, and tape recorders, which it sold illegally on the domestic market. Its activities flourished to such an extent that out of its US$95 million in foreign contracts between May 1980 (the date it started operations) and the end of 1981, only 4.5% actually concerned electronic equipment (*RMRB*, 11 March and 22 April 1982). The ministry on which this company was dependent (called the Fourth Ministry of the Mechanical Engineering Industry at the time) was, of course, in cahoots with the company and therefore turned a blind eye to the use of its facilities for the disposal of the enormous quantity of imported consumer goods. For example, in September 1980, a company dependent on the same ministry, the Nanking Radio Equipment Company, spent US$1 million of its foreign exchange quota on television sets, which it obtained illegally from the above mentioned company in Shenzhen. Apart from needing a bit of welding, these sets were already assembled, but this did not prevent the Nanking company from selling them as if they had just come off its production lines.[31] From the explanations given by the 'departments concerned' to the Central Commission for Discipline Inspection, the sector-based interests involved are quite clear. For them, the whole problem lay in the conflict between the 'great collective' (the state, the nation) and the 'small collective' (themselves), that is to say, between public interests at large and their own interests.

## Localism

Localism is based on a fragmentation of the administrative apparatus and is the exact counterpart of departmentalism, the only difference being that it develops horizontally and not vertically. This fragmentation depends on a certain reversal of the power flow: the cadres (*ganbu*) of an administrative district no longer act as local agents of the central authorities; their authority takes on a pseudo-representative function of their citizens, reports prepared for their superiors will be filled with abridged or erroneous information, and they will tone down the decisions they are supposed to implement, retaining only the aspects that do not directly conflict with local interests and eliminating the rest.[32] Moreover, to strengthen their position, local cadres, like their departmental colleagues, will insure themselves of the greatest possible degree of economic independence.

The most visible manifestation of this phenomenon is the blind duplication of production capacities, which makes the local administration resemble an enormous nest of Russian dolls with each one seeking its own economic self-reliance. The following is a flagrant example, concerning the salt lakes of Yuncheng, in southwest Shanxi. Here the state exploits salt and saltpetre through a group of enterprises that depend directly on the ministry responsible. But the local bureaucracy at each level (regional, county and people's commune) has illicitly demarcated its own salt marshes. And each of them in turn is the starting point for an integrated complex of chemical industries accountable only to the corresponding administrative level. The productivity of these industrial complexes decreases, of course, as one goes down the bureaucratic ladder. Not to be left out, production brigades and even individuals go and gather salt for themselves, knocking down the walls around the marshes and committing acts of vandalism to discourage the building up of a public infrastructure (*RMRB*, 24 May 1982).

Regions not only want to have their own industries, but they try, by all possible means, to protect these against external competition. This local protectionism may go as far as a complete blockade. Local governments, and provincial ones in particular, set up control organisms at banks, forcing them to refuse payments of orders contracted to enterprises outside their domain of jurisdiction when the goods in question can be manufactured on the spot. That this practice is widespread may be seen by the fact that the ban imposed on it by the central authorities is accompanied by one notable exception: branches manufacturing consumer goods and light industry in 'economically underdeveloped regions' are exempt from this rule (*Gongren Ribao*, 22 March 1982 and *RMRB* 21 April 1982). The most developed form of localism is certainly the veritable toll gates which are set up on public highways. This is commonplace not only at the county level, where it is semi-legal, but also at the former commune and brigade level. In the latter case it verges on banditry, for the peasants prevent traffic from passing by digging ditches across the roads, for example, and then demand excessive 'repair fees' from the vehicles stuck in the mud.[33]

Horizontal autarchic spaces may be found at numerous points of the economic circuit in direct competition with the vertical autarchic corridors (the departments) for the exploitation of the same natural resources. This competition results in a form of economic crime in which a whole locality, that is to say a village, a commune, or even a whole administrative district, goes in for widespread and systematic plundering of a state enterprise set up on its territory, or of the natural resources over which the state, in theory at least, has the monopoly. The vast number of such cases denounced in the press seems to imply that the local bureaucracy is, at the very least, a passive accomplice to these actions. Not infrequently the cadres themselves organized bands of people which might number as many as 200 or 300 people to take over anything that can be re-used such as cement, construction material, steel cables, electric wiring, pylons, etc., from state building sites, mines, foundries, or oil wells. When high voltage cables crossed their territory, communes linked up to them illegally and protected their installations by force if necessary.[34] Railway lines are particularly vulnerable: peasants will remove ballast from the railway bed, take apart the sleepers for firewood, or even remove steel rails. In the vicinity of oil wells, the theft of this fuel is so widespread that it has given way to a veritable illicit refining industry, the existence of which is confirmed by the fact that the police periodically announce the closure of illegal small-scale cracking furnaces. In south-west China, communes intercepted tree trunks which are floated down rivers and canals, and whole production teams, led by the cadres, set upon any surveillance body which interfered.[35] An even more serious problem exists when peasants take on the illegal exploitation of mineral resources which are in theory under state monopoly. In Gejiu in Yunnan province, a major tin production centre, the peasants (individually or collectively), the inhabitants of the town, the unemployed, and even the factory workers, all encouraged by the Municipal Committee cadres, spread out over the ore containing mountains and, as in the good old days of the American Far West, dug their own mines. The ore thus extracted represented a loss for the state of a thousand tons in a two-year period.[36] It might be a fair assumption that the clandestine exports of tin to which we referred above originated in part from this source. The same phenomenon of anarchic mineral extraction (*luanwa, lancai*) has been observed elsewhere. Coal, for example, was plundered to such an extent by the communes that state mines complained regularly that their galleries were flooded or permeated with fire-damp as a result of this. It is the same with marble, which is extracted by peasants using dynamite, or gypsum from state quarries, which is used by communes and brigades to supply their lime kilns and calcium carbide plants. Wood is particularly coveted by the peasants who cut it down at random in the country's few remaining forests.[37]

As in the case of departmentalism, the objectives of the enterprises which lead them to economic misappropriation are not necessarily incompatible with localist tendencies. On the contrary, because enterprises under regional administration are at one and the same time the last link in the chain and the real power base of the feudalities of which they are part, the despoiling of the central state is undeniably grounds for agreement between the two. This is shown in the case of tax evasion for which enterprises frequently take the precaution of requesting the consent of the local authorities to which they are accountable. Thus in Huainan city in Anhui province, nine enterprises illegally withheld revenue from the state between 1980 and 1981, for a total of 5.4 million yuan. An enquiry revealed that for 80% of this sum, the companies in question had acted after consultation with the Finance Bureau (*ju*) and the Economic Commission of the town, and that the latter, in connivance with the Bureau of Light Industry, had given its approval (*RMRB*, 10 February 1980).

Let us go one step further: the interests of the enterprises, the ministries, and the regions may very well all coincide. Let us imagine an enterprise which depends on a ministry and which, with the latter's blessing, 'removes' goods from the central distribution circuit. To sell these goods the enterprise will first turn to the local market where there will probably be no shortage of buyers among the collective enterprises, or those enterprises under 'the ownership of the whole people' which are run by the local administration. In addition, the enterprise might also contact a township with which it could exchange manufactured goods for agricultural produce.[38]

## Conclusion: A Dislocated Economy

The numerous articulations that exist between the different levels of the second economy could be equated with a kind of centrifugal force that the central authorities, at least in their present phase, seem to be unable to check. The problem of over-investment clearly shows this. Although since 1979, the year 'readjustment' began, the emphasis has been on limiting 'basic level construction',[39] in 1981 the country's total investment figure nevertheless exceeded 42% of the year's estimate.[40] In actual fact only 48% of this figure was really covered by the national budget, the remaining 52% coming from extra-budgetary sources of financing. In point of fact an enterprise has no shortage of choice in the matter of financing an investment for which no credits have been allocated by the state. A few accounting tricks will enable it to transfer funds set aside for other purposes, such as the provision for depreciation or technical renovation. Failing this, the financing may just as likely come from a bank loan, or, more frequently, be in the form of an advance drawn on a local budget or from the financial resources of one or the other of the numerous interlocked departments with which it has dealings. At the end of 1980, a 'special commentator' of the *People's Daily* enumerated 'eight different ways of financing an investment' (*RMRB*, 30 December 1980). Shortly before that, another writer remarked that in 1979 there were 34 different ways for an enterprise to obtain financing in Shanghai, and 30 in Shandong province. Hence a dyeing factory with an investment project requiring 2.8 million yuan, which the state refused to grant, turned to 'the departments concerned' and obtained credit worth 4.8 million yuan, 70% more than it actually needed (*RMRB*, 31 January 1980).

This investment race falls under a power logic that is contrary to all notions of economic viability. Indeed, if we admit that the different branches, vertical or horizontal, of the administration are as many little independent 'kingdoms' each following its own objectives, it is not difficult to see that what matters to each one is not so much the growth of the nation's economy, but its own. And since no economic constraints really apply to these 'kingdoms', there is no structural means for eliminating redundant projects that have no real economic utility. The result is that there is sometimes considerable over-investment, and an investment propensity that grows in reverse proportion to the decrease in the productivity of enterprises. This is the case with the car industry, which in 1978 was working at only 43% of its projected production cpacity. Of the 106 car factories to be found in China at the time, nine alone accounted for 68.6% of total car production. The production costs of the 97 other factories were far too high and some were incapable of producing more than one or two dozen cars per year. Nevertheless, they planned to multiply their production capacity by a factor of three, while the nine most productive factories only planned to double theirs (*RMRB*, 31 January 1980). In fact, each region of any importance would like to have its own car factory because this is important for its independence and its weight in relation to the other regions, so rather than close down their non-productive factories, local authorities prefer to encourage them to enter into a frenetic investment policy. In principle, nothing can slow down this process because any deficit will normally be covered by subisidies.

It is only recently that the existence of 'economic crime' in China has been recognized with any frankness. This does not mean that it never existed in Maoist times. Despite the shortage of available source material, it is clear that the three temptations we have shown – the capitalist, the sectoral, and the localist – all existed well before 1976, although to a degree and in forms not necessarily the same as those in existence today.[41] But the difficulties in making an analysis over a long period of time make it nearly impossible to answer a number of vital questions, among them possibly the following: Is the present campaign due to a recent 'great leap forward' in the second economy, which previously had been better contained? Or was it the absolute priority recently given to economic development that made the present Chinese leadership aware of the urgent need to overcome a phenomenon that has not really varied in magnitude from 1976 to the present day?[42] Or else, a question covering both of the above: How much of the second economy may be attributed to structural factors and how much to the disorganization that all attempts at reform inevitably bring in their wake?[43] As an indication, a comparison with other socialist countries suffering from the same blight would ascribe the dominant role to the structural aspect, even if the presence of purely circumstantial factors cannot be denied.

Western countries know from experience that any legal regulations concerning the economy give rise to incitement to transgress the same. A case in point is undeclared labour, a typical economic transgression generated by social legislation. But in Western countries, the very fact that the market remains the pulse of the economy serves to reduce such irregularities to a secondary social and economic problem, albeit one that cannot be ignored. In a socialist country like China, on the contrary, where the market is officially recognized as having a subsidiary role at best, there is a symmetric progression of economic crime. It is as if, strange irony, the entropy of a given economy increases in direct proportion to how far the state removes the economy from the laws of the market, and how much it tries to control it through planification and centralization.

## Notes

1. In March 1982, following an 'urgent recommendation' of the Central Committee dated January of the same year, the Permanent Committee of the National People's Assembly adopted a modification to the recent penal code which increased sentences for cadres found guilty of 'economic crimes'. Then in April the State Council (*Guowuyuan*) and the Party published a 'joint decision' inaugurating the actual campaign (*RMRB*, 10 March and 14 April 1982) .

2. *QSND*, April 1982.

3. The pre-1949 'compradores' being less greedy: according to the *RMRB* of 17 April 1982, they were satisfied with a commission of a mere 0.125%.

4. According to rumours prevalent in Hong Kong (see *Baixing* [The Plebeians], 1 July and 10 October 1982), Ye Xuanping, son of the ageing Ye Jianying, was implicated in a number of 'economic crimes', and Zhao Ziyang and Zhang Caiqian are supposed to have made self-criticisms because their sons had been involved in a number of dubious dealings. According to the *Hong Kong Standard* of 6 April 1982, the grandson of the prestigious Zhu De was arrested for 'smuggling and illegal economic activities'.

5. On questions pertaining to economic reforms, see Aubert and Chevrier, 1982–83.

6. See also *RMRB*, 5 June 1982, in which a Guangdong regulation forbidding these practices is published.

7. In 1981 the production of chemical fertilizer, at only 12.39 million tons, remained stationary in comparison with 1980 *XH*, 29 April 1982).

8. According to a circular (*tongzhi*) from the General Buying and Selling Cooperative to its provincial branches (*RMRB*, 24 February 1982).

9. The association of only two persons is often enough to set up a permanent supply line for the black market: a cadre from one of the state commercial departments who issues coupons for goods that are not on the free distribution circuit and a private 'entrepreneur' to unload them. For an example of this type of association, see *FBIS*, 26 August 1982.

10. *RMRB*, 26 June 1982; see also *RMRB*, 7 June 1982, for an example in Shanxi province; *FBIS*, 3 June 1982, for another in Henan; and *FBIS*, 5 May 1982, for one in Yunnan. According to *RMRB*, 1 January 1982, there are regulations against the sale of land in every province. *RMRB*, 19 April 1982, points out that illegally occupied land must be returned.

11. According to *RMRB*, 13 May 1982, 370 hectares of agricultural land in the suburbs of Hangzhou were in this way leased or sold illegally for construction purposes since 1979.

12. Examples of this kind of 'fiddling' appear in *JJGL*, August 1980, and *RMRB*, 5 June 1982.

13. A good description of this phenomenon may be found in *RMRB*, 2 August 1982. To remedy the situation, the article suggests, among other things, that the state undertake not to take back any surplus raw materials an enterprise might have accumulated, and not to alter its supply quotas. In fact this problem is partly responsible for the decision made at the beginning of 1981 to slow down the reforms. (See *JJGL*, February and July 1981, on the order of priorities adopted by the Chengdu conference in April of the same year.)

14. Statistical information on commune and brigade enterprises (*she-dui qiye*) is to be found in *RMRB*, 10 May 1982. The case of the Shenyang ceramic factory (*RMRB*, 11 August 1981 and 29 August 1982) is typical: a good portion of its

production (glazed tiles, earthenware tiles, bathroom fittings) was sold illegally to a people's commune in Fujian province, enabling the latter to make a net profit of one million yuan.

15. See the anxieties manifested by Gu Mu, member of the State Council, in *RMRB*, 13 July 1982.

16. For an example, see *Minzhu Yu Fazhi*, December 1981.

17. According to the *Liaoning Ribao* of 9 May 1982, the losses incurred by the cereal companies of that province due to 'breach of financial discipline' amounted to four million yuan in 1981.

18. *XH*, 12 February 1982. In Tianjin the total amount paid out in bonuses in 1981 was 150 million yuan, that is to say 4.3 times the salary increases for that year (*JJYJ*, April 1982).

19. See examples in *RMRB*, 5 June, 12 June and 17 July 1982. In Heilongjiang, 567 work units (*danwei*) spent 13 million yuan in this way within a year (*RMRB*, 21 April 1982).

20. *XH*, 14 December 1982 (report on the budget by Wang Bingqian). In March 1982 the first results of this financial investigation revealed that 2.5 billion yuan had not been paid into the state treasury, this without counting the 1.3 billion yuan in tax evasion discovered at the end of the previous year (*XH*, 7 March 1982). Two months later, in May, it was announced that 'violation of economic and financial discipline' had cost the state a total of 3.5 billion yuan (*RMRB*, 22 May 1982). On the basis of this figure the total amount for the period corresponding to the investigation at the end of 1981 and the one at the beginning of 1982 should have amounted to at least 4.8 billion yuan, which does not fit in with Wang Bingqian's estimate of 4.5 billion yuan. It might be that the latter did not take the results of the first financial investigation into account. If this were the case the grand total in financial fraud brought to light from both inquiries should be 5.8 billion yuan. For the purpose of comparison, the cases discovered during the second investigation were as follows: 220 million yuan in Shanghai (*Wenhuibao*, 7 May 1982); 254 million yuan in Shandong province (*FBIS*, 29 March 1982); 97 million yuan in Tianjin (*Tianjin Ribao*, 10 May 1982) where in 1981, 12,600 cases of tax evasion were discovered and 32% of the *danwei* were evading taxes or behind on their payments (*FBIS*, 9 June 1982); and 343 million yuan in Sichuan province (*FBIS*, 11 March 1982).

21. This objective is clearly confirmed in Yao Yilin's 'Report on the Social and Economic Development Project,' in *XH*, 5 May 1982. On the new role of banks, see also *RMRB*, 24 July and 13 August 1982.

22. This was a complaint brought up by the Harbin General Sewing Machine Factory in *RMRB*, 28 August 1982.

23. According to Gu Mu (*RMRB*, 13 July 1982), banks open accounts for 'criminals' and grant loans to non-registered, and therefore illegal, enterprises. The problem is particularly serious in Guangdong, the province with the most 'open' economy (*NFRB*, 1 April 1982, and *XH*, 26 August 1982). See also *RMRB*, 18 August 1982, on the regulations concerning industrial and commercial licences. The role of banks in the second economy is well illustrated by the case of the 'automobile kings of Anyang' (*RMRB*, 2 March and 22 March 1982): the agents of two local commodity centres made a speciality of the illegal resale of cars, an activity for which the Henan branch of the Agricultural Bank gave generous loans, discounted their drafts and advanced funds.

24. In 1981, there were 26 million urban unemployed (*Le Monde*, 5 March 1981) for a working population of 98 million in 1978 (*JJYJ*, September 1980). According to

the recent census (*XH*, 27 October 1982), the urban population is 206.6 million.

25. On the employment problem, see Cartier (1982–83). On the subject of unemployment, see Feng Lanrui and Zhao Lükuan (1982). To help solve the unemployment problem, labour service companies/centres (*laodong fuwu gongsi/zhan*) were set up throughout China (see *RMRB*, 7 July 1982). These companies (or centres) are in fact a revival of those set up in the early 1950s and after the Great Leap Forward (see Lynn T. White III, 1976.) See also Volume 1 of this work, Chapter 8.

26. Howe (1973, p. 107) reckons that in 1958 the temporary workforce numbered some 12 million representing 26.5% 'of all workers and staff'. Lynn T. White III (1976) considers that during the same period in Shanghai they were as numerous as the regular industrial employees.

27. *Yancheng Wanbao*, 3 August 1982. According to incomplete statistics, there were at the same time 167,000 such 'semi-legal' workers in Hunan province employed in sectors suffering from labour shortage, such as transport and construction (*RMRB*, 23 June, 1982).

28. *Difang zuzhifa*, in *RMRB*, 17 July 1979. According to this law, local sectors of the administration are 'led' (*lingdao*) by the local governments, while the corresponding sectors of the central administration have to make do with a 'guiding' (*zhidao*) role.

29. See Fang Dan's argument in *Baixing* from 16 December 1982, to 16 March 1983.

30. See Lin Zili (1980, p. 187). A metallurgical equipment factory used its inactive machines to make bicycles and sewing machines. The provincial bureau of mechanical engineering therefore refused to pay the factory workers and employees. There was also a case in which there was a refusal to deliver the means of production.

31. *RMRB*, 25 May 1982. Thanks to this operation the enterprise made an illegal profit of 424,000 yuan.

32. *RMRB*, 1 July 1979, and, three years later, *Hebei Ribao*, 6 August 1982, for example.

33. According to readers' letters in the *RMRB*, 10 July 1982, these 'customs barriers' are commonplace in Ningxia, Hebei, Henan, and Anhui. Another expression of this peasant particularism is the plundering of primary and secondary schools run by communes (*RMRB*, 18 June 1982, and *XH*, 8 June 1982) and the peasants' refusal to pay the teachers (*RMRB*, 5 August 1982). The destruction of hydraulic works by the peasants (e.g., *RMRB*, 8 July 1982) could also be included under this heading.

34. According to the complaint of one oil exploiting company in a district of Henan province (*RMRB*, 5 June 1982), the electricity misappropriated by the peasants amounted to one third of the total used by the company!

35. *RMRB*, 12 July 1982. In one district crossed by the Dadu River, theft of wood during the floating season of 1981 represented over two million yuan (*RMRB*, 16 June 1982).

36. *RMRB*, 16 June 1982. The article mentions the loss of one million tons but this is clearly a typographical error.

37. See *RMRB*, 13 April and 8 May 1982, for cases in Inner Mongolia and the Wuhan region; *RMRB*, 29 May 1982, for a case of illegal marble extraction; *RMRB*, 21 February 1982, for a case of illegal exploitation of gypsum. In an interview given to the *RMRB*, 17 July 1982, the Minister for Mines and Geology expresses his concern over these phenomena. For an example in Shanxi in the erosion zone of the

Yellow River, see *RMRB*, 24 July 1982. *RMRB*, 24 April 1982, gives interesting details about the random cutting down of trees in a forest district of Hunan. In 1980 the State Council passed a decree to control the felling of trees, but it is clear that this has largely gone unheeded.

38. Example in *RMRB*, 4 December 1978. The fact that agriculture has now tilted in favour of the private economy has removed the major raison d'être of this traffic, except of course for foodstuffs such as cereals, which continue to be distributed through the state.

39. The readjustment (*tiaozheng*) agreed upon at the Third Plenum in December 1978 was officially announced in March 1979. The limitation of 'basic level construction' is an urgent necessity: from 1953–7 to 1978 the capital formation rate went from 24.2% to 36.6% of the national revenue and was still at 33.6% in 1979 (*JJYJ*, September 1980; *JJGL*, December 1980).

40. 'Rapport sur le réadjustement du plan d'économie nationale et du budget d'État pour 1981', *Beijing Information* (French translation of the *Beijing Review*), no. 11, 16 March 1981; 'Communiqué on the fulfilment of the National Economic Plan for 1981', *XH*, 29 April 1982. See also 'A Few Provisions Concerning the Prevention of Blind and Duplicated Construction', a document translated and reprinted in *Issues and Studies*, August 1982.

41. The falsified production figures, so widespread during the Maoist period, would seem to be a case in point, right down to the well known model brigade, Dazhai, whose phenomenal results were reported to be a cleverly arranged scenario (*Beijing Information*, no. 29, 21 July, 1980)! For an account of a factory that had 'usurped' the then much coveted title of 'Daqing type enterprise', see *RMRB*, 15 December 1978. But this is not always the case. For example, the practice by which a coal mine subcontracts part of its production quota to a commune, which as we have seen is still common today, is precisely that followed between 1969 and 1978 by Wang Shouxin, the head of a fuel company in a district of Heilongjiang province. She was shot in early 1980 for having accumulated secret funds totalling 500,000 yuan (*Beijing Wanbao*, 28 February 1980). See the 'literary reportage' of Liu Binyan (1983 and 1981).

42. The author personally would favour this second alternative: in the criticism of the system brought up by the advocates of reform in 1979–80, one of the major arguments was precisely these symptoms of a second economy that the system generates. Certainly the absence of a legal system, which was the case in China before 1979, most probably resulted in a fertile breeding ground for 'economic crime'. If this hypothesis is correct, the fact that there was no mention of this before 1979 might simply be that, as the authorities did not then have veritable criteria and norms of economic efficiency, they were unaware of the magnitude of the problem, or else that they were too preoccupied with other problems (factional disputes, for example) to concern themselves with this matter.

43. Such is the case with smuggling, a serious problem in the coastal regions of Guangdong, Fujian, and Zhejiang provinces, the upsurge of which is recent. See *Hongqi*, No. 6, 16 March 1982, and *Minzhu Yu Fazhi*, June 1982, for example.

# Bibliography

Aguignier, P. (1984), 'Politique économique et disparités régionales en Chine de 1949 à 1982', Doctoral thesis, 3rd cycle, University of Paris – III.

Aubert, C. (1982), 'Chine rurale: la révolution silencieuse', *Projet*, September–October.

Aubert, C. and Chevrier, Y. (1982–3), 'Réformer ou ne pas réformer? Le dilemme de l'expérience chinoise (1979–1981)', *Révue française de gestion*, Winter.

Balawdyer, A. (ed.), (1980), *Co-operative Movements in Eastern Europe*, Macmillan, London.

Balcerowicz, L. (1980), 'Organisational Structure of the National Economy and Technical Innovations', *Acta Oeconomica*, vol. 24, nos. 1–2.

Barnett, A. D. (1967), *Cadres, Bureaucracy and Political Power in Communist China*, Columbia University Press, New York.

Barnett, A. D. (ed.), (1971), *Chinese Communist Politics in Action*, University of Washington Press, Seattle.

Barnett, A. D. (1985), *The Making of Foreign Policy in China*, I.B. Tauris, London.

Bartke, W. (1981), *Who's Who in the People's Republic of China*, Harvester Press, Brighton.

Bartke, W. and Schler, P. (1985), *China's New Party Leadership: Biographies and Analysis of the Twelfth Central Committee of the Chinese Communist Party*, Macmillan, London.

Bauer, T. (1976), 'The Contradictory Position of the Enterprise under the New Hungarian Economic Mechanism', *Eastern European Economics*, 15.

Bauer, T. (1981), *Tervgazdasag, Beruhazus, Ciklusok*, Kozgazdasagi es Jogi Könyvkiado, Budapest.

Berend, I. and Rankin, G. Y. (1985), *The Hungarian Economy in the Twentieth Century*, Croom Helm, London.

Bettelheim, C. (1975), *The Transition to Socialist Economy*, Harvester, Brighton.

Birch, D. L. (1979), *The Job Generation Process*, MIT Centre for Policy Alternatives, Cambridge, Mass.

Blecher, M. (1981), 'Peasant Labour for Urban Industry: Temporary Contract Labour, Urban-Rural Balance and Class Relations in a Chinese County', *World Development*, vol. II, no. 8.

Brus, W. (1972a), *The Economics and Politics of Socialism*, Routledge and Kegan Paul, London.

Brus, W. (1972b), *The Market in a Socialist Economy*, Routledge and Kegan Paul, London.

Brus, W. (1975), *Socialist Ownership and Political Systems*, Routledge and Kegan Paul, London.

Bukharin, N. and Preobrazhensky, E. (1920) (1969), *The ABC of Communism*, Penguin Books, Harmondsworth.

Byrd, W. (1983), *China's Financial System: The Changing Role of Banks*, Westview, Boulder, Co.

Campbell, A. (1981), *Producer Cooperatives in Eastern Europe*, Industrial Common Ownership Movement, London.

Campbell, A. (n.d.), *Polish Mondragon*, Scottish Cooperatives Development Committee, Glasgow.

Cartier, M. (1982–83), 'Les contraintes démographiques de l'emploi en Chine', *Revue française de gestion*, Winter.

Cave, M. and Hare, P. G. (1981), *Alternative Approaches to Economic Planning*, Allen and Unwin, London.

Central Committee (1984), *Decision of the Central Committee of the Communist Party of China on Reform of the Economic Structure* (adopted by the twelfth Central Committee of the CCP at its third planning session, 20 October 1984), *BR*, vol. 27, no. 44, 29 October.

Chevrier, Y. (1983), 'Les politiques économiques de la démaoisation (1977–1982)', *Revue d'études comparatives est-ouest*, vol. 14, no. 3, September.

China Quarterly (1984), *The Readjustment in the Chinese Economy* (special issue), no. 100, December.

Communist Party of China (1984), *Decision of the Central Committee of the Communist Party of China on Reform of the Economic Structure*, Joint Publishing Co., Hong Kong.

Dai Yuanchen (1981), 'The Socialist Economy Can Effectively Check Inflation', *JJYJ*, no. 8 (20 August) in *SWB*, W 1153.

Deng Jie (1958), *Initial Summary of the Socialist Transformation of China's Handicraft Industry* (in Chinese), Renmin Chubanshe, Beijing.

Engels, F. W. (1947), *Anti-Dühring*, Progress Publishers, Moscow.

Erlich, A. (1960), *The Soviet Industrialisation Debate, 1924–1928*, Harvard University Press, Cambridge, Mass.

Feng Sheng (1982), 'The Revival of Individual Economy in Urban Areas', in Lin Wei and A. Chao (1982).

Feng Lanrui and Zhao Lukuan (1982), 'Urban Unemployment in China', *Social Sciences in China*, January.

Feuchtwang, S. and Hussain, A. (eds), (1983), *The Chinese Economic Reforms*, Croom Helm, London.

Feuerwerker, A. (1970), *China's Early Industrialisation*, Atheneum, New York.

Franklin, B. (ed.), (1973), *The Essential Stalin: Major Theoretical Writings*, Croom Helm, London.

Gendai (1972), *Gendai Chogoku Jinmei Jiten* (Collection of biographies of contemporary China), Kazankai, Tokyo.

Gibelli, M-C. and Weber, M. (eds), (1983), *Una Modernizazione Difficile: Economica e Societa in Cina dopo Mao*, F. Angelli, Milan.

Gold, T. B. (1980), 'Back to the City: The Return of Shanghai's Educated Youth', *China Quarterly*, 84.

Goodman, D. (1980) 'The Provincial First Secretary in the People's Republic of China, 1949–78: A Profile', *British Journal of Political Science*, 10.

Goodman, D. (1986), 'The National CCP Conference of September 1985 and China's Leadership Changes', *China Quarterly*, 105, March.

Gray, J. and Gray, M. (1983), 'China's New Agricultural Revolution', in S. Feuchtwang and A. Hussain (1983).

Hare, P. G. (1983a), 'The Beginnings of Institutional Reform in Hungary', *Soviet Studies*, vol. 35, no. 3, July.

Hare, P. G. (1983b), 'China's System of Industrial Economic Planning', in S. Feuchtwang and A. Hussain (1983).

Hare, P. G., Radice, H. K. and Swain, N. (1981), *Hungary: A Decade of Economic Reform,* Allen and Unwin, London.

Hare, P. G. and Wanless, P. T. (1981), 'Polish and Hungarian Economic Reforms – A Comparison', *Soviet Studies*, vol. 33, no. 4, October.

He Jianzhang (1979), 'Problems in the Planned Management of the Economy Owned by the Whole People and the Orientation of Reform', *JJYJ*, 5 (20 May) in *CREA*, 5 (3 August).

He Jianzhang and Zhang Weimin (1982), 'The System of Ownership: A Tendency Toward Multiplicity', in Lin Wei and A. Chao (eds), (1982).

Hinton, W. (1966), *Fanshen*, Monthly Review Press, New York.

Howe, C. (1973), *Wage Patterns and Wage Policy in Modern China – 1919–1972*, Cambridge University Press, London.

Howe, C. (1978), *China's Economy: A Basic Guide*, Granada Publishing, London.

Hu Qiaomu (1978), 'Observe Economic Laws, Speed Up the Four Modernizations', *Peking Review*, nos. 45–47, November.

Huan Xiang (1980), 'From Mandarin to Manager' (in Chinese), *JJGL*, 11.

Shigeru, Ishikawa (1983), 'China's Economic Growth Since 1949: An Assessment', *China Quarterly*, .

Ji Chongwei and Rong Wenzuo (1979), 'How Are We to Reform the System of Industrial Administration?', *JJGL*, no. 6, 25 June, in *CREA*, no. 18.

Ji Long (1984), 'Contracting and Reform in Collective Enterprises of the Light Industry', *JJYJ*, 11 in *CREA*, 85–009.

Jiang Nan (1980), 'The Method of Favouring Ownership by the Whole People and Slighting Collective Ownership Should be Changed', *RMRB*, 21 August, in *CREA*, 84–76425.

Jiang Weijun (1984), 'Forum on Reforming Bank Interest', *RMRB*, 13 August, in *FBIS*, 161.

Jiang Yiwei (1979), 'A Discussion of "The View that the Enterprise is the Fundamental Unit" . . .', *JJGL*, 6, 25 June, in *CREA*, 18.

Jiang Yiwei (1980), 'The Theory of an Enterprise-based Economy', *Social Sciences in China*, 1.

Jiang Yiwei (1985), 'If all Staff and Workers are on the Contract System, it will not suit the Socialist Nature of Enterprises' (in Chinese), *Jingji Tizhi Gaige*, 1.

*Jingjixue Zhoubao* (Economic Review), 'Table of the Eight-Level Progressive Tax Rates for Urban Collective Industry' (in Chinese), 10 January 1983.

Kapralov, P., Krugulov, A. and Ostrovsky, A. (1981), 'Some Trends in the Chinese Leadership's Social and Economic Policies', *Far Eastern Affairs*, 1.

Kau Ying-Mao (1971), 'The Urban Bureaucratic Elite in Communist China: A Case Study of Wuhan, 1945–65', in A. D. Barnett (ed.), (1971).

Klein, D. W. (1962a), 'Sources for Elite Studies and Biographical Material on China', in R. Scalapino (ed.), (1962).

Klein, D. W. (1962b), 'The Next Generation of Chinese Communist Leaders', *China Quarterly*, 12, October–December.

Klein, D. W. and Clark, A. B. (1971), *Biographic Dictionary of Chinese Communism 1921–1965*, 2 vols, Harvard University Press, Cambridge, Mass.

Kornai, J. (1959), *Overcentralisation in Economic Administration*, Oxford University Press, Oxford.

Kornai, J. (1980a), *Economics of Shortage* (Vol. A), North Holland Publishing Company, Amsterdam.

Kornai, J. (1980b), 'The Dilemmas of a Socialist Economy: the Hungarian Experience', *Cambridge Journal of Economics*, 4.

Korzec, M. and Whyte, M. K. (1981), 'Reading Notes: The Chinese Wage System', *China Quarterly*, 86.

Koves, A. (1981), 'Socialist Economy and the World Economy', *Review*, vol. V, no. 1, Summer.

Kowalak, T. (1981), 'Work Cooperatives in Poland: Basic Information and Critical Review of the Last Decade', paper presented to International Conference on Producer Cooperatives, Gilleleje, Denmark.

Laky, T. (1984), 'Small Enterprises in Hungary – Myth and Reality'.

Lange, O. (1936–7) (1972), 'On the Economic Theory of Socialism', in A. Nove and M. Nuti (eds), (1972).

Lange, O. with Taylor, F. (1938), *On the Economic Theory of Socialism*, University of Minnesota Press, .

Lardy, N. R. (1978), *Economic Growth and Distribution in China*, Cambridge University Press, Cambridge.

Lardy, N. R. (ed.), (1978), *Chinese Economic Planning*, M. E. Sharpe, White Planes, N.Y.

Lardy, N.R. and Lieberthal, K. (eds), (1983), *Chen Yun's Strategy for China's Economic Development: A Non-Maoist Alternative*, M. E. Sharpe, New York.

Lardy, N. R. (1984), 'Consumption and Living Standards in China 1978–83', *China Quarterly*, 100.

Lee Hong-Yung (1983), 'China's Twelfth Central Committee: Rehabilitated Cadres and Technocrats', *Asian Survey*, vol. 23, no. 6, June.

Lee Hong-Yung (1984), 'Evaluation of China's Bureaucratic Reforms', *Annals of the American Academy of Political and Social Science*, November.

Lemoine, F. (1984), 'Réformes économiques et finances publiques en Chine', *Économie prospective internationale*, 13, January.

Lenin, V. I. (1967), (original 1897), *A Characterisation of Economic Romanticism*, Progress Publishers, Moscow.

Lenin, V. I. (1918), 'The Immediate Tasks of the Soviet Government', in *Questions of Socialist Organization of the Economy*, Progress Publishers, Moscow (n.d.).

Lenin, V. I. (1960), *The Development of Capitalism in Russia*, Progress Publishers, Moscow.

Li Chengrui (1985), 'An Important Question in Macro-Economic Management – Strict Control of Issuance of Currency by the State', *RMRB*, 26 April, in *FBIS*, 087.

Li Chengrui (1985), 'Economic Reform Brings Better Life', *BR*, vol. 28, no. 29, 22 July.

Li Fuyu (1983), 'Start from readjusting distribution to modify the financial system' (in Chinese), *Caizheng*, 5.

Li Shuren and Huang Yinzhu (1979), 'Several Questions which Urgently Await Solution in the Development of Collectively Owned Industries in Cities and Towns', *JJYJ*, 9, in *CREA*, 28–74598.

Li Yue and Chen Shengchang (1981), 'Exploratory Discussion of the Scale Structure of Industrial Enterprises' (in Chinese), *SHKX*, 1.

Li Zongwei and Wu Wenzao (1980), *Jijigaohao gongye gaizu gongzuo* (carry through the industrial reorganisation), Zhongguo Shehui Kexue Yuan Chubanshe, Beijing.

Liang Chuanyun (1984), 'Development of China's Individual Commerce and Industry' (in Chinese), *JJNJ*.

Lin Wei and A. Chao (eds), (1982), *China's Economic Reforms*, University of Pennsylvania Press, Philadelphia.

Lin Zili (1982), 'Initial Reform in China's Economic Structure', *Social Sciences in China*, March.

Liu Binyan (1983), edited by Perry Link, *People or Monsters? And Other Stories and Reportage from China after Mao*, Indiana University Press, Bloomington; and (1981) in W. Zafanolli (ed.), *La Face Cachée de la Chine*, Pierre Emile, Paris.

Liu Guoguang (1980), 'The Question of the Reform of the Chinese Economic Management System', *Wan Hui Bao*, 8 March, in *FBIS*, 20 March.

Liu Guoguang (ed.), (1981), *Guomin Jingji Zonghe Pingheng de Ruogan Lilun Wenti* (Principal Theoretical Problems Concerning the Global Balance of the Chinese Economy), Chinese Social Science Research Publications, Beijing.

Liu Shinian (1980), 'Discussions on the Orientation for Restructuring China's Economic System', *JJYJ*, 1, 20 January, in *CREA*, 54, 8 April.

Liu Wenzhu (1979), 'Letter', in *Liaoning Ribao* (Liaoning Daily), 7 September, in *CREA*, 16–74251.

Lockett, M. (1983), 'Producer Cooperatives in China: 1919–1981' (in Italian), *Rivista della Cooperazione*, 15.

Lockett, M. (1986), 'Small Business and Socialism in Urban China', *Development and Change*, .

Lu Baifu and Qian Zhongtao (1984), 'Establish a New Socialist Banking System in Our Country', *RMRB*, 1 February, in *FBIS*, 033.

Ma Hong (1981), 'On Several Questions of Reforming the Economic Management System' (in Chinese), *JJYJ*, 7, 20 July.

Ma Hong (ed.) (1981), *Zhongguo Jingji Jiegou Wenti Yanjiu* (Analysis of the Structural Problems of the Chinese Economy), People's Publishing House, Beijing.

Mackintosh, M. (1984), 'Economic Tactics: Commercial Policy and the Socialisation of African Agriculture', in special issue, edited by G. White and E. Croll, on 'Agriculture in Socialist Development', of *World Development*, January 1985.

Mandel, E. (1968), *Marxist Economic Theory*, Merlin, London.

Mao Tsetung (1977), transl. M. Roberts, *A Critique of Soviet Economics*, Monthly Review Press, New York.

Mao Zedong (1977), *Mao Zedong Xuanji* (Selected Works of Mao Zedong), vol. 5, People's Publishing House, Beijing.

Marer, P. (1984), 'Hungary's Economic Reforms: From Traditional Central Planning to Market Socialism', in *A Compendium of Studies on the Economies of Eastern Europe*, prepared for the Joint Economic Committee, US Congress, US GPO, Washington, DC.

Marx, K. (1976), *Capital*, vol. 1, Penguin, Harmondsworth.

MITI (Ministry of International Trade and Industry, Japan) (1985), White Paper on Small and Medium Enterprises in Japan 1985, Tokyo.

Mills, W. De B. (1983), 'Generational Change in China', *Problems of Communism*, November–December.

Mills, W. De B. (1985), 'Leadership Change in China's Provinces', *Problems of Communism*, vol. 34, no. 3, May–June.

Naughton, B. (1985), 'False Starts and Second Wind: Financial Reforms in China's Industrial System' in E. Perry and C. Wong (eds), (1985).

Nove, A. (1972), *An Economic History of the USSR*, Penguin, Harmondsworth.

Nove, A. (1983), *The Economics of Feasible Socialism*, Allen and Unwin, London.

Nove, A. and Nuti, M. (eds), (1972), *Socialist Economics: Selected Readings*, Penguin, Harmondsworth.

Oksenberg, M. (1971), 'Local Leaders in Rural China, 1962–65', in A. D. Barnett (ed.), (1971).

Pairault, T. (1980), *Les Politiques Économiques Chinoises*, La Documentation Française, Paris.

Pairault, T. (1982), 'La loi de la valeur en Chine: aspects théoriques, pratiques et politiques actuels', *Revue Française de Science Politique*, 6 December.

Pairault, T. (1983a), *Politique Industrielle et Industrialisation en Chine*, La Documentation Française, Paris.

Pairault, T. (1983b), 'La Riforme Economiche', in Gibelli and Weber (eds), (1983).

Peng Baoquan (1985), 'Development and Reform in Commerce'. *BR*. 29. July.

Peters, V. and Schädler, M. (1983), 'The Urban Individual Enterprises in China: 1978–1982. A Revival of the Private Economic Sector?', *Asia*, 1.

Perry, E. and Wong, C. (eds), (1985), *The Political Economy of Reform in Post-Mao China*, Harvard University Press, Cambridge, Mass.

Qiao Rongzhan (1982), 'How to maintain a basic stability in commodity prices and currency value' (in Chinese). *Jingji Wenti*. 9. in *CREA*. 305.

Rawski, T. G. (1979), *Economic Growth and Employment in China*, World Bank and Oxford University Press, Oxford.

Rong Zihe (1983), 'Some views on current work in the area of finance' (in Chinese), *Caizheng*, 8 (also translated in *FBIS*, 178).

Rothwell, R. and Zegveld, W. (1982), *Innovation and the Small and Medium Sized Firm*, Frances Pinter, London.

Scalapino, R. A. (1962), 'The Transition in Chinese Party Leadership: A Comparison of the Eighth and Ninth Central Committees', in R. A. Scalapino (ed.), (1962).

Scalapino, R. A. (ed.), (1962), *Elites in the People's Republic of China*, University of Washington Press, Seattle.

Shambaugh, D. L. (1984), *The Making of a Premier – Zhao Ziyang's Provincial Career*, Westview Press, Boulder, Co.

Shanghai (1983), *Shanghai Jingji 1949–1982* (Shanghai's Economy 1949–1982), People's Publishing House, Shanghai.

Skinner, G. W. (1964–5), 'Marketing and Social Structure in Rural China: Parts I, II and III', *Journal of Asian Studies*, vol. 24. nos. 1–3, November 1964, February 1965, May 1965).

Stalin, J. (1931), 'The Tasks of Business Executives', in *Leninism* (1940). Lawrence and Wishart, London.

Stalin, J. (1952), 'Concerning the Errors of Comrade L. D. Yaroshenko', in J. Stalin (1952).

Stalin, J. (1952), *Economic Problems of Socialism in the Soviet Union*, Progress Publishers, Moscow and also (1972), FLP, Beijing.

Stalin, J. (1977), *Les Questions du Léninisme*, Foreign Languages Press, Beijing.

State Statistical Bureau (1985), 'Communique on Fulfilment of China's 1984 Economic and Social Development Plan', *BR*, 25 March.

*Statisztikai Evkönyv* (1983), (Hungarian Statistical Yearbook), Central Statistical Office, Budapest.

Sun Xiaoliang (1980), 'Motivating Force, Initiative and Market Economy', *JJGL*, 3. 15 March, in *CREA*, 66.

Swain, N. (1985), *Collective Farms Which Work?*, Cambridge University Press, Cambridge.

Thomas, A. R. and Lockett, M. (1983), *Choosing Appropriate Technology*, (T361 Units 15–16, 2nd Edition) Open University, Milton Keynes.

Teiwes, F. C. (1967), *Provincial Party Personnel in Mainland China 1956–1966*, Occasional Papers of the East Asian Institute, Columbia University, New York.

Tretiak, D. (1980), 'Political Movement and Institutional Continuity in the Chinese Ministry of Foreign Affairs, 1966–1979', *Asian Survey*, 20, 9 September.

UN (1981), *Classification of the Functions of Government*. Statistical Studies, Series M, no. 70. United Nations, New York.

Walker, K. R. (1984), 'Chinese Agriculture During the Period of the Readjustment, 1978–83', in *China Quarterly*, 100.

Wan Dianwu (1983), 'An Inquiry into the Question of Separating Government Administration from Enterprise Management in Commerce', *RMRB*, 20 April, in *FBIS*, 81.

Wang Bingqian (1982), 'Certain Questions of Financial Work', *RMRB*, 26 November, in *FBIS*, 229.

Wang Chuanbun (1984), 'Some Notes on Tax Reform in China', *China Quarterly*, 97, March.

Wang Jiye (1983), 'Appropriately Strengthen the Degree of Centralisation in Financial Work', *RMRB*, 26 August, in *FBIS*, 170.

White, G. (1982), 'Urban Employment and Labour Allocation Policies in Post-Mao China', *World Development*, vol. 10, no. 8.

White, G. (1983a), *Industrial Planning and Administration in Contemporary China*, transcript of a research trip June–July 1983, Institute of Development Studies, University of Sussex.

White, G. (1983b), 'Socialist Planning and Industrial Management', *Development and Change*, 14.

White, G. (1984), 'Urban Bias, Rural Bias or State Bias? Urban–Rural Relations in Post-Revolutionary China', *Journal of Development Studies*, vol. 20, no. 3.

White, G. (1985), 'Labour Allocation and Employment Policy in Contemporary China', *IDS Research Report*, University of Sussex.

White, L. T. III (1976), 'Workers' Politics in Shanghai', *Journal of Asian Studies*, November.

*Who's Who in Communist China* (1969), 2 vols, Union Research Institute, Hong Kong.

Wong, P. (1976), *China's Higher Leadership in the Socialist Transition*. The Free Press, New York.

World Bank (1981), *China: Socialist Economic Development*, World Bank, Washington, DC.

Wu Jiapei and Li Wenrui (1979), *The Path of Changzhou's Industrial Development* (in Chinese), Renmin Chubanshe, Beijing.

Wu Renjian (1983), 'National Forum to Discuss Comprehensive Planning of Finance and Credit', *RMRB*, 20 May, in *SWB*, 7344.

Wu Yuanfu (1979), 'The Practice of Uncompensated Transfer of Assets Must Be Stopped', *RMRB*, 21 August, 2, in *CREA*, 13, 74099, pp. 62–64.

Xiao Daiyun (1956), *Wo Guo Guodu Shiqi Zhong Congye Fazhan Sude de Jige Wenti* (Some Problems Concerning the Growth Rate of Industry During the Transition Period in our Country), People's Publishing House, Shanghai.

Xiao Liang (1982), 'The Rehabilitation Collective Enterprises in Urban Areas', in Lin Wei and A. Chao (eds), (1982).

Xiao Liang, Tang Zongku and Zhang Tianxin (1980), 'Weihai Municipality's Big Collective Industry' (in Chinese), *SHKX*, 1.

Xiao Weixiang (1984), 'Several Questions Concerning the Reform of Collective Enterprises in Light Industry', *JJGL*, 10, in *CREA*, 85–007.

Xin Ling (1985), 'China Promotes Innovative Jobs Policy', *BR*, 11 November.

Xu Yi and Chen Baosen (1982), *Zhongguo de Caizheng* (The Finances of China), Renmin Chubanshe, Beijing.

Xue Muqiao (1980), *Dangqian woguo jingji ruogan wenti* (China's economic problems today), Renmin Chubanshe, Beijing.

Xue Muqiao (1981), *China's Socialist Economy*, FLP, Beijing.

Xue Muqiao, Su Xing and Lin Zeli (1960), *The Socialist Transformation of the National Economy in China*, FLP, Beijing.

Yeh, K. C. (1984), 'Macroeconomic Changes in the Chinese Economy During the Readjustment', in *China Quarterly*, 100.

Yu Guangyuan (1980): 'The Basic Approach to Socialist Ownership', *BR*, 8 December, pp. 13–15.

Zhao Yang (1980), 'Autonomy of Collectives Must Be Respected', *Tianjin Ribao* (Tianjin Daily), 18 March, p. 3, in *CREA*, 63 75812: 37; 40.

Zhao Yiwen (1957), *Industry in New China* (in Chinese), Tongji Chubanshe, Beijing.

Zhao Ziyang (1985), 'The Current Economic Situation and the Reform of the Economic Structure' (Report to the Third Session of the Sixth National People's Congress), *BR*, 22 April.

Zhong Zhang and Dong Yan (1983), 'The Tax Burden of Collectively Owned Industrial Enterprises Has Still to be Lightened' (in Chinese), *JJXZ*, 10 January, p. 3.

*Zhonggong Renminlu* (1982), (Biographical collection of Chinese Communists), Institute of International Relations, Taibei.

Zhu Chuan (1980), 'Collective Ownership in Cities and Towns and Several Questions on Economic Policy', *JJYJ*, 2, pp. 3–11, in *CREA*, 62, 75735: pp. 20 – 35.

Zhu Ling (1985), 'Auditors Pinpoint Irregularities Worth $2.9 Billion', *China Daily*, 18 December, p. 1.

Zhuang Qidong, Shen Jiyan and Wu Yan (1980), 'The Economy of the Collective Ownership in Cities and Towns Must be Developed Energetically', *JJYJ*, 4, pp. 10–16, in *CREA*, 64, 75888: pp. 38–49.

# Index

Page references followed by 't' refer to tables.